The Dialectics of Globalization

The Dialectics of Globalization

Regional Responses to World Economic Processes:
Asia, Europe, and Latin America
in Comparative Perspective

Edited by

Menno Vellinga

Westview
PRESS
A Member of the Perseus Books Group

Latin America in Global Perspective

Copyright © 2000 by Westview Press, A Member of the Perseus Books Group

Published in 2000 in the United States of America by Westview Press, 5500 Central Avenue, Boulder, Colorado 80301-2877, and in the United Kingdom by Westview Press, 12 Hid's Copse Road, Cumnor Hill, Oxford OX2 9JJ

Find us on the World Wide Web at www.westviewpress.com

A CIP catalog record for this book is available from the Library of Congress.
ISBN 0-8133-3781-X

The paper use in this publication meets the requirements of the American National Standards for Permanence of Paper for Printed Library Materials Z39.48–1984.

10   9   8   7   6   5   4   3   2   1

For my three sons:
Michiel, Bouke and Willem,
born global adventurers

Contents

Tables and Figures

Preface

Globalization has become an essential part of the analyses of present-day societal change, conceptualizing processes of scale expansion and increasing transnational interaction. This includes interfirm relations, operations within internationalized market-structures, as well as the emergence of transgovernmental networks and policy communities, transnational cause groups and many other international networks. Most studies of the economic dimensions of globalization emphasize their homogenizing effects and tend to present these processes as operating with a great degree of autonomy. Globalization is pictured as an unstoppable force moving along uncontrollably by individual actors: corporations as well as nation states. The state in particular is being viewed as losing out to globalizing processes, its policies becoming more and more driven by external forces that dictate the options. It cannot be denied that state actors and different agencies within particular jurisdictions, together with private sector partners, are increasingly integrated into transgovernmental networks and policy communities. The state's traditional reach and authority and its capability to act as a developmental state is being challenged by global transformations from above and emerging regionalisms and inter-regional coalitions from below. But do these developments result in a downright surrender of sovereignty, as the radical "globalizers" do suggest?

The image of homogenization—supposedly the result of such a steamroller-type process—should be rejected and replaced by a more realistic picture. Globalization processes, as we observe around us, tend to have contradictory effects. They both homogenize and fragment within and between countries. Rather than creating one big economy or one big polity, globalizing processes also divide, fragment and polarize. Real differences do persist and often reflect conscious choices in the "global" political economy. Further, globalization is not the exclusive result of the "blind" mechanisms of world economic development. It is based in the concrete actions and interactions of actors involved in a myriad of decisionmaking processes on the various scale levels: supra-national, national and local. Also, it is a multifaceted phenomenon.

Along with the economic aspects, social, political, and cultural dimensions are important.

Subnational levels of analysis have become more and more important while investigating the nature, scope and impact of "globalization" in concrete situations. Globalizing processes and the ensuing focus on supranational levels of action and problem resolution have produced a resurgent affirmation of regional identities and an emphasis on locality. There is a growing awareness among analysts and policymakers that only by enhancing the comparative strength—in an economic, as well as political (through decentralization), social and cultural sense—of subnational regions, will national governments be able to mediate global processes successfully and boost national economies.

The characteristics of globalization as a social, political, and cultural process indicate an important role for an actor-oriented analysis. This approach is especially fruitful in the study of the impact of globalizing processes on the regional and local levels and their interaction with regional and local economic, sociopolitical, and sociocultural idiosyncrasies. In individual cases, the response on these levels may take the form of counter movements, where the politics of identification based on a regional cultural dynamics will make the mobilization possible of purposive, politically significant actions that may include references to projects of regional economic development.

In the present volume we have joined a number of studies that address themselves explicitly to this dialectical dimension of globalization: the interaction—and sometimes the contradiction—that develops between global processes and regionally based production systems, giving rise to a new process conceptualized by the term *glocalization.* This issue is dealt with through the study of a number of cases drawn from East and Southeast Asian countries, from Latin America and the Caribbean, as well as from Western Europe, deepening our insight into the workings of glocalization under different economic, social, political and cultural conditions.

The authors come from different disciplines: economics, economic geography, political science, sociology, and anthropology. As editor I wish to express my great appreciation to our colleagues who responded enthusiastically to the invitation to participate in the project. The chapter's first versions were discussed at a conference organized at Utrecht University in June 1997. They have all been rewritten substantially since then. I thank my colleague Otto Verkoren for his support of the project and the valuable comments made on earlier versions of the manuscript. I gratefully acknowledge the help of Paula Duivenvoorde in preparing the manuscript. The Institute for Development Studies Utrecht (IDSU) and the Faculty of Geographical Sciences at Utrecht University have all been very supportive of my research endeavours. I am grateful for the space they have given me to pursue these interests.

Menno Vellinga
Utrecht University

PART ONE

Introduction

Fo2

lqlobal *org*

1

The Dialectics of Globalization: Internationalization, Regionalization, and Subregional Response

Menno Vellinga

Globalization has become the buzzword of the 1990s. Numerous publications have presented the idea of an increasing global interdependence, conveying the image of a genuine world economy with transnational corporations as its most important actors, deploying resources across economic sectors and national boundaries. In this view, the specific dynamics of national economies and economic management at the national level have become increasingly irrelevant in a truly global economy, where these transnational corporations manufacture parts of a commodity in one country, assemble it elsewhere, put on the finishing touches in a third country, and sell it in yet another. Their marketpower derives from the mobility of capital, but also from the relative immobility of labor.[1] Extreme views on globalization, like those presented by Kenichi Ohmae,[2] picture these international economic processes as a juggernaut rolling along, uncontrolled and uncontrollable by individual governments. The state, in this perspective, has increasingly become a nominal participant on the world economic stage. Its ability to define a course independent from these pressures toward international coordination has been decisively undermined by the increasing global economic interdependence.

Besides the processes pushing toward global integration, globalization addresses widely different developments within the international political economy, including social, political, and cultural-ideological factors. In this way, globalization interrelates multiple levels of analysis in the economic, political, social, and cultural spheres.[3]

3

However, the explanatory strength of the globalization paradigms has remained unclear, as have the nature, causes, mechanisms, and transformative power of the processes it is meant to conceptualize. Globalization is proving difficult to pin down conceptually and to demonstrate empirically.[4] It has the characteristics of a "theoretical umbrella," much like dependency theory in the 1970s. Whether globalization does refer to a historically new phenomenon, a watershed in the history of world economic development, and not to some conjunctural development has remained subject to debate. In various publications, Paul Hirst has maintained that the present dynamics of the international economy has important historical antecedents that go back to the second half of the last century and that the suggestion of a structurally "new" development should be rejected.[5]

The Dimensions of Globalization

When using a "container" theory like globalization, the object of analysis has to be precisely defined. The dimensions of the processes covered by the theory are so many and so manifold that careful systematization is required.[6] A very basic dimension obviously concerns the inner workings and "logic" of capital as manifest in the functioning of the world economy, but this dimension is already a "container" in itself.

A second major dimension refers to the actors involved—their strategies and the objectives and means used while attempting to realize them. Actors include multinational corporations, national states, and supranational organizations—including trade blocs—to which national decisionmaking powers have been delegated, but also social classes and class organizations. Obviously, the inner workings and logic of capital are not viewed as anonymous processes that dictate conditions to the actors. On the contrary, these workings are considered the outcome of a myriad of decisionmaking processes. Some of these processes are directed toward the optimization of positions as defined by neoclassical theory, and others are pursuing the optimization of satisfaction in other terms. Thus considered, the logic of capital will have different meanings in different situations and would certainly not always be defined on the basis of pure capitalistic criteria.

A third dimension concerns the complex interaction between the processes of globalization and those of regionalization through the formation of regional blocs. In addition, the way these tendencies toward economic internationalization interact with processes generated subregionally and locally would be object of analysis. Finally, the social, political, and ideological consequences of the economic processes indicated above should be considered in relation to the role of the actors involved and their response to globalizing processes.

Globalization is a multifaceted phenomenon of an inherently contradictory nature, as developments on the regional, subregional, and local levels show.[7] On the one hand, some observers emphasize the all-encompassing nature of the global economic, social, political, and ideological processes, with the suggestion of inevitable homogenization. On the other hand, others note a strong movement that runs contrary to this trend toward integration and convergence. This gives globalization a dialectical appearance, in particular on the regional, subregional, and local levels.[8] The trends towards homogenization through investment, trade, technology, modern communications, and transport meet with regionally generated production, innovation, and knowledge systems.[9] In addition to a whole body of regional experiences in production, trade, and doing business in general, these systems often constitute a counterpoint to global trends, one that—paradoxically enough—is continuously being reinforced by global trends. Not only in economics but even more so in the social and cultural fields, this manifestation of the global-local nexus, of the global thrust feeding the subnational and the subregional project, can be observed.[10] On the one hand, under the influence of globalization we observe the disembedding of social relationships from locally bound contexts of interaction, and on the other hand, under the influence of locally or regionally based patterns of behavior and regional ideological-cultural complexes, we see the re-embedding of interaction in local contexts.[11] This counterthrust to globalization may even seek political expression at the subregional and local levels. The study of these interactions between global trends and subregionally embedded production and service systems, supported by social, political, and cultural-regional idiosyncrasies, is essential to our understanding of the movements and countermovements that form part of the globalization process.

State and Region

The role of the state has changed considerably under the circumstances of globalization. Traditionally, the state was responsible for protecting the national economy from disrupting influences emanating from international economic processes. Its new role entails facilitating the adaptation of the economy to the new realities created by the processes of internationalization and globalization. Often these activities will include the integration of the national economy into a supranational economic context.[12] Inevitably, this process has undermined the state's decisionmaking powers over areas that traditionally belonged to its sphere of authority. Its active cooperation in the formation of economic blocs has fed supranationalist tendencies, while on the domestic front, state policies are increasingly disrupted by sub-state actors who are seeking advantage through regionalization. The state is caught in the middle and its role has undoubtedly become rather complex. However, as the various contributions to this volume show, it has retained an important role in guiding and regulating domestic economic and social policies and still has considerable decisionmaking power with regard to national resources. The state has not in the least become obsolete as an actor in its own right on the national and international economic scenes, as the radical "globalizers" are proclaiming. Even an institution like the World Bank has come around on this point. In its 1997 World Development Report, the bank underlines the important role of the state in mediating the integration of the domestic economy into an international economic context.[13] At the same time, however, the report emphasizes the state's responsibilities in mitigating globalization's polarizing effects with regard to regions, subregions, and social classes on the domestic front.

Globalization has its own winners and losers, both among and within nations. Certain sectors of economy and society and—above all—certain regions and subregions will undergo the effects of a growing economic and social interdependence more intensively than others. As a result, the interregional and intraregional differences in economic growth, income distribution, and access to resources are becoming more pronounced. The accompanying shifts in sociopolitical influences between regions at the subnational level may affect their potential for interest promotion at the national and supranational levels. The tensions between core and peripheral regions, a permanent issue in many countries, may increase in scope and intensity. The "winners" among the major European regions have begun to take affairs into their own hands, opening their own embassy in Brussels in order to promote their interests directly on the supranational level. A similar process of interest promotion can be observed in Monterrey in northern Mexico, where the forces of globalization and the demands of global competitiveness have proven to be powerful vehicles for the industrial bourgeoisie in their efforts to shape local conditions to their needs and to defend their interests directly and aggressively within NAFTA (North American Free Trade Agreement).[14]

Regionalization at the supranational and at the subnational level are two different processes, although they closely influence each other.[15] Regionalization on the supranational level involves organized political cooperation within a particular group of states. It requires a multilateral arrangement with formal membership and institutions that form the decisionmaking structures providing the basis for cooperation. Initially this basis usually is trade and the flow of goods, people, and money. As cooperation develops, as in the case of the European Union (EU), policies in the social, cultural, defense, and monetary fields may be coordinated. Regionalization on the subnational level involves a different process. On this level, regions are mostly products of history, processual spaces that have emerged over the course of time through the projects of various economic and social actors seeking to secure a territory of their own. These spaces cannot always be defined in a strict geographical sense. The boundaries are often not clearly delimited and may shift with changes in the development process. The formation of these regions results from the development of material interests and related social classes and power relations in a socio-spatial context. This process will often also involve the formation of communities of belief and identity. These may turn the region into an object of identification, competing with loyalties to one's local community, social class, or the nation state.[16] These sentiments and identifications can be mobilized and manipulated by regional power holders—a frequent historical phenomenon, as exemplified in northern Italy, Catalonia, and Basque Country, to mention a few spectacular cases. In this way, cultural-ideological complexes may become a driving force in regional development projects, may "style" the region's response to globalizing tendencies and projects of economic integration, and may form a crystallization point for movements emphasizing regional identities.

The following chapters present examples of subregional development, each meeting the challenges of globalization in its own way. We mention:

1. the old traditional industrial regions, hit hard by global competition and the internationalization of capital and forced to change their industrial and institutional structures (the *Ruhrgebiet* in Germany and northeast England are obvious examples);
2. traditional industrial regions with a still flourishing industry and solid institutions; (for example, northern Italy and southern Germany); add the reagglomeration of older industries, strongly embedded in regional networks of an economic, social, political and cultural nature (examples are found in the traditional industrial regions in Western Europe;
3. regions with a manufacturing sector and supporting institutions that for more than half a century have followed the model of import-substituting industrialization, are presently forced to restructure and have to find ways to insert themselves into the international economy (many examples can be found in Latin America);
4. regions with longer established nuclei of export-led industrialization, at present restructuring the manufacturing sector to medium-tech or high-tech production (examples are found in Southeast Asia and East Asia);
5. regions without a longstanding industrial tradition, launching themselves on the road toward labor–cost intensive production—

often concentrated in export-processing zones—and with a weak institutional structure, not capable of supporting higher level production processes (examples abound in Central America, the Caribbean, and Southeast Asia);

6. regions with an economic base in the knowledge and service sectors and with a highly flexible institutional structure (examples can be found in Southeast England and in Singapore).[17]

The institutional structures that form part of the context for regional development differ considerably in their capacity to promote, empower and guide innovative entrepreneurial activity, private as well as public. The above-mentioned cases refer to distinctive production milieus. At the same time, they represent most significant regional responses to globalizing processes as we observe them today. The institutional solutions to the challenge of trying to sustain regional economic vability in the face of market developments and technological change will differ in each individual case. Comparative analysis will produce knowledge on those variables that in the various production milieus build an innovating environment with ability to mediate successfully the impact of world economic processes.

In addition to these experiences, we see the growing importance of "global" cities—strategic sites for the operation of global networks with a specific geography that often cuts across old divides (like those that used to exist between the industrialized world, developing countries, and Eastern Europe) and connects centers of wealth and power around the globe: New York, São Paulo, Tokyo, London, Paris, Budapest, etc.[18]

In all these cases firms are participating in a process of "global localization" or *glocalization*, a term which in itself expresses the dimensions of convergence and divergence, of homogenization and fragmentation, that form part of the dialectical nature of a globalizing world. "Think globally, act locally" is the often-heard slogan, expressing the essence of the strategies behind the globalization process. Localized or regionalized production complexes are firmly embedded in a regional production milieu. At the same time they are highly internationalized and globalized both organizationally and in terms of trade and other networks.[19] They are simultaneously intensely local and intensely global.[20]

Regional Responses to Globalization

The various contributions to this volume argue quite convincingly that global market forces have not been able to homogenize the world to the extent that globalization theorists would want us to believe. More than two-thirds of the trade conducted by the industrialized countries (EU,

North America, Japan) is moving within this industrialized region. The intraregional trade in other markets is increasing rapidly.[21] The trend toward regionalization has reinforced these tendencies. Latin America is still very much dependent on trade with partners outside the region, but this situation is changing rapidly under the influence of the regionalization projects that are in force (NAFTA, Mercosur). It may change even more in the near future, when efforts to revive the older regionalization schemes, like the Andean Pact and the Central American Common Market (MCCA), will succeed. The thesis that the process of globalization is not as pervasive or total as many make it out to be is most forcefully defended in this volume by Paul Hirst. The international economy, he asserts, is perfectly governable, given the political will and cooperation of the major powers. His argument is convincing: That the position of the state has become more complex, that the state inevitably has been implicated in these globalizing developments, that its role has been profoundly transformed by this participation, but that it has maintained its status as a viable and strategic institution. Nation states are still able to manage significant dimensions of the national economies. Further, on the subregional level the state has remained an important actor despite the decentralization schemes that are so much in vogue in recent years and that are empowering the social actors on the regional and local levels. In Asia, where globalization trends have inspired development projects in many countries, the role of the state has proven to be of crucial importance, certainly now when it is mediating the effects of the financial crisis.

In Latin America, the neoliberal offensive of the 1980s and early 1990s had radical consequences for the state role in many countries without, however, sidelining it. State reform in recent years—as recommended by the multilateral agencies—does entail a strategy that, under the banner of "good governance," defines important state responsibilities in infrastructure, in the field of social policy, and in technology development; it is a strategy that even indicates the necessity of state support for certain strategic industrial developments—though cautiously and while following strict market criteria.[22]

Gary Gereffi goes beyond this state-market debate and presents the organization of production as the crucial factor behind the processes of economic transformation resulting from globalization. International production and trade networks incorporate hierarchical divisions of labor that determine the regional location and relocation of the various phases in global commodity chains. He makes this point through an analysis of the most internationalized of all branches of industry—the apparel industry. Yet he also shows the importance of regionally based divisions of labor. Asia, North America, and Europe tend toward the development of intraregional trade and production networks in the commodity chain of this industry, creating new patterns of interaction between the local and the global.

Cases from Asia

This trend toward regionalization is reaffirmed by Sam Ock Park in his chapter on Asia. A process of economic integration along the lines of the European Union is not within reach in Southeast and East Asia, a region divided by historical enmities, political conflicts, differences in levels of economic development, and—as seen more recently—in ways of handling the effects of the economic-financial crisis. However, integration between regions in neighboring economies is a phenomenon of increasing importance and includes the formation of growth triangles or subregional economic zones. Regional industrial networking has further added to these trends. The result has been a sharp increase in intraregional trade. These processes entail the active participation of the social actors (governments, entrepreneurs) and often involve elaborate planning.

In this respect, Tak-Wing Ngo indicates that in the cases of pre-1997 Hong Kong and Taiwan, regionalization was not a product of "blind" market forces. It was the result of the combined effects of business strategy and state intervention. The large firms were competing for state action in support of their economic interests, while the state was trying to manipulate private capital investment for political ends. It remains to be seen whether these trends will continue during the process of industrial and financial restructuring most countries in the region are presently experiencing. This applies most certainly to Malaysia and Singapore, both hit hard by these developments, as Leo van Grunsven and August van Westen show. Of these two, Singapore has been more successful in riding out the storm. Its financial sector has remained relatively stable. Its manufacturing activities, which over the last decades have been moving toward higher-value-added and skill and technology intensive operations, appear reasonably capable of coping with the crisis. The regionalization trend among Singapore firms will undoubtedly slow down as a result of the contraction of regional markets.

Malaysia's project to upgrade its economic structure and to move toward technologically advanced endeavors has been (temporarily?) cut short by the crisis. In its future growth the export sector will very much depend on developments in East Asia, a major destination of Malaysian exports. This is another result of the advanced regionalization in the region. Economic booms as well as economic downturns will leave few economies unaffected. This will also apply to Vietnam, with an economy that in trade and investment is also strongly oriented toward the East

Asian countries. On the other hand, Vietnam presents an interesting example of engagement with global capital on one's own terms—as Stephanie Fahey notes—and the outcome of the transition process experienced by its economy and society is as much the result of internally generated impulses toward change as it is a reaction to global pressures. It shows again the importance of considering regional contextual factors of a sociopolitical and sociocultural nature while assessing the impact of globalization processes.

Cases from Latin America and the Caribbean

Developments in Latin America have been decisively influenced by neoliberal policies in combination with regionalization. In the course of the 1990s most national economies have been integrated with the global economy. However, the formation of trade blocs has created a situation in which trade liberalization—the rules of foreign investment, technology transfer, and so on conforming to neoliberal strategies—have remained limited to those joining the bloc.

Bloc formation and membership were clearly indicated by developments in the global economy, but political considerations also figure prominently. Robert Gwynne indicates that in the case of Mercosur, the Argentine government was very much motivated by the desire to restructure its economy and to reform industrial labor relations; the Brazilian government, on the other hand, had approached the challenges presented by Mercosur more from a geopolitical standpoint and, initially at least, was less motivated by the desire for industrial reform. Political considerations were also prominent when NAFTA was formed, although the economic dynamics between the countries concerned created the initial impetus for the formation of the free trade agreement.

Regionalization has a long history in the Central American and Caribbean countries. The first initiatives were motivated by the desire to overcome the drawbacks of the small domestic markets and were undertaken in the late 1950s. These initiatives did not fare well in subsequent years. Not until the recent waves of neoliberal reform and bloc formation was the interest in regionalization rekindled.

The region has become a location for *maquiladora*-type industries. The socially polarized character of these societies, coupled with a lack of political stability, has made it difficult—as Helmut Nuhn points out—to construct a role in the global economy other than one based on inexpensive exports and cheap labor. In traditional exports Central American and Caribbean countries are often each other's competitors in international markets. Local identities and sentiments run strong in the small Central American countries and even more so in the Caribbean island states.

In the Caribbean region, the polarizing effects of the processes of globalization are again apparent. Globalization has its own winners and losers and the Caribbean has not been on the winning side—at least until now. Their small domestic markets and high production costs in virtually any activity they may engage in has not given them any leverage in dealing with international capital. The formation of NAFTA has brought to several Caribbean nations the logic behind the formation of economic blocs: to maximize the advantages for the participants while keeping others out. But Mexico has become a more attractive location for producers selling in the U.S. market and this situation is not likely to change in the future. NAFTA threatens to continue to lure foreign investment and production away from locations in the Caribbean. The Lomé treaty, which gives sixteen Caribbean countries preferential access to the market of the an Union, will expire in the year 2000 and a renewal of this foreign assistance to the region is not expected.[23] In his chapter, Terry McCoy is not optimistic about the prospects for the Caribbean under intensifying conditions of global economic expansion. The solution may lie not with regionalization but rather with creatively developing individual niches in the international economy.

In the case of the southern cone countries regionalization works, if only because of the sheer size of the two major participating economies. Mercosur helped ease some of the problems resulting from the restructuring of the importsubstituting industrialization model and provided a means for managing their integration into the global economy. Within this common market—like in the case of NAFTA and the EEC—sub-regions are manouvring to take positions. Kees Koonings analyzes the interesting case of the southernmost Brazilian state of Rio Grande do Sul and its participation in the regionalization process, strongly conditioned by federal and state politics.

Cases from Europe

In Europe, globalization is having a considerable impact, though it has not been able to change substantially the economic landscape in the EU member countries. As Egbert Wever shows, areas that have traditionally been economically strong have generally been able to retain their positions and continue to prosper. Europe is a continent of regions and subregions with strong identities, rooted in history, ethnicity, language, or other cultural factors. Firms are a part of this scenery. The large firms in particular create regions through their locational behavior, but at the same time these firms are also products of the institutional and cultural environment of their locations.[24] In the chapters written by Eike Schamp and Ray Hudson, this type of interaction between regions or subregions and firms figures prominently. Globalization is shown to be a process that is not an alien force, external to the national state, the national economy, and society or to the economy and society at the local and regional levels. At all institutional levels, social actors and decisionmaking processes have played key roles in bringing about the institutional arrangements that opened the door to the economic processes conceptualized as *glocalization*. The national state has retained a core position in mediating the relations between these processes and its internal regional patterns of socioeconomic change. On a supranational level, pressure is being exercised to mobilize the regional funds of the EU in support of those regions that are declining or having difficulties catching up with global trends and need to restructure their economies. Several old industrial regions that experienced radical de-industrialization in the 1970s are re-emerging as industrial powers. Northeastern England presents an interesting case, analyzed by Hudson. Here a radical restructuring of the economy resulted in part from the deliberate policy of the United Kingdom to allow global political-economic forces to have a greater influence in shaping the sectoral and spatial patterning of the economy in order to increase general international competitiveness. But Hudson concludes that domestic political forces—including present socio-spatial inequalities resulting from the polarizing effects of globalization—also played a decisive role in determining the ultimate outcome of the process.

This coordination between state policies and global market forces is also a central theme dealt with by Schamp in his analysis of three subregions in southern Germany. He shows that in very few cases can a direct link be shown between these global market forces and specific economic changes in a particular region or subregion. In practice, such changes result from an intricate complex of factors, of which market developments and the changing criteria of international competitiveness are only one element to consider. State regulation, regional politics, and the actions of other social actors (e.g., chambers of commerce, labor unions) have remained important influences mediating the effects of globalization. In the European context, northern Italy is another fascinating case in which the impact of political institutions and political struggles involving regional and local government, the regional elites, labor, and other interest associations, has created a complex environment for regional and local production systems. The specific characteristics of these systems— the presence of large numbers of small firms, spatially concentrated, sectorally specialized, and organized in a local, vertical dimension of labor— makes them cater to specific market niches in the domestic and international economy that are less vulnerable to general globalizing influences.[25] Southern Italy has lagged behind and runs the risk of entering the ranks of the "losers" left by the globalization process.

Conclusion

Globalization and localization are two closely interwoven processes; in fact, they may be considered as two sides of the same coin. The presence of one implies the presence of the other. This global-local nexus has been conceptualized by the term *glocalization*. Like globalization, glocalization is a very general concept. It lacks precision and has heuristic qualities rather than precise empirical connotations. Glocalization processes result from the interaction between the global restructuring of production and developments of a political or sociocultural nature that appear to be connected with a specific region or locality. Basically, glocalization concerns the regional/local conditioning of global processes. The concept stems from the assumption that economic behavior is rooted in territorially articulated social, cultural, and institutional settings and that this embeddedness does influence economic outcomes.[26]

It appears that in recent years analysts of international economic developments have become more aware of the importance of these factors.[27] In current analysis, deterritorialization is slowly being replaced by reterritorialization. The exclusive attention on globalization as an all-encompassing, all-powerful process that crushes regionally embedded production systems is fading, and the emphasis is shifting from an analysis of global forces, based on macroeconomic data, to the dynamics on a regional and/or local level.

In analyzing this dynamic, obvious core points of attention are the competitiveness of the regional production system—as determined by its level of technological development—the mobilization of resources, and the possibility for accumulation of wealth. In addition, political, sociocultural, and institutional variables will come into play. As such, this approach offers a far richer analysis and a better insight into the workings of globalizing processes than do the more general surveys and the high level of abstraction that until now have dominated the globalization debate.

Notes

1. James H. Mittelman and Mustapha Kamel Pasha, *Out from Underdevelopment Revisited: Changing Structures and the Remaking of the Third World* (New York: St. Martin's Press, 1997), p. 65.
2. Kenichi Ohmae, *The End of the Nation State: The Rise of Regional Economies* (London: Harper Collins, 1995).
3. James H. Mittelman, "The Dynamics of Globalization," in *Globalization: Critical Reflections*, ed. James H. Mittelman (Boulder: Lynne Reinner), p. 2.

4. Alan Harding and Patrick Le Galès, "Globalization, Urban Change, and Urban Policies in Britain and France," in *The Limit of Globalization*, ed. Alan Scott (London: Routledge, 1997), p. 181.

5. See, for example, Paul Hirst and Grahame Thompson, *Globalisation in Question* (Cambridge: Polity Press, 1996).

6. Mittelman, "The Dynamics of Globalization," pp. 1–19.

7. François Chesnais, *La Mondialisation du Capital* (Paris: Syros, 1994), p. 14; Claire Turenne Sjolander, "The Rhetoric of Globalization: What's in a Wor(l)d?" in *International Journal* 51, no. 4 (1996): 603–616.

8. Ash Amin and Nigel Thrift, "Globalization, Socio-Economies, Territoriality," in *Geographies of Economies*, ed. Roger Lee and Jane Wills (London: Arnold, 1997), pp. 147–149.

9. See Michael Storper, *The Regional World, Territorial Development in a Global Economy* (London: The Guilford Press, 1997).

10. Robert W. Cox, "A Perspective on Globalization," in Mittelman, *Globalization: Critical Reflections*, p. 27.

11. Anthony Giddens, *The Consequences of Modernity* (Cambridge: Polity Press, 1990), p. 21.

12. Sjolander, "The Rhetoric of Globalization," p. 608.

13. The World Bank, *The State in a Changing World, World Development Report 1997* (Washington, D.C.: The World Bank, 1997).

14. Menno Vellinga, "The Monterrey Industry and the North-America Market: Past and Present Dynamics," *Journal of Borderlands Studies* 10, no. 2 (1995): 45–65.

15. Van R. Whiting, "The Dynamics of Regionalization: Road Map to an Open Future?" in *The Challenge of Integration: Europe and the Americas*, ed. Peter H. Smith (London: Transaction Publishers, 1993), pp. 18–23.

16. Bryan Roberts, "The Place of Regions in Mexico," in *Mexico's Regions, Comparative History and Development*, ed. Eric Van Young (San Diego: Center for United States-Mexican Studies, University of California at San Diego, 1992), pp. 228–229.

17. See also Martin Heidenreich, "Regional Innovation Systems in Global Competition" (paper presented at the international conference, *Globalization and the New Inequality*, Utrecht University, November 1996).

18. Cf. Saskia Sassen, *Cities in a World Economy* (Thousand Oaks, Calif.: Sage, 1994).

19. Philip G. Cerny, "Globalization and Other Stories: The Search for a New Paradigm for International Relations," *International Journal* 51, no. 4 (1996): 619.

20. Eric Swyngedouw, "The Local in the Regional in the National and in the Global: The Re-Configuration of Scale and the Process of "Globalisation" (paper presented to the international conference, *Globalization, the Formation of Economic Blocs, National States and Regional Responses*, Utrecht University, June 1997), p. 13.

21. Sheila Page, *How Developing Countries Trade. The Institutional Constraints* (London: Routledge, 1994), pp. 19–20.

22. Menno Vellinga, "The Changing Role of the State in Latin America," in *The Changing Role of the State in Latin America*, ed. Menno Vellinga (Boulder: Westview Press, 1998), pp. 18–19.

23. Menno Vellinga, "The European Community and Latin America: A Search for Direction," *Journal of Third World Studies* 12, no. 1 (1995): 238–264.

24. See Storper, *The Regional World*, p. 50.

25. Ibid., pp. 137–147.

26. Amin and Thrift, "Globalization, Socio-Economics, Territoriality," p. 151.

27. See Storper, *The Regional World*; Paul Krugman, *Development, Geography and Economic Theory* (Cambridge, Mass.: M.I.T. Press, 1995).

2

The Myth of Globalization

Paul Hirst

The notion that an integrated global economy has developed in recent decades has become part of the new common sense. It is widely believed that nations, firms, and individuals have no option but to adapt to the intensifying global competitive pressures or go under. Distinct national economies, it is claimed, have dissolved into the world system, and with them has gone the possibility of macroeconomic management by national governments. The new global system is driven by uncontrollable international market forces and is dominated by transnational companies that produce and sell wherever economic advantage dictates. States cannot govern world markets and if they are not to disadvantage their societies, they have to accept that the only role remaining to them is to help make their territory attractive to internationally mobile capital.

Governance and the Market

Globalization is not just a trendy concept; its acceptance by politicians, media commentators, and academics is politically highly consequential. The question is whether globalization is indeed the case, whether world market forces that are beyond all governance have in fact developed. We shall consider the evidence for and against the existence of a process of globalization. But first we need to spell out the social and political issues at stake, for if globalization is occurring then we face a very bleak future indeed. A truly global economy will make the expectations developed in the advanced world during the long boom after 1945 completely obsolete.

Some commentators see the process of globalization as an entirely positive development. In his influential book *The Borderless World*, the management guru Kenichi Ohmae argues that globalization means that at last markets have developed on a scale that allows them to escape from the inefficient and interventionist grasp of governments. Global free markets facilitate the allocation of resources to maximize benefits for the consumer.[1]

Others less convinced of the inherent wisdom of the market, like the bulk of the moderate left, nevertheless feel powerless before the logic of globalism. They can see no policy alternative to meeting the demands of international competition. At best public policy can strive to maintain national competitiveness by promoting training and investing in the public infrastructure that business requires. This, broadly speaking, is the view of the United States secretary of labor in Clinton's first administration, Robert Reich, as advanced in his book *The Work of Nations*.[2] The left has become convinced that states can neither tax too heavily to achieve this nor can they sustain overextensive welfare states. If they do, they will become uncompetitive and global capital will move elsewhere. Thus even the left holds that many of the policies of post-1945 social democracy are now unsustainable in the face of globalization. It has become the victim of a widespread and pathological tendency to over-diminish expectations.

If the left feels thus constrained, then the free-market right regards globalization as a godsend. They are convinced that both between societies and within societies there will be no option but a brutal competitive struggle for existence. The civilizing of capitalism by public policy and state action, countering and regulating market forces at the national level, will have to be abandoned. Globalization means a return to the savage capitalism of the nineteenth century and the social Darwinist belief in the supreme value of the survival of the fittest.

The dominance of global market forces means that market failures can now occur on a colossal scale and that they are virtually uncorrectable because they are beyond the scope of national governments acting singly or in concert to control them. A global economy is in fact fragile and highly vulnerable to the unintended effects of markets. For example, it is vulnerable to a major slump brought on by the crash of volatile and interconnected financial markets and vulnerable to irreversible environmental damage caused by extensive and unregulated industrial development in poorer countries fuelled by foreign direct investment (FDI) seeking the advantage of lower wages.

In such an ungoverned and unstable economic system the lives of all but the super-rich are extremely insecure. If states are unable to alter their macroeconomic environment and if their welfare spending is constrained by international competitive pressures, then public and collective forms of response to and protection against such internationally generated uncertainty are undermined. As states become able do less, so individuals will expect less of them and desert weakening forms of common security. Individuals will thus increasingly seek to protect themselves, investing in their own competitiveness and privately insuring themselves against such risks as they can afford to cover. The need for self-protection will reinforce the tax aversion of the successful and tend to make them hostile to welfare spending on others. Those who fail in the competitive struggle for existence will increasingly be judged inadequate rather than unfortunate—they fail to strive, to invest in their skills, and to make provision for contingencies.

In such a climate social solidarity would collapse; not only will the rich and the successful be motivated by self-interest but they will no longer be part of a national community. Society will divide not only on the basis of wealth but of mobility. Thus the key division will be between an internationally mobile elite of managers and highly skilled professionals, whose first loyalty is to their transnational corporate employers or to their own careers, and a nationally bound mass whose skills are easily replicated. The constraints of competitiveness will ensure that the interests of the elite and of mobile capital will tend to prevail, and if they do not, then the country in question will become an impoverished backwater.

This conception of society is not pure speculation. In a globalized world atomized individualism and highly local loyalties make more sense to the successful than continued commitment to communities based on what appear to be increasingly powerless national states. Not only the right but most of the international technocratic elite and many business leaders believe they have economic logic on their side in preferring the market to the state and in seeking to limit the activities and the cost of government.

In a globalized economy, mainstream politics—political parties competing to control the policies of the nation state—matter less and less. In this context, it is exceedingly difficult for the moderate left to sustain mass interest in an alternative politics that amounts to public spending in order to make the country attractive to business. Necessary as this might be, it will seem like municipal politics—providing essential services in the same way as local authorities deliver street lighting and sewers. This task will undoubtedly bore the talented and alienate the committed, who will desert professional politics for business, the media, and issue-based activism. Thus the weakening of the capacities of the state brought about by global markets will become self-reinforcing, and people will expect less of national politics.

At the international level too, politics will matter less and less in comparison to the power of the global markets. Economic activity will become independent of political power and military force will become secondary to the muscle of the markets. Of course, advanced states will have the military means to render themselves invulnerable to direct threats and will find direct military conflict pointless and self-defeating. States that try to threaten the interests of world business will be crushed by devastating, if unplanned, economic sanctions—collapsing exchange rates, capital flight or boycott, and plunging trade balances. The dream of free-market liberals will at last be realized, free trade will over political authority. Only authoritarian societies willing to pay the price of economic backwardness for religious or ethnic reasons will stand outside this logic. As the world becomes more integrated economically, it becomes more polycentric politically, but politics will cease to have central importance in most people's lives.

Globalization in Question

Most of these consequences would certainly follow in a globalized economic system. But the question that needs to be posed first is, *has* globalization taken place? For all the vigor with which the new conventional wisdom is being presented as fact, evidence and rigorous conceptual arguments for it are in short supply. Most globalizers, rhetoric aside, are unclear about what a truly global economic system would look like and therefore have little idea what could count as decisive evidence for or against its existence or development. For example, it is clear that some important aspects of economic activity have further internationalized since the early 1970s, but is this sound evidence for globalization? Not necessarily, since most of these trends prove neither that national economies are dissolving nor that the international economy is inherently ungovernable. Most of the evidence is compatible with something very different, an open *international* economy in which trade and investment take place between the distinct national economies of the advanced countries and in which companies, although they are active multinationally, remain committed to national bases and conduct the bulk of their business within their home region. Such a system is quite different from a *global* economy, in which national economies have been subsumed, in which markets have autonomized themselves on a world scale, and in which stateless transnational corporations predominate.

It may be that after a decade of making the rounds in the media, globalist rhetoric is running up against inconvenient facts. Some mainstream commentators are now denying that the state is as powerless before global pressures as we have been led to believe. Martin Woolf has pointed out that the current degree of international openness to trade among the major economies is no greater than it was before 1914 and few people thought the state was powerless then.[3] This point is reinforced with the following table:

Table 2.1   Ratio of Commodity Exports Plus Imports to GDP at Current
Market Prices (in percentages)

	1913	1950	1973	1994
France	30.9	21.4	29.2	34.2
Germany	36.1	20.1	35.3	39.3
Japan	30.1	16.4	18.2	14.6
Netherlands	100.0	70.9	74.8	89.2
UK	47.2	37.1	37.6	41.8
US	11.2	6.9	10.8	17.8
Arithmetic Average	42.6	28.8	34.3	39.5

Source: Paul Hirst and Graham Thompson, Globalization in Question, revised and updated
(Cambridge: Polity Press, 1996), p. 27.

Moreover, despite all the evidence of highly internationalized financial trading, most capital remains within national boundaries and capital markets retain distinct national peculiarities. In the case of the United Kingdom, David Miles has shown that despite policies designed to attract FDI, some 90 percent of capital formation in the last decade has been from domestic sources.[4] The household sector still generates the vast majority of savings and, as Miles pointed out, few countries invest abroad more than 5–10 percent of the financial assets derived from households (see Figure 2.1).

Further, an editorial in the Economist in October 1995 argued that global economic forces are not causing states to converge in their policies, citing the wide variation in the proportion of public spending to GDP, which ranges from 20 percent in Singapore to 68 percent in Sweden.[5]

Needless to say, globalizers like Andrew Marr reject such claims.[6] They contend that such high proportions of public spending to national income are an index of economic failure and high unemployment. For the moment, the state has the capacity to meddle—it can still tax and spend—but in the long term, it will have to conform to global economic realities or take the punishment inflicted by internationally mobile capital.

However, the level of public spending is not in itself an index of economic failure. Societies have different characteristics and public spending ratios reflect distinct political choices. Thus Sweden has had a high level of public spending relative to GDP for a long time, including the period when it was seen as a model of high-tech competitiveness and had very low unemployment. Swedes have accepted public social provision as both economical and efficient, spending very little on private health insurance, schools, or pensions.

Figure 2.1   Percentage of Financial Assets Ultimately Owned by Households Held in Overseas Bonds and Equities at the End of 1995

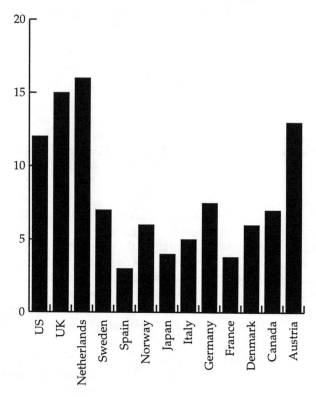

Source: David Miles, "Globalization, the Facts Behind the Myth," *Independent,* December 22, 1997, p. 19.

Such things have to be paid for in a mature economy, whether in the public or private sectors. Much of the obsession with the balance between public and private spending assumes that taxes are a deduction from the public welfare rather than a form of collective consumption. High levels of public spending relative to GDP, far from "crowding out" the public sector, may actually help to sustain it—providing infrastructure, training, and insurance against risk more cheaply, efficiently, and equitably than equivalent market spending. Singapore's low level of public spending is an artifact of its very rapid recent growth; it has been an industrializing rather than a mature economy. It will not be able to get away with 20 percent public spending forever; spending on items such as health and social services will rise considerably in due course as the population ages. Singapore's system of compulsory pensions works at present because the country has enjoyed rapid growth and full employment. What is crucial is not the level of public spending per se but that the internationally tradable sectors of a country remain competitive, that competitiveness is by no means hindered by a developed welfare state.

Moreover, Sweden's economic difficulties are neither the cause of its high level of public spending—it was at the top of the league table of public expenditure to GDP *before* the crisis of the early 1990s—nor did public spending per se cause these difficulties; they are the result of a complex of structural and conjunctural factors. Other high-spending internationally exposed European countries, like Denmark or the Netherlands, have not encountered the same difficulties—both have high rates of growth, falling unemployment, and healthy external balances.[7]

It is time to turn to the relevant facts about the international economy that argue against the credibility of the globalization thesis. The first point that Woolf makes about globalization is right: the protagonists of a rapid and recent process of globalization have short memories. They tend to talk as if national economies were almost closed systems until the 1970s. Yet the international economy has changed frequently and radically since a modern industrial trading system was first developed in the 1870s. One does not want to be bogged down in history and statistics, but the evidence is striking and surprising. In many ways the international economy was *more* open in the period leading up to 1914 than it is today. Indeed, if globalization ever existed, it was during the Belle Époque. Several major states had high trade to GDP ratios, and these were not exceeded in the period of rapid growth after 1945—France's ratio in 1913 was 35.4 percent and in 1973 it was 29.0 percent; Germany's was 35.1 percent in 1913 and 35.2 percent in 1973. Capital was highly mobile, levels of FDI were high, and the ratio of total capital flows to GDP was higher for major international rentier states like Britain and France than in any subsequent period. The nineteenth century was the age of mass migration, with European labor flowing freely to new growing economies abroad, whereas today economic migrants are feared and discriminated against. Finally, of course, the gold standard ensured that the international monetary system was beyond the control of any state, even Britain. States had to adapt to monetary movements but they could not directly control exchange rates.

The point can also be made that the supposed golden era of national economic management from 1945–1973 was in fact dependent on an *international* trading system controlled by *international* institutions that promoted growth and made the macroeconomic or industrial policies of the nation states possible. The liberal managed multilateralism of the post-1945 world was largely an Anglo-American creation. It was sustained by the hegemony of the United States and by its willingness to bear the costs of underwriting the system. The Bretton Woods system of fixed exchange rates, Marshall Plan aid, GATT (General Agreement on Tariffs and Trade), large-scale U.S. corporate investment abroad, and massive U.S. military aid all helped to promote domestic growth in allied states and boost world trade. Indeed, in 1950–1973, international trade grew faster than did domestic output and grew at a faster rate relative to domestic output than in the supposed era of globalization after 1973. The point to emphasize here is that national controls over exchange rates, foreign exchange transactions, and capital movements were made possible by a system of international institutions underwritten by a hegemonic state. The dismantling of this system was driven largely by national and often short-term policy considerations; states deregulated and abandoned exchange controls from the late 1970s, mainly because of internal political agendas rather than as a result of the pressure of international markets.

Financial Markets

The ungovernability of major financial and other markets is consistently overemphasized by the globalizers. The greatest economic turbulence in modern times was caused by deliberate acts of price-fixing by nation states—the OPEC price hikes in 1973 and 1979. It is certainly true that the 1970s and early 1980s were a period of intense volatility in currency markets and free floating exchange rates. Given the intensity of the inflationary crisis of the 1970s, it is difficult to see how any international monetary regime could have survived. Yet efforts were being made to re-regulate the major financial institutions at the micro level in the 1980s, especially through the cooperation of the central banks of the major industrial states. Equally, the Plaza Agreement of 1985 and the Louvre Accord of 1987 did effect some stabilization in exchange rates among the G-3—Europe, Japan, and the United States. Similarly, the EMS (European Monetary System) served to stabilize exchange rates in Europe from 1979 to 1992. At present the battles between public policy and the major currency markets are far from settled, one reason being that no one state is willing to underwrite the system and the major players have divergent interests.

It is true that the volume of international financial trading is so great as to limit market-making by central banks, which dwarfs the real economy of international trade. Yet these volumes represent short-term and repeated market transactions by financial institutions, and these casino-like trading patterns could be rapidly "cooled" by a modest turnover tax on short-term transactions, such as that proposed by James Tobin.[8] The problem here is not merely in getting governments to agree to plug loopholes and the like, but in changing the perceptions in the international financial community that institutions use these transactions to *avoid* risk and that there is no shortage of capital to finance trade or fixed investment. Thus unless volatility becomes a real concern to financial institutions and major companies it is unlikely that the major states could be persuaded to act in concert to limit short-term international financial trading and to plug loopholes. Speculators aside, business has no direct interest in high levels of market volatility or states of uncertainty about major financial movements. Such conditions make it more difficult to trade or to meet commitments arising from financial assets like pensions or insurance policies. Incalculable risks created by volatile markets kill investment and trade and, therefore, growth. This is self-evident in the current Asian crisis, in which countries like Korea and Thailand, having been overheated by easy access to foreign capital, now face severe deflation as part of the international rescue packages fronted by the IMF.

The internationalization of newly industrializing countries' capital markets, without incurring the adequate supervision of lending by the national banks, was clearly a folie à deux between elites in these countries and the forces in the advanced world promoting financial globalization as a positive agenda. The IMF rescue packages in effect subsidize imprudent international investors, as also was the case in Mexico in 1994–1995. Investors can wreak havoc if they know their risks are limited—a clear point in favor of greater restriction and regulation.[9]

The present international currency and other financial markets are thus too lightly governed, but they are not beyond control in principle. What prevents greater governance is not market forces per se but the divergent interests of the major nation states and the belief in business circles that current risks do not justify the inconvenience of greater regulation. The notion that even given their combined authority, the major states are in principle powerless in the face of global markets is thus highly exaggerated. The difficulties of the EMS in 1992–1993 do not gainsay this judgment. The policies of several nation states, but especially the United Kingdom, provoked the markets by being stubbornly committed to unrealistic and unsustainable rates against the deutsche mark. Stupidity in public policy is reason to believe, not that all governance is ineffective, but simply that it should not grossly violate the interests and expectations of economic actors.

The Role of Transnational Companies

Thirdly, true transnational companies are relatively rare. Most multinational companies are based in a major industrial state, and they conduct the majority of their business within their home region, such as North America, Asia-Pacific, or Europe; typically the figure is around 60–70 percent of sales and about the same for assets.[10] This does not mean that companies are not internationally oriented, but that they have a recognizable national/regional "base" from which they operate and in which they keep the key value-adding parts of their activities, such as R&D and core manufacturing. Companies use FDI in subsidiaries and branch plants in other countries to facilitate trade, but they remain distinctly "national"—Ford is unmistakably an American company despite its global reach, and Sony is distinctly Japanese despite its large acquisitions in the United States. Firms continue to derive substantial benefits from being nationally based, even if the days of interventionist state industrial policy and "national champions" are over. Companies benefit from the complex of institutions that form a national business system, particularly with nationally rooted financial institutions that provide the bulk of their capital. They also benefit from the cultural intangibles that generate common attitudes and expectations, something a supranational company will lack. There is little sign that companies are shifting from such nationally based patterns of multinational trading to a truly transnational scale of activity; the current national/regional concentration is not just an historic artifact. The existence of national companies shows that distinct national economic systems remain, demonstrating the relevance of national policy in promoting corporate performance and in ensuring regulations of companies through their national home bases. Will Hutton's influential book, *The State We're In*, shows what happens when the complex of national institutions fails to sustain the manufacturing sector; national policy is not an irrelevancy, but in no country has the myth of globalization and of the impotence of the state taken stronger root than in Britain.[11]

Foreign Direct Investment in the Third World

Further supposed evidence of globalization is to be found in the twin processes of FDI in less developed countries and the rapid growth of a large part of the Third World, in countries such as China and India, which will alter western dominance and create a truly global economy in the early twenty-first century. But at present, trade and investment remain distinctly lumpy; the rich world of North America, Japan, and Europe accounted for 14 percent of the world's population, but 75 percent of investment flows in the period 1980–1991; in 1992 the same countries accounted for approximately 70 percent of export trade.[12] Capital is not fleeing the developed world to low-wage countries. Foreign direct investment has been flowing to a select minority of developing countries—Singapore, Malaysia, Mexico, and the coastal provinces of China taking the lion's share. At face value the volumes of FDI flowing to less developed countries seem huge—for example, they surged from US$31 billion in 1990 to US$80 billion in 1993. But this increase is closely correlated with a severe recession in the developed world and a downturn in investment opportunities there. Moreover, even large numbers can be misleading out of context—$80 billion appears an enormous sum until one considers that in 1992 the total population of India and China alone amounted to some two billion, and that if the whole of FDI to the Third World in 1993 were invested in these two countries it would amount to US$40 per capita. Paul Krugman has calculated that the entire net outflow of investment between 1990 and 1994 has reduced the total capital stock of the advanced world by a mere 0.5 percent.[13]

It is possible that China and India will grow rapidly into the twenty-first century, but it is by no means certain. They will need to, since it is estimated that both will have populations of 1.5 billion by 2025. At that point China may well have to support 300 million people over sixty and perhaps up to 250 million unemployed. The truth is that prospects for growth in the Third World are uncertain. Latin American growth rates have been notoriously volatile since the 1960s. Now Asia has also experienced volatility, once it became open to large external capital movements, as Latin America had been for some time. Growth rates have been spectacular in some East Asian countries, such as Singapore and South Korea, but they are unlikely to continue to grow at rates of 9 percent p.a. indefinitely. The current crisis will have varied effects. Some countries, such as Korea, will probably recover; others, such as Indonesia, face serious economic dislocation. However, the myth of Asia's miracle is well and truly shattered. In part these rapid growth rates in the most successful Asian newly industrialized countries (NICs) were investment driven, once-and-for-all processes, part of the process of conversion to a modern market society. Singapore, for example, doubled its labor participation ratio from 27 percent to 51 percent in just over two decades and invested something like 40 percent of its output.[12] Moreover, countries like Singapore have staggeringly high export to GDP ratios—185 percent in 1991—proving its role as an entrepôt and confirming that the growth of such Tigers depends directly on First World prosperity.

The odds are, therefore, that the three most wealthy regions in the world will retain their dominance of output, investment, and trade. That means they will continue to dominate the world economy and to have the capacity to regulate it effectively if they choose to do so and can agree. The EU and NAFTA (United States, Canada, and Mexico) remain, moreover, much less internationalized than smaller states. They still exported only about 10 percent of their GDP in 1990, and even Japan exported only

11 percent. If they wished, the major regional trade blocs of the EU and NAFTA could go it alone, imposing distinct regional policies and maintaining distinct regimes of welfare and labor rights. This would involve a measure of protectionism, and apart from its likely effects in constraining the growth of world trade, a world divided into regional economic blocs is likely to be more politically uncertain and unstable than one in which the major powers act to sustain an open world economy and to help its weaker members.

Conclusion

The examples presented above show that the scope of national policy in the advanced world has not been diminished to the degree the globalizers believe. However, even if we are not at the mercy of uncontrolled market forces, the managed multilateralism and the activist macroeconomic steering at the national level that characterized the period between 1947 and 1973 are unlikely to return. The world economy is governable to a degree—curbing the volatility of world financial markets, promoting free trade through the World Trade Organization (WTO), attempting to impose social and environmental conditions on investment in poorer countries through home regulation in the advanced world, and so on. States need to coordinate national policies and to act in concert to support international forms of regulation. States will be more effective if they act to promote international regulation, cooperating to pursue common goals and to pool their powers. Thus the national policies of economic management will be increasingly concerned with international issues; states will be effective as representatives of their populations at the supranational level. This will require a new outward-looking orientation on the part of national politicians and informed publics. The problem with the notion of globalization is that it denies this international orientation of national policy by insisting that the world market system is beyond all control. Globalization is a myth, unsustained by the evidence. It is a myth that serves the interests of neither business nor labor. Companies need a calculable degree of risk if they are to invest and promote growth, and uncertainty can only be contained by the governance of markets and by an effective framework of regulation at national and international levels. In such a context labor can defend its welfare and its rights. A regulated international environment in which the advanced states feel secure is more likely to benefit the bulk of less developed economies than a volatile free-for-all. Globalization is a myth that the left and those conservatives concerned with maintaining social stability and solidarity should never have fallen for in the first place. Never have ill-founded and ill-substantiated ideas been so pernicious. It is time they were abandoned and we returned to exploring the practical possibilities of active economic governance at national and international levels.

Notes

1. Kenichi Ohmae, *The Borderless World* (London: Collins, 1990).
2. Robert Reich, *The Work of Nations* (New York: Vintage, 1992).
3. Martin Wolf, "A Liberal World Restored," *Financial Times*, October 9, 1995, p. 24.
4. David Miles, "Globalisation: the Facts behind the Myth," *Independent*, December 22, 1997, p. 19.
5. "The Myth of the Powerless State," editorial, *Economist*, October 7, 1995, pp. 13–14.
6. See Andrew Marr, "Globalization and Public Spending," *Independent*, October 19, 1995.
7. See, for Denmark, *OECD Economic Surveys—Denmark 1997* (Paris: OECD, 1997); and for the Netherlands, Jelle Visser and Anton Hemerijcks, *A Dutch Miracle: Job Growth, Welfare, Reform and Corporatism in the Netherlands* (Amsterdam: Amsterdam University Press, 1997).
8. James Tobin, "Speculator's Tax," *New Economy*, 1994, pp. 104–109.
9. On the Asian crisis and the role of the IMF, see Jeffrey Sacks, "The IMF and the Asian Flu," *The American Prospect*, March-April 1998, pp. 16–21.
10. Paul Hirst and Grahame Thomson, *Globalisation in Question* (Cambridge: Polity Press, 1996), especially ch. 4.
11. Will Hutton, *The State We're In* (London: Cape, 1995).
12. Paul Hirst and Grahame Thomson, "Globalisation, Foreign Direct Investment, and International Economic Governance," *Organisation* 1, no. 2 (1994): 294–296.
13. Paul Krugman, "Does Third World Growth Hurt First World Prosperity?" *Harvard Business Review*, July-August 1994, p. 119.
14. Paul Krugman, "The Myth of Asia's Miracle," *Foreign Affairs* 74, no. 6 (1994): 63–75.

3

The Regional Dynamics of Global Trade: Asian, American, and European Models of Apparel Sourcing

Gary Gereffi

During the past several decades, East Asia's export industries have become increasingly diversified, internationalized, and regionally integrated. Whereas industrial upgrading from labor-intensive to capital- and technology-intensive industries has clearly occurred within Japan and the East Asian newly industrializing economies (NIEs), the notion of industrial upgrading by itself is inadequate to explain this process. It retains the national economy as the central unit of analysis and thus it neglects the ways in which tiered production involving interfirm networks between and within regions has shaped economic change. Related perspectives such as the "flying geese" model of East Asian development and product life cycle theory, while more dynamic than comparative advantage explanations of economic growth, also fail to capture the significance of a network-centered view of the world economy.

The industrial upgrading question is often framed as a debate about the relative importance of market forces and state policies in the development process. The significance of both states and markets is widely acknowledged in recent discussions of the most dynamic region of the world, East Asia.[1] But neither perspective directly addresses the question of how East Asian nations have been able to *sustain* their high rates of export-oriented growth since 1960, especially in the face of a variety of adverse factors such as several oil price hikes, rising wage rates, labor shortages, currency appreciations, a global recession, and growing protectionism in their major export markets.

To understand industrial upgrading, one needs to move beyond the states versus markets debate and focus instead on the organization of production as a major determinant of economic transformation in areas such as East Asia. The successful export industries of Japan and the East Asian NIEs are part of a broader process of globalization in which international production and trade networks create hierarchical divisions of labor within and between regions. An economic organization perspective reveals that East Asian firms have mastered the art of using networks as a strategic asset, and these networks are a key form of social capital in their regional context. The technological and organizational learning that accompanies these networks is an essential feature of East Asia's ability to endogenize its international competitive edge.

In making these arguments and extending them to other regions, I utilize a global commodity chains approach. Industrial upgrading has created an increasingly differentiated regional division of labor within Asia, with Japan playing the lead role in producer-driven commodity chains and China becoming the production center for buyer-driven chains. The East Asian NIEs play significant intermediary roles in both types of industries, as information brokers and producers of intermediate inputs in buyer-driven chains and as direct manufacturers of assorted inputs and low-cost finished goods in producer-driven chains. These changes have propelled East Asia to shift from being an export platform for goods sent to North America and Europe to become instead a major market for its own output. Even though interregional trade and investment ties between Asia, Europe, and the Americas are still strong, it is striking to see that North America and Europe are also developing newly integrated regional divisions of labor, with Central America and the Caribbean, and Eastern Europe and North Africa, respectively, being drawn more closely into the sourcing orbits for the lead economies of each region. Evidence in support of these assertions will focus on the structure and dynamics of regional divisions of labor in the apparel sector, which paradoxically combines some of most traditional and modern forms of economic organization in what is arguably the most global of all industries.

Global Commodity Chains

In global capitalism, economic activity is not only international in scope, it also is global in organization. *Internationalization* refers to the geographic spread of economic activities across national boundaries. As such, it is not a new phenomenon; indeed, it has been a prominent feature of the world economy since at least the seventeenth century, when colonial empires began to carve up the globe in search of raw materials and new markets for their manufactured exports. *Globalization* is much more recent than internationalization because it implies the functional integration and coordination of internationally dispersed activities.

Industrial and commercial capital have promoted globalization by establishing two distinct types of international economic networks, which we call "producer-driven" and "buyer-driven" commodity chains[2] (see Figure 3.1).

Producer-driven commodity chains are those in which large, usually transnational manufacturers play the central roles in coordinating production networks (including their backward and forward linkages). This is characteristic of capital- and technology-intensive industries, such as automobiles, aircraft, computers, semiconductors, and heavy machinery. The automobile industry offers a classic illustration of a producer-driven chain, with multilayered production systems that involve thousands of firms (including parents, subsidiaries, and subcontractors). The average Japanese automaker's production system, for example, comprises 170 first-tier, 4,700 second-tier, and 31,600 third-tier subcontractors.[3] Richard Florida and Martin Kenney have found that Japanese automobile manufacturers actually reconstituted many aspects of their home country supplier networks in North America.[4] Richard Doner extended this framework to highlight the complex forces that drive Japanese automakers to create regional production schemes for the supply of auto parts in a half dozen nations in East and Southeast Asia.[5] In their studies of the internationalization of the U.S. and Japanese semiconductor industries, Jeffrey Henderson and Michael Borrus also support the notion that producer-driven commodity chains have established an East Asian division of labor.[6]

Buyer-driven commodity chains refer to those industries in which large retailers, designers, and trading companies play the pivotal role in setting up decentralized production networks in a variety of exporting countries, typically located in the Third World.

This pattern of trade-led industrialization has become common in labor-intensive, consumer goods industries such as garments, footwear, toys, housewares, consumer electronics, and a variety of handcrafted items (e.g., furniture, ornaments). Production is generally carried out by tiered networks of Third World contractors that make finished goods for foreign buyers. The specifications are supplied by the large retailers or designers that order the goods.

One of the main characteristics of the firms that fit the buyer-driven model, including retailers—such as Wal-Mart, Sears Roebuck, and J. C. Penney—athletic footwear companies—such as Nike and Reebok—and fashion-oriented apparel companies—such as Liz Claiborne and The Limited—is that these companies design and/or market, but do not make, the branded products they order. They are part of a new breed of "manufacturers without factories" that separate the physical production

34

Figure 3.1   The Organisation of Producer-Driven and Buyer Driven Global
Commodity Chains

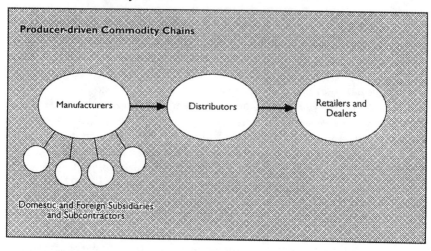

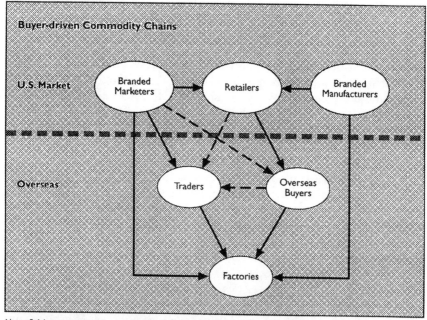

Notes: Solid arrows are primary relationships; dashed arrows are secondary relationships.
    Retailers, branded marketers, and traders require full-package supply from overseas factories.
    Branded manufacturers ship parts for overseas assembly and re-export to the manufacturer's home market.

of goods from the design and marketing stages of the production process. Profits in buyer-driven chains derive not from scale, volume, or technological advances, as in producer-driven chains, but rather from unique combinations of high-value research, design, sales, marketing, and financial services that allow the retailers and designers to act as strategic brokers in linking overseas factories and traders with evolving product niches in the main consumer markets.

Profitability is greatest in the relatively concentrated segments of global commodity chains characterized by high barriers to the entry of new firms. In producer-driven chains, manufacturers making advanced products like aircraft, automobiles, and computers are the key economic agents not only in terms of their earnings, but also in their ability to exert control over backward linkages with raw material and component suppliers and forward linkages into distribution and retailing. The transnationals in producer-driven chains usually belong to global oligopolies. Buyer-driven commodity chains, by contrast, are characterized by highly competitive and globally decentralized factory systems. The companies that develop and sell brand-name products exert substantial control over how, when, and where manufacturing will take place and how much profit accrues at each stage of the chain. Thus, whereas producer-driven commodity chains are controlled by industrial firms at the point of production, the main leverage in buyer-driven industries is exercised by retailers and branded merchandisers at the marketing and retail end of the chain.

The main characteristics of producer-driven and buyer-driven commodity chains are highlighted in Table 3.1. Producer-driven and buyer-driven chains are rooted in distinct industrial sectors, they are led by different types of transnational capital (industrial and commercial, respectively), and they vary in their core competencies at the firm level and their entry barriers at the sectoral level. The finished goods in producer-driven chains tend to be supplied by core country transnationals, while the goods in buyer-driven chains are generally made by locally owned firms in developing countries. Whereas transnational corporations establish investment-based vertical networks, the retailers, designers, and trading companies in buyer-driven chains set up and coordinate trade-based horizontal networks.

The Power Shift to Big Buyers in Developed Countries

Several sets of factors help to explain the growing prominence of buyer-driven commodity chains since the 1960s. On the supply side, there has been a marked increase in the industrial capability of Third World nations. Particularly in East Asia, the prevalence of export-oriented development strategies gave rise to a multitude of export manufacturers,

Table 3.1   Main Characteristics of Producer-Driven and Buyer-Driven Global
Community Chains

	Producer-Driven Commodity Chains	*Buyer-Driven Commodity Chains*
Drivers	Industrial capital	Commerical capital
Core competencies	Research & development; production	Design; marketing
Barriers to entry	Economics of scale	Economics of scope
Economic sectors	Consumer durables; intermediate goods; capital goods	Consumer nondurables
Typical industries	Automobiles; computers, aircraft	Apparel; footwear; toys
Ownership of manufacturing firms	Transnational firms	Local firms, predominately in developing countries
Main network links	Investment-based	Trade-based
Predominant network structure	Vertical	Horizontal

especially for labor-intensive consumer goods. The evolution of Asian manufacturing capability spread rapidly from Japan in the late 1950s and 1960s to the East Asian NIEs—South Korea, Taiwan, Hong Kong, and Singapore—during the late 1960s and 1970s, then to Southeast Asia and the People's Republic of China in the 1980s, and currently to a wide range of less developed countries including Bangladesh, Pakistan, Sri Lanka, and Vietnam in the 1990s. The sourcing networks for buyer-driven commodity chains extend to virtually all world regions, although the export volumes and variety of consumer goods are greatest in Asia.

On the demand side, there has been a remarkable consolidation of power in the hands of the biggest discounters, department stores, and specialty chains in the United States. Between 1987 and 1991, the five largest soft-goods companies increased their share of apparel sales in the United States from 35 to 45 percent of the retail market.[7] By 1995, the five largest U.S. retailers—Wal-Mart, Sears, Kmart, Dayton Hudson, and J. C. Penney—accounted for 68 percent of all apparel sales in publicly held retail outlets. The next top twenty-four retailers, all billion dollar corporations, represented an additional 30 percent of these sales.[8]

A fundamental restructuring is underway in the retail sector in the United States and the developed world more generally. The global retailing industry is becoming dominated by large organizations that are moving toward greater specialization by product (the rise of specialty stores) and price (the growth of high-volume, low-cost discount chains). Furthermore, the process of filling the retail distribution pipeline is leading retailers to develop strong ties with global suppliers, particularly in low-cost countries. Nowhere are these changes more visible than in apparel. Collectively, traditional retailers, which accounted for nearly 60 percent of the value of U.S. apparel sales in 1995, have lost ground to the nontraditional retail outlets—discount stores, off-price retailers, factory outlets, mail order houses, warehouse clubs, and so on—that feature a broad selection of merchandise at low prices. Discount stores have been the biggest winners among this group. Whereas discounters represent 20 percent of the U.S. apparel market in dollar sales, they control over 40 percent of the unit volume of clothes sold in the United States (see Table 3.2). The two top discount giants, Wal-Mart and Kmart, by themselves control one-quarter of all apparel units sold in the United States.

Table 3.2   U.S. Distribution Channels for Apparel, 1995

Distribution Channels	*Units 1995*	*Dollars 1995*
Total volume (billions)	16.1	152.4
Channel share (percent)		
1. Department stores	9.7	19.0
2. Speciality stores	11.6	22.0
3. Major chains	14.8	16.7
Traditional retail outlets (subtotal)	36.1	57.7
4. Discount stores	41.1	19.7
5. Off-price retailers	5.4	6.3
6. Factory outlets	4.3	4.3
7. Mail order	3.8	5.6
8. Other outlets	9.4	6.3
Nontraditional retail outlets (subtotal)	64.0	42.2
Total share	100.1	99.9

1. Includes Dillards, Nordstrom, Macy's, and Bloomingdale's, as well as regional department stores.
2. Includes The Limited, The Gap, and small independently owned stores.
3. Includes retail and catalog sales for Sears, J.C. Penney, Montgomery Ward, Mervyn's, and Kohl's.
4. Includes large outlets such as Wal-Mart, Kmart, and Target.
5. Includes T.J. Maxx, Burlington Coat Factory, Loehmann's, and other similar stores.
6. Includes VF Outlets, Levi's Outlet, Van Heusen Direct, Hanes Mill Outlet, and others.
7. Includes L.L. Bean, Spiegal, Land'sEnd, Patagonia, and others.
8. Includes warehouse clubs such as Sam's Club and Price/Costco, Sporting good stores. and all other outlets
Source: National Purchase Dairy Group,Inc., Port Washington, N.Y.

From the vantage point of buyer-driven commodity chains, the major significance of growing retailer concentration is its tendency to augment global sourcing, which is the practice of buying goods from overseas suppliers—goods made according to the specifications issued by the buyer from inputs procured by the manufacturer. In 1975, only 12 percent of the apparel sold by U.S. retailers was imported; a decade later, retail stores had doubled their use of imported apparel. According to unpublished data of the U.S. Customs Service's Net Import File, in 1993 retailers accounted for 48 percent of the total value of imports of the top 100 U.S. apparel importers (who collectively represent about one-quarter of all 1993 apparel imports); U.S. apparel merchandisers, which perform the design and marketing functions but contract out the actual production of apparel to foreign or domestic sources, represent 22 percent of the value of these imports;[9] and domestic producers make up an additional 20 percent of the total.[10]

The picture in Europe is strikingly similar. A 1991 study carried out by KSA/Texco reports that 51 percent of the European Community's apparel imports go to retailers, while 29 percent are channeled via manufacturers or designers. Only 20 percent of EC imports were controlled by "other parties," such as wholesalers or importers, and the share of imports controlled by developing country exporters was marginal.[11] In both the United States and Europe, then, retailers account for fully one-half of all apparel imports, and merchandisers or designers add roughly another 20 percent. Given that foreign production can often provide similar quantities, qualities, and services as domestic producers but at lower prices, the decision of many manufacturers is no longer *whether* to engage in foreign production, but how to organize and manage it.

The growth of big buyers has led to a shift in power from the production to the consumption side of commodity chains, and it has given retailers and designers unprecedented scope to reshape international supply networks. New information technologies are to a large degree responsible for this shift, since they provide retailers and distributors with real-time information about what customers want to buy. These changes have allowed big retailers to push inventories back on manufacturers and to be the primary beneficiaries of quick response networks that link retailers, manufacturers, and their component suppliers. In 1995, 72 percent of U.S. textile and apparel manufacturers reportedly had quick response programs with their customers, up from 60 percent in 1994.[12]

Finally, buyer-driven commodity chains reflect an increasing specialization of companies, which are now emphasizing "core competencies" and "strategic capabilities" as a key to achieving maximum flexibility, reduced risk, and higher profits. One of the most notable features of buyer-driven chains is the creation since the mid-1970s of prominent design firms whose brands are extremely well known, but that carry out no production whatsoever. These "manufacturers without factories" include companies like Liz Claiborne, Nike, and Reebok, who literally were "born global" since their sourcing has always been done overseas. In the 1980s, many retailers began to compete directly with these national brands by expanding their sourcing of "private label" (or store-brand) merchandise, which is sold more cheaply than the national brands but also is more profitable to the retailers since they cut out one of the main middlemen in the chain.

National Variations in Buyer-Driven Chains

Although the degree of market power that is concentrated in U.S. retailers and merchandisers may be extreme owing to the recent spate of mergers and acquisitions in the U.S. retail sector, a similar shift in power from manufacturers to distributors and retailers appears to be underway in most developed economies. Retailing across the EU has been marked by a process of substantial concentration in recent years. In Germany, the five largest clothing retailers (C&A, Quelle, Metro/Kaufhof, Karlstadt, and Otto) account for 28 percent of the EU's largest national market, while the United Kingdom's two top clothing retailers (Marks & Spencer and the Burton Group) control 25 percent of the UK market.[13] In both France and Italy, the role of independent retailers in the clothing market has declined since 1985, while the share of specialty chains, franchise networks, and hypermarkets is rising rapidly. In Japan, the 1992 revision of the Large Retail Store Law, which liberalized restrictions on the opening of new retail outlets, has caused a rapid increase in the number of large-volume retailers and suburban chain stores. The Japanese government predicts there will be 20 percent fewer retailers in Japan in the year 2000 than in 1985, mainly because of attrition among the small and medium retail stores.[14]

Because there are differences in the degree of retail concentration among industrialized nations, the relative weight of retailers and designers as "drivers" in buyer-driven commodity chains varies. The United States has the largest and most powerful retailers, and the various types of retailers (e.g., discount chains, department stores, specialty shops) and designers follow distinct patterns in terms of how and where they source their goods. Historically, the United Kingdom and the Netherlands have had large retail organizations as well. Whereas in the Netherlands retailers were quick to switch to direct imports, as happened in the United States, the major UK retailers (led by Marks & Spencer, whose mission statement included a commitment to source in Britain) exerted tight control over their domestic suppliers and obliged them to produce exclusively in the United Kingdom. Marks & Spencer, Britain's largest and most successful retailing firm with over 260 stores in the United Kingdom plus stores in other parts of Europe and Canada, itself buys about 20 percent of all the clothing made in Britain.[15] When the UK retailers did loosen their buying policies in the 1980s, UK manufacturers were unable to adjust. In Belgium and France, the largely independent retailers were in a weak bargaining position relative to the manufacturers, who had their own brands and eventually started their own retail operations. Germany has a tradition of regionally based retailers; the manufacturers used to be dominant because production was more centralized than retailing. Now in Germany both retailers and manufacturers are engaged in extensive offshore sourcing.

At the opposite end of the spectrum, Italy and Japan have notoriously fragmented retail institutions and strong craft and quality orientations within their manufacturing sectors. This has led manufacturers to retain a strong bargaining position vis-à-vis retailers and distributors. However, recent evidence suggests that Japan is undergoing a "distribution revolution." The consumerization of the Japanese economy is shifting the focus from upstream manufacturers to downstream retailers—the sector in the best position to gain information and knowledge of consumer needs—with a drastic reduction in the number of wholesalers. In both Japan and Italy, small manufacturers and retailers alike are being squeezed out by mergers and acquisitions among larger companies.[16]

Global Sourcing in the Apparel
Commodity Chain: The Asian Pattern

The world textile and apparel industry has undergone several migrations of production since the 1950s and they all involve Asia. The first migration of the industry took place from North America and Western Europe to Japan in the 1950s and early 1960s, when Western textile and clothing production was displaced by a sharp rise in imports from Japan. The second supply shift was from Japan to the "Big Three" Asian apparel producers—Hong Kong, Taiwan, and South Korea—which permitted the latter group to dominate global textile and clothing exports in the 1970s and 1980s. During the past ten to fifteen years, there has been a third migration of production—this time from the Asian Big Three to a number of other developing economies. In the 1980s, the principal shift was to mainland China, but it also encompassed several Southeast Asian nations and Sri Lanka. In the 1990s, the proliferation of new suppliers included South Asian and Latin American apparel exporters, with new entrants like Vietnam waiting in the wings. This most recent shift is seen in sharp relief in Table 3.3, which looks at apparel imports to the United States. Between 1987 and 1996, the U.S. market share of Northeast Asian apparel suppliers fell dramatically from 56 to 30 percent. Southeast Asian and South Asian nations improved their position from 17 to 24 percent of the U.S.

Table 3.3   Trends in U.S. Apparel Imports by Region and Country (in millions of U.S. dollars)

Country Source	1987 Values		1996 Values	
Northeast Asia				
Hong Kong	3,370		3,861	
China	1,790		3,769	
Taiwan	2,702		1,974	
South Korea	2,245		1,381	
Total	10,107	56%	10,985	30%
Southeat Asia				
Philippines	578		1,503	
Indonesia	373		1,326	
Thailand	280		1,049	
Malaysia	298		647	
Singapore	472		326	
Total	2,001	11%	4,851	13%
South Asia				
India	416		1,187	
Bangladesh	276		1,125	
Sri Lanka	337		1,007	
Pakistan	133		561	
Total	1,162	6%	3,880	11%
Central America & the Caribbean				
Dominican Republic	376		1,753	
Honduras	n/a		1,220	
Guatemala	n/a		796	
El Salvador	n/a		721	
Costa Rica	182		704	
Jamaica	182		505	
Other CBI nations	309		310	
Total	1,049	6%	6,009	17%
Mexico	365	2%	3,560	10%
All other countries	3,352	19%	7,104	20%
Total apparel	18,036	100%	36,389	100%

Source: Major Shippers Report, Office of Textiles and Apparel, U.S. Department of Commerce (Washington, D.C,:GPO, 1987 and 1986).

market, but the big gainers were the Caribbean Basin nations and Mexico, whose share of the U.S. market more than tripled from 8 to 27 percent. While the trans-Pacific apparel trade still accounts for over one-half (54 percent) of the U.S. market, the linkages within North America are becoming increasingly significant.

Basic economic and political factors help to explain this shift. Neoclassical economics has the simplest prediction: The most labor-intensive segments of the apparel commodity chain should be located in countries with the lowest wages. This theory is supported by the sequential shifts of textile and apparel production from the United States and Western Europe to Japan, the Asian Big Three, and China, since the entrants into each new tier of the production hierarchy had significantly lower wage rates than their predecessors. The neoclassical cheap labor argument does not hold up as well, however, when we get to the proliferation of new Asian and Caribbean suppliers, whose U.S. market share expanded even though their wage rates are often considerably higher than China's. Furthermore, although the share of U.S. apparel exports represented by Hong Kong, South Korea, and Taiwan has declined during the past decade, these NIEs still ranked among Asia's top apparel exporters to the United States in 1996, despite having the highest apparel labor costs in the region (excluding Japan).

The statist perspective, which argues that government policies will play a major role in shaping the location of apparel export activities, helps to explain these discrepancies. A critical factor in the sharp decline of Taiwan's and South Korea's apparel exports in the late 1980s was not only their rising wage rates, but the sharp appreciation of their local currencies vis-à-vis the U.S. dollar after the Plaza Agreement was signed in 1985. Between 1985 and 1987, the Japanese yen was revalued by close to 40 percent, the New Taiwan dollar by 28 percent, and from 1986 to 1988 the Korean won appreciated by 17 percent.

The most important policies to shape U.S. apparel imports from Asia, the Caribbean, and elsewhere, however, are quotas and preferential tariffs. Quotas on apparel and textiles items continue to be regulated by the Multifiber Arrangement (MFA) of the early 1970s. The MFA has been used by the United States, Canada, and various European nations to impose quantitative limits on imports in a wide variety of product categories. Although the clear intent of these policies was to protect developed-country firms from a flood of low-cost imports that threatened to disrupt major domestic industries, the result was exactly the opposite; protectionism heightened the competitive capabilities of developing-country manufacturers, who learned to make sophisticated products that were more profitable than simple ones. Protectionism by core countries also diversified the scope of foreign competition, as an ever widening circle of exporters was needed to meet booming North American and European demand. In recent years, the creation of the EU and the NAFTA has led to the imposition of preferential tariffs within regional markets, which has generated a major shift in the global sourcing dynamics of these regional markets.

Specification Contracting in East Asia

The East Asian NIEs are generally taken as the archetype for industrial upgrading among developing countries. They made a rapid transition from the initial assembly phase of export growth, typically utilizing export processing zones located near major ports, to a more generalized system of incentives that applied to all export-oriented factories in their economies. The next stage for Taiwan, South Korea, Hong Kong, and Singapore was original equipment manufacturing (OEM), also known as specification contracting. It has the following features: the supplying firm makes a product according to the design specified by the buyer; the product is sold under the buyer's brand name; the supplier and buyer are separate firms; and the supplier lacks control over distribution. East Asian firms became full-range "package suppliers" for foreign buyers and thereby forged an innovative entrepreneurial capability that involved the coordination of complex production, trade, and financial networks.[17]

The OEM export role has many advantages. It enhances the ability of local entrepreneurs to learn the preferences of foreign buyers, including prevailing international standards for the price, quality, and delivery of export merchandise. It also generates substantial backward linkages in the domestic economy because OEM contractors are expected to develop reliable sources of supply for many inputs. Moreover, expertise in OEM production increases over time, and it contributes to the development of local conventions (norms and practices) that are the glue in agglomeration economies. Particular places such as the East Asian NIEs thus retain an enduring competitive edge in export-oriented development. However, East Asian producers confront intense competition from lower-cost exporters in various parts of the Third World, and the price of their exports to Western nations has been further elevated by sharp currency appreciations during the past decade. Under these circumstances, it is advantageous to establish forward linkages to developed-country markets, where the biggest profits are made in buyer-driven commodity chains. Therefore, a number of firms in the East Asian NIEs that pioneered OEM are now pushing beyond it to the original brand name manufacturing (OBM) role by integrating their manufacturing expertise with the design and sale of their own branded merchandise.

South Korea is the most advanced of the East Asian NIEs in OBM production, with Korean brands of automobiles (Hyundai), electronic devices, and household appliances (Samsung and Goldstar), among other items, being sold in North America, Europe, and ,apan. Taiwanese companies have pursued OBM in computers, bicycles, sporting equipment, and shoes, but not in apparel. Hong Kong has only been successful in apparel OBM. There have been significant reversals, however. Taiwan's Mitac Corporation, the main competitor to Acer in Taiwan's personal computer market, reduced its own name brand computers from 70 percent of its total sales in 1990 to 40 percent in 1993,[18] and Daewoo, Korea's third largest appliance and consumer-electronics company (after Samsung and Goldstar), moved from years of brand-building back to the OEM game.

Why has the OEM role proved so resilient? To a large degree, the answer lies with core competencies and networks. C. S. Ho, the president of Mitac, says that his firm was more profitable when it concentrated on its core competencies: "We asked ourselves: What functions are we best at? Our strengths are in R&D, design and manufacturing. We are now focusing on designing and supplying products and key components for major OEM customers, whose brands are better-known but which have withdrawn from fully integrated manufacture."[19] S. H. Bae, chairman and chief executive officer of Daewoo, says, "Our strength is in manufacturing. If our margins are adequate, we don't mind making products for others."[20] Bae expects a shakeout in appliances and consumer electronics by the year 2000, and he concludes that companies will have to become dominant producers in core products.

To keep OEM profitable under conditions of intense wage competition among developing countries and protectionism in western markets, East Asian NIE companies have set up elaborate offshore production networks. Daewoo, for example, has sixteen offshore plants in China, Vietnam, Central Asia, Europe, and Mexico. It is building more, even as it upgrades its factories in Korea. Through worker training programs, Bae claims that "[Daewoo's] Vietnam plant is almost as efficient as local ones."[21] Thus, the key to profitability in OEM production for East Asian NIEs seems to be manufacturing expertise—including substantial spending in research and development—and learning how to flexibly manage overseas production networks. This can be seen in Hong Kong's apparel manufacturers, Taiwan's footwear companies, and Singapore's computer firms. Network flexibility thus has become one of the major organizational assets utilized by the NIEs in their internationalization strategies.

One of the most important mechanisms facilitating the shift to higher-value-added activities for mature export industries like apparel in East Asia is the process of "triangle manufacturing."[22] The essence of triangle manufacturing, which was initiated by the East Asian NIEs in the 1970s and 1980s, is that U.S. or other overseas buyers place their orders with the NIE manufacturers they have sourced from in the past, who in turn shift some or all of the requested production to affiliated offshore factories in low-wage countries (e.g., China, Indonesia, or Guatemala). These offshore factories can be wholly owned subsidiaries of the NIE manufacturers, joint-venture partners, or simply independent overseas contractors. The triangle is completed when the finished goods are shipped directly to the overseas buyer under the U.S. import quotas issued to the exporting nation. Triangle manufacturing thus changes the status of NIE manufacturers from established suppliers for U.S. retailers and designers to "middlemen" in buyer-driven commodity chains that can include as many as fifty to sixty exporting countries.

The Shift of Buyer-Driven Commodity Chains Out of the East Asian NIEs

In each of the East Asian NIEs, a combination of domestic supply side constraints—labor shortages, high wages, and high land prices—and external pressures—currency revaluation, tariffs, and quotas—led to the internationalization of the textile and apparel complex by the late 1980s and early 1990s. Typically, the internationalization of production was sparked first by quotas, but the process was greatly accelerated as supply-side factors became adverse. Quotas determined *when* the outward shift of production began, while preferential access to overseas markets and social networks determined *where* the firms from the East Asian NIEs went. In this international division of labor, labor-intensive activities are relocated and skill-intensive activities are retained. In the apparel sector, the activities associated with OEM production that tended to remain in the NIEs were jobs such as product design, sample making, quality control, packing, warehousing, transportation, quota transactions, and local financing through letters of credit. These provided relatively high gross margins or profits.

The internationalization of Hong Kong's firms was triggered by textile import restrictions imposed by the United Kingdom in 1964, which led Hong Kong manufacturers in the late 1960s to shift production to Singapore, Taiwan, and Macao. The Chinese population in these three countries had cultural and linguistic affinities with Hong Kong investors. In addition, Macao benefitted from its proximity to Hong Kong, while Singapore qualified for Commonwealth preferences for imports into the United Kingdom. In the early 1970s, Hong Kong apparel firms targeted Malaysia, the Philippines, and Mauritius. This second round of outward investments again was prompted by quota restrictions, coupled with specific host-country inducements. For example, Mauritius established an export processing zone in an effort to lure Hong Kong investors, particularly knitwear manufacturers who directed their exports to European markets that offered preferential access in the form of low tariffs.

The greatest spur to the internationalization of Hong Kong's textile and apparel companies was the opening of the Chinese economy in 1978. At first, production was subcontracted to state-owned factories, but eventually an elaborate outward-processing arrangement with China was set up that relied on a broad assortment of manufacturing, financial, and commercial joint ventures. The relocation of industry to the Chinese mainland led to a hollowing out of Hong Kong's manufacturing sector during the late 1980s and early 1990s. In 1991, 47,000 factories were employing 680,000 workers in Hong Kong, a figure 25 percent below the peak of 907,000 manufacturing jobs recorded in 1980.[23] The decline was particularly severe in textiles and apparel. Employment in the Hong Kong textile industry fell from 67,000 in 1984 to 36,000 in 1994—a drop of 47 percent. Meanwhile, Hong Kong's clothing jobs plummeted from 300,000 in 1984 to 137,000 in 1994—a decrease of 56 percent.[24]

While manufacturing declined, trading activities in Hong Kong grew to encompass approximately 70,000 firms and 370,000 jobs in 1991, a fivefold increase in the number of firms and a fourfold increase in the number of workers in the trading sector compared to 1978.[25] Thus, to a large extent, trading companies have replaced export-oriented factories as the key economic agent in Hong Kong's internationalization. In 1995, Hong Kong entrepreneurs operated more than 20,000 factories employing an estimated four and a half to five million workers in the Pearl River Delta alone in the neighboring Chinese province of Guangdong.[26] Considering that total employment in Hong Kong industry had shrunk to 386,000 in 1995 (15.3 percent of the Hong Kong workforce), Hong Kong manufacturers increased their domestic labor force well over ten times through their outward processing arrangement with China.[27]

As in Hong Kong, the internationalization of South Korea's and Taiwan's apparel producers began as a response to quota restrictions. Korean garment firms lacking sufficient export quotas initially set up production in quota-free locations like Saipan, a U.S. territory in the Mariana Islands. More recent waves of internationalization have been motivated by the domestic constraints of rising wages and worker shortages. The low-wage regions that have attracted the greatest number of South Korean companies are Latin America, Southeast Asia, and South Asia. The preference of Korean firms for investment in Latin America (Guatemala, Honduras, the Dominican Republic, etc.) is stimulated by its proximity to the U.S. market and easy quota access. The pull of Asian nations such as Indonesia, Sri Lanka, and Bangladesh comes mainly from their wage rates, which are among the lowest in the world. When Taiwanese firms moved offshore in the early 1980s, they also confronted binding quotas. While Taiwan's wages in the late 1970s and early 1980s were still relatively low, quota rents were high. Firms had to buy quotas (whose value in secondary markets fluctuated widely) in order to be able to expand exports, thereby causing a decrease in profitability for firms without sufficient quotas.[28] This led to a growing emphasis on nonquota markets by Taiwan's textile and apparel exporters. Quota markets, which include the United States, the European Community, and Canada, accounted for over 50 percent of Taiwan's textile and apparel exports in the mid-1980s, but this ratio declined to 43 percent in 1988 and fell further to 35 percent in 1991. The United States, which had been Taiwan's largest export market for years, claimed one-quarter of Taiwan's textile and apparel exports in 1991, the European Community 8 percent, and Canada just 2 percent. The main nonquota markets, which absorbed nearly two-thirds of Taiwan's textile and apparel exports in the early 1990s, are Hong Kong, with 30 percent, Japan, with 6 percent, and Singapore, with 3 percent.[29] Hong Kong, now Taiwan's leading export market, is mainly a conduit for shipping yarns, fabrics, and clothing to China for further processing and re-export.

Two trends—the shift from OEM to OBM and the growing importance of nonquota markets for the NIEs—point to an important fact: production and trade networks in the apparel commodity chain are becoming increasingly concentrated in Asia. There has been a sharp decline in Asian clothing exports to North America (from 27 percent of the global total in 1984 to 17 percent in 1995), a leveling off in Asian apparel exports to Western Europe (just under 12 percent of global trade), and a striking increase in intra-Asian trade in apparel (from 4 percent in 1980 to 13 percent in 1995). This rise in intra-Asian trade is even stronger in textiles, where it increases from 13 percent of the world total in 1980 to 28 percent in 1995 (see Table 3.4).

Asia's growing prominence as a market for its own textile and apparel output, and the continuing migration of production to low-cost supply sites around the world, suggest a general movement may be underway toward a regionalization of the apparel commodity chain within Asia, North America, and Europe. The emerging supply relationships that are being fashioned with nearby low-cost producers in each area (South Asia and Vietnam in Asia, Central America and the Caribbean vis-à-vis North America, and North Africa and Eastern Europe for the EU) are likely to strengthen intraregional trade and production networks in the apparel commodity chain, thereby giving rise to new forms of economic coordination and competition among local as well as global firms.

Table 3.4 Regional Trade Patterns in World Exports of Textiles

Textiles	1980	1984	1987	1990	1993	1995
World (US $ billions)	55.6	53.9	80.2	104.8	115.4	152.6
World (percentages)	100.0	100.0	100.0	100.0	100.0	100.0
Intra-Western Europe	40.1	34.9	40.0	41.4	32.8	20.9
Intra Asia	13.1	17.4	18.2	20.6	26.6	28.4
Asia to Western Europe	1.6	4.6	5.9	5.6	5.8	5.5
Western Europe to Central/ Eastern Europe/Baltic States/CIS*	n/a	n/a	n/a	2.3	3.1	4.0
Asia to North America	2.9	5.4	4.9	3.6	4.3	3.7
Asia to Middle East	n/a	n/a	n/a	2.2	3.0	2.9
Western Europe to Asia	1.6	2.0	2.0	3.0	2.6	2.9
Western Europe to North America	1.6	2.9	2.9	2.4	2.3	1.9
Other	39.1	26.1	26.1	18.9	19.5	19.8

Source: GATT, *International Trade,* and WTO, *Annual Report,* various years.

China's Central Role in East Asia's Buyer-Driven Commodity Chain

The growth of China as an export power is one of the major reasons for the greater centrality of Asia within a wide range of buyer-driven commodity chains. Mainland China has now become the center of gravity for Asia's exports of an extensive array of consumer goods. Table 3.5 provides a list of U.S. import products for which China was the major source in 1995. These include footwear and apparel, toys and dolls, sporting goods and luggage, housewares and handtools—all soft goods and hard goods that rely on the retailer-dominated sourcing networks we have referred to as buyer-driven commodity chains. Thus, China has developed a considerable stock of social capital in learning how to exploit the networks on which these exports are based. For most products on this list, China provides between one-third and two-thirds of total U.S. imports. When we look at China's nearest competitors in these product categories, we see three kinds of rivals: developed countries that supply top quality, high-priced "fashion" merchandise (such as Japan, Italy, and the United Kingdom); the relatively high-cost East Asian NIEs that are exiting the finished goods segment of these commodity chains (Taiwan, Korea, and Hong Kong); and low-priced suppliers that are increasing their U.S. market share in these industries (such as Mexico and the Southeast Asian nations).

There are several important qualifications that need to be made to this picture of Chinese dominance. First, while Japan and the East Asian

Table 3.5   Products in which China Is the Leading Suplier of U.S. Imports,1995

Product	Total Value of U.S. Imports in 1995 (in millions of US $)	Percentage of Total U.S. Imports in Product Catagory							
		#1 Supplier	%	#2 Supplier	%	#3 Supplier	%		
Footwear	12,095	China	48.1	Brazil	9.3	Italy	8.4		
Toys	4,526	China	72.6	Mexico	4.7	Taiwan	3.0		
Electrical household appliances	4,074	China	22.1	Mexico	14.8	Korea	11.5		
Luggage and handbags	3,332	China	48.2	Italy	7.7	Taiwan	7.7		
Sporting goods	2,956	China	26.7	Taiwan	23.2	Canada	8.9		
Lamps	2,198	China	49.8	Taiwan	15.5	Mexico	9.0		
Microphones/loudspeakers	2,001	China	19.1	Japan	17.1	Mexico	14.5		
Sweaters	1,750	China	36.6	Hong Kong	27.5	Italy	5.9		
Ceramic household articles	1,658	China	31.6	Japan	9.6	U.K.	8.6		
Laether apparel and accessories	1,199	China	56.5	Korea	9.3	India	5.9		
Dolls	1,167	China	74.4	Malaysia	6.8	Indonesia	4.8		
Brooms and brushes	610	China	32.8	Taiwan	13.1	Korea	10.3		
Costume jewelry	493	China	31.3	Koea	26.5	Taiwan	11.1		
Portable electrical handtools	481	China	20.7	Japan	19.6	Mexico	11.4		
Clocks	430	China	34.9	Taiwan	13.9	Japan	13.2		
Children's vehicles	266	China	50.1	Taiwan	17.7	Italy	8.5		
Umbrellas	198	China	64.8	Taiwan	16.2	Thailand	5.7		

Source: Compiled from official statistics of the U.S. Department of Commerce, 1995

NIEs have lost international competitiveness in the downstream, or finished goods, segments of buyer-driven commodity chains, they frequently retain a strong position in the midstream and upstream segments that supply intermediate and capital goods. Japan, for example, continues to be the major supplier of textile and apparel machinery (spinning, weaving, and sewing) throughout Asia, using the trading houses, or *sogo shosha*, as conduits. In addition, several of the East Asian NIEs are making the transition from finished apparel exports to textile and fiber supply for their triangle manufacturing partners in China, Southeast Asia, and South Asia. Taiwan is a classic example of this process. Between 1985 and 1995 Taiwan's exports of clothing declined, from 56 percent of its textile and apparel total to 20 percent, while the share represented by intermediate goods (textile fibers, yarn, and fabrics) rose from 44 to 80 percent.[30] The trend in South Korea is the same as in Taiwan; textiles have displaced apparel as the export leader in the apparel commodity chain.[31]

Second, many of the export factories in China are actually owned, managed, or controlled by firms in the East Asian NIEs, especially Hong Kong and Taiwan. This can be clearly seen in the case of China's leading export sector, footwear. In the late 1980s, as currency appreciations and supply side constraints began to hinder the competitiveness of the world's two leading footwear exporters, South Korea and Taiwan, Taiwanese shoe factories began to shift to Thailand, the Philippines, Indonesia, and especially mainland China. In the city of Dongguan in the Pearl River Delta in southern China, the number of Taiwanese shoe companies mushroomed from the first plant, which was built in 1987, to more than 400 shoe factories by 1990.[32] With Chinese wages at one-tenth the Taiwanese level and labor productivity in China about 50 percent of that in Taiwan, overall labor costs in China were five times lower than in Taiwan.

Taiwanese investors took advantage of this favorable economic situation by re-establishing their production networks in southern China in two main ways: shipping major materials and components across the straits from Taiwan to the mainland and building "local" supplier networks with other Taiwanese firms that also moved to southern China. While the mother company in Taiwan controlled product development and design, marketing, sales, and high-value-added production, the manufacturing operations in China focused on routine, low-value-added activities. Local Chinese managers, foremen, and college graduates are now acquiring the technological and organizational skills needed to move into a controlling position in the footwear industry in the near future, but to date much of China's export success has served as a "Second Spring" for Taiwanese businesses.

Third, the Chinese government is following the lead of Japan and the East Asian NIEs in actively promoting industrial upgrading to more technology-intensive sectors. Land prices and rents in China's major cities rival those in Hong Kong and the other East Asian capitals, wage rates have soared in southern China and the coastal regions, and the government is pursuing policies that would require traditional industries like textiles and apparel to relocate to lower-wage areas in China. This is creating opportunities for the newest entrants in Asia's production hierarchy—Vietnam, Laos, and Cambodia. The Asian industrial model is one in which success in buyer-driven commodity chains pushes toward a deepening of the regional division of labor by adding new layers of producers, while the previous exporters either move upstream or make the transition to more technology-intensive sectors.

Apparel Sourcing in the Americas and Europe

Production Sharing in Mexico and the Caribbean Basin

Production sharing in Latin America is centered in Mexico and the Caribbean Basin because of this area's low wages and proximity to the U.S. market, where over 90 percent of their exports are sold. Virtually all of the production in the region is of a very low-value-added nature, which is a direct result of U.S. policy. Under U.S. tariff schedule provision HTS 9802.00.80 (formerly clause 807), enterprises engaged in production sharing have an incentive to minimize locally purchased inputs because only U.S.-made components are exempt from import duties when the finished product is shipped back to the United States. This constitutes a major impediment to increasing the integration between the activities in the export production zones and the local economy, and it limits the usefulness of production sharing as a stepping stone to higher stages of industrialization.

Mexico's *maquiladora* industry, which was established in 1965, is made up of assembly plants known as *maquilas* that use mainly U.S. components to make goods for export to the U.S. market. In 1993, the maquiladora industry generated US $ 22 billion in exports and employed 540,000 Mexicans. By 1996, after the enactment of the NAFTA on January 1, 1994, and a 50 percent devaluation of the peso in December 1994–January 1995, employment in the maquiladora sector had grown by 50 percent to 811,000, while exports rose by 54 percent to $34 billion.33

Caribbean Basin venues are also popular for export-oriented assembly in Latin America. By the early 1990s, export production zones (EPZs) had become a leading source of exports and manufacturing employment in various Caribbean nations. The Dominican Republic is a prime example. There are 476 companies employing 176,000 workers in the country's thirty-one free trade zones; three-quarters of the firms are involved in textiles and apparel.[34] In terms of employment, the Dominican Republic is the fourth largest EPZ economy in the world (the fifth if China's Special Economic Zones are included). The Dominican Republic is especially dependent on EPZs, whose share of official manufacturing employment on the island increased from 23 percent in 1981 to 56 percent in 1989; by this latter year, EPZs also generated over 20 percent of the Dominican Republic's total foreign exchange earnings.[35] U.S. investors account for more than half (54 percent) of the companies operating in the zones, followed by firms from the Dominican Republic itself (22 percent), South Korea (11 percent), and Taiwan (3 percent).[36]

While EPZs in Mexico and the Caribbean have been associated with undeniable gains in employment and foreign exchange earnings, these benefits are offset by a picture of immiserizing employment growth which is contingent on falling real wages and a decline in local purchasing power. In Mexico the real minimum wage in 1989 was less than one-half (47 percent) of its 1980 level, and in El Salvador workers in 1989 earned just 36 percent of what they did at the beginning of the decade.[37] These trends exacerbate the polarization between the rich and the poor in Latin America, where close to 50 percent of the population lives in poverty, with 25 percent considered destitute.

The rivalry among neighboring EPZs to offer transnationals the lowest wages fosters a perverse strategy of "competitive devaluation," whereby currency depreciations are seen as a means to increase international competitiveness. Export growth in the Dominican Republic's EPZs skyrocketed after a very sharp depreciation of its currency against the dollar in 1985; similarly, Mexico's export expansion was facilitated by recurrent devaluations of the Mexican peso, most recently in 1994–1995. Devaluations heighten already substantial wage differences in the region. Hourly compensation rates for apparel workers in the early 1990s were US $ 1.08 in Mexico, US $ 0.88 in Costa Rica, US $ 0.64 in the Dominican Republic, and US $ 0.48 in Honduras, compared to US $ 8.13 in the United States.[38] Although it may make sense for a single country to devalue its currency in order to attract users of unskilled labor to their production sites, the advantages of this strategy quickly evaporate when other nations simultaneously engage in wage-depressing devaluations, which lower local standards of living while doing nothing to improve productivity.

Despite its current recession, the lure of Mexico's nearly 100 million consumers, half of whom are under the age of twenty, has proved irresistible for U.S. retailers. Spurred by NAFTA, the Americanization of

Mexican retailing is in full swing. Sears Roebuck, for years the largest department store chain in Mexico, is being joined by other prominent U.S. department stores, such as J. C. Penney, Dillards, and Saks Fifth Avenue. More significant is the incursion of giant U.S. discount chains, which augment retail consolidation by establishing joint ventures with Mexican partners; Wal-Mart, the largest retailer in the United States, and Cifra, Mexico's biggest retailing organization, entered into a fifty-fifty partnership.[39] Strategic alliances have also been formed between Kmart and Liverpool, and Price Club and Commercial Mexicana.

Although the ambitious expansion plans of the U.S. retailers may be put on hold or slowed somewhat because of Mexico's current slump, two longer-term implications of the U.S. retail invasion are likely to be quite significant. First, Mexico's informal distribution outlets, made up primarily of street markets *(tianguis)*, have been the dominant retail channel for many consumer items, including about one-third of all apparel sales. Giant U.S. discount chains, like Wal-Mart or Price Club, are likely to erode sales first and foremost in the informal sector, with negative consequences for employment and income among these small vendors. Second, the relocation of U.S. retailers to Mexico may increase the incentive to establish local supplier networks for buyer-driven commodity chains. By 1994, the Mexican government had already established vendor certification schemes that issued quality ratings and made recommendations for improvement to small and medium-sized manufacturers that hoped to supply large foreign retailers in Mexico and eventually the United States.

Outward Processing Trade in Europe

Outward processing trade (OPT) in the European clothing sector is the practice by which companies export fabrics or parts of garments to be further processed in a third country and then re-import them as finished garments in an EU country.[40] OPT is analogous to the U.S. production sharing system (sometimes known as 807 or 9802 trade) and similar to outward processing arrangements that cover a portion of Hong Kong's trade regime in apparel with mainland China. OPT, which has been regulated within the EU since 1982, is widely recognized as accelerating the process of delocalization, or the shift of apparel production to low-wage countries. Trade policy discourages textile firms from delocalization, however. If non-EU fabrics are used in OPT, they are penalized by a tariff of 14 percent levied on their re-imports. The level of tariff duties offsets the advantage of lower production costs.

The main lure of OPT is to reduce labor costs, which account for up to 60 percent of production costs in the clothing industry. Given the EU's relatively high cost of labor, the share of the market that can be supplied by EU-made products is reportedly quite small; only 10 percent of men's shirts, 15 percent of men's suits, 25 percent of women's blouses, and 30 percent of bras can be made at a profit in the EU.[41] "Buy European" slogans, although widely advertised, are not representative of the general policies of retailers, who are rapidly increasing their offshore sourcing.

In 1995, OPT accounted for 14 percent of total EU clothing imports. This is considerably less than the 80 to 90 percent of U.S. imports from Mexico and the Caribbean Basin Initiative (CBI) countries that qualifies as production sharing or 9802 trade. However, the extent of OPT trade is much more significant than this overall figure of 14 percent might indicate. More than 80 percent of OPT imports in clothing are concentrated in only four member states of the EU: Germany, Italy, France, and the United Kingdom. The share of OPT in total clothing imports is highest in Germany, with 21 percent, followed by Italy with 17 percent, France with 7 percent, and the United Kingdom with 5 percent.[42] By the year 2000, it is predicted that imports—including OPT garments and imported apparel secured by large volume retailers—will account for 70 percent of EU apparel consumption.[43]

For France, it is estimated that 80 percent of direct imports from North Africa, Southern Europe, and Eastern Europe qualify as forms of international subcontracting, even if locally produced fabric or fabric made in other non-EU countries is used. In the case of Germany, more than 90 percent of textile and clothing trade with Central and Eastern Europe also falls in the subcontracting category.[44] Triangular trade is frequently employed in this type of international subcontracting. Thus, a German client may supply fabrics sourced in India for garments to be made up in Bangladesh, or Malaysian fabrics may be made up in Indonesia. Thus, as in the case of U.S. production sharing, European manufacturers are moving production offshore to neighboring countries in North Africa, Eastern and Central Europe, or countries in the former Soviet Union. This facilitates the flexibility of European retailers and manufacturers, but it also contributes to an integrated form of domestic production in the supplying nations. Since integrated apparel manufacturers are still stronger in Europe than in the United States, OPT is of greater importance for the EU than are direct imports from Asian producers.

Comparing North American and European Regional Divisions of Labor in Apparel Sourcing

The apparel sourcing structures for the United States and the EU are compared in Figures 3.2 and 3.3. They reveal substantial differences not only in the geographical locations of their sourcing activities, but also in the way each region's sourcing networks are organized. In 1995, apparel imports totaled US $ 39.7 billion for the United States and US $ 25.6 billion for the twelve member states of the European Union (EU12). The five rings in Figure 3.2 correspond to different levels of importance by the supplying nations; each of those in the central circle account for 10 percent or more of the total value of clothing imports in 1995, while those in the outer ring each make up 1.0–1.9 percent of total imports. In other

Figure 3.2   The Regional Structure of U.S. Clothing Imports, 1995

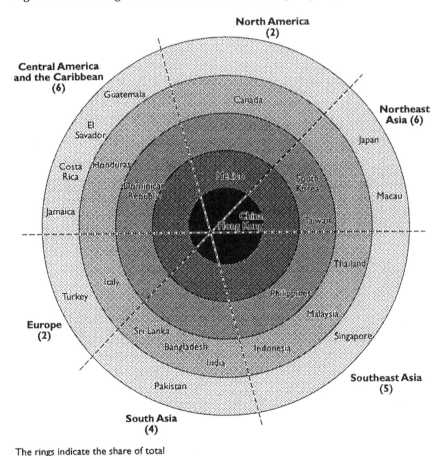

The rings indicate the share of total
U.S. imports in U.S. dollars by partner country

| ■ > 10% | ▦ 4.0% - 5.9% | ▨ 1.0% - 1.9% |
| ▦ 6.0% - 9.9% | ▨ 2.0% - 3.9% | Total value = US$39.7 billion |

words, as we move from the inner rings to the outer ones, the relative importance of the clothing suppliers decreases.

The two key apparel suppliers for the United States are China and Hong Kong, followed by only Mexico in the second ring (6.0–9.9 percent of apparel imports). Of the twenty-five countries that account for at least 1 percent of U.S. clothing imports, fifteen are located in Asia: six in Northeast Asia, five in Southeast Asia, and four in South Asia (Figure 3.2).

Figure 3.3   The Regional Structure of E.U. Clothing Imports, 1995

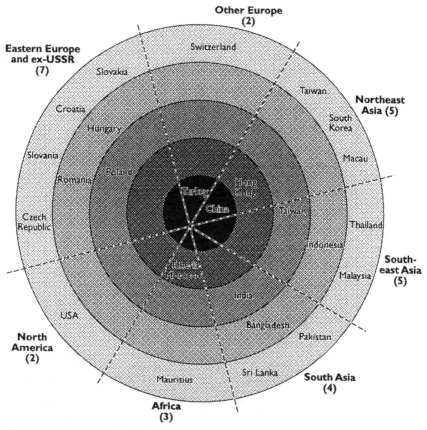

The rings indicate the share of total
EU imports in ECU by partner country

■ > 10%   ▦ 4.0% - 5.9%   ▢ 1.0% - 1.9%

▩ 6.0% - 9.9%   ▦ 2.0% - 3.9%   Total value = ECU 33.5 billion, 1 US$ = 0.765 ECU

Although the Northeast Asian economies are still the most significant suppliers from their region in aggregate terms, we know from Table 3.4 that the Northeast Asian economies are moving toward the outer rings, that is, they are becoming less important, while the South Asian suppliers are becoming more central. The other major cluster of U.S. apparel suppliers are located in North America (two), and the Caribbean and Central America (six nations). Thus, U.S. apparel supply networks have two primary axes: Asia and greater North America, including the Caribbean Basin.

The EU has a different apparel sourcing mix. It has two primary Asian suppliers—China in the first ring and Hong Kong in the second—and three primary Mediterranean suppliers—Turkey in the first ring, and Morocco and Tunisia in the second. Of the twenty-five countries that account for at least 1 percent of EU12 clothing imports in 1995, twelve are from Asia, nine from Europe, three from Africa, and one from North America (Figure 3.3). The seven supplying nations located in Eastern Europe and the former Soviet Union, plus nearby Turkey, are analogous to the cluster of U.S. apparel suppliers located in the Caribbean Basin and Mexico; they are geographically proximate, relatively low-wage countries that enjoy a preferential tariff in their exports to the EU and the United States because of their membership in regional customs unions.

There is a deeper implication of the regional sourcing patterns highlighted by Figures 3.2 and 3.3. They represent two very different types of sourcing networks within the U.S. and EU buyer-driven commodity chains. The apparel imports that are coming into the United States and the EU via the Asian axis are typically supplied by the "specification contracting" or OEM mode, whereby the sourcing agents are retailers and branded marketers that place orders with East Asian manufacturers, who either fill the orders themselves or shift them to lower-wage nations in the region via a process of triangle manufacturing. In contrast, the apparel imports that come into the United States via Mexico and the Caribbean or into the EU via Eastern Europe and the Mediterranean suppliers follow a distinct sourcing channel, known in the United States as "production sharing" and in Europe as "outward processing trade."

Conclusions

The answer to the question "Who drives global industries?" depends on what kind of industry we are considering. The power of large transnational manufacturers in a range of capital- and technology-intensive industries is well known, and thus their controlling position in producer-driven commodity chains is relatively easy to understand. These transnational corporations were the key force that countries in Latin America, Eastern Europe, and India had to deal with when they were pursuing their strategies of import-substitution industrialization from the 1950s until the 1980s. However, the shift to export-oriented industrialization strategies in the developing world ushered in by the East Asian NIEs in the 1960s brought to the forefront the importance of big buyers based in the developed-country markets of North America and Europe. These large retailers and designers have actually been the key agents in buyer-driven commodity chains in two regards: they helped fuel globalization by their increasingly prominent role as importers to their home markets, and they orchestrated shifts in overseas production networks through the policies implemented by their overseas buying offices. There has been a dramatic consolidation of the retailer segment of buyer-driven commodity chains in the United States and a growth in the strength of retailers versus apparel manufacturers in the EU and Japan as well. While retailing and marketing is becoming more concentrated, manufacturing is splintering. To a certain degree, this trend is propelled by the information revolution that is permitting retailers to have far better day-to-day market information about consumer purchasing decisions. This allows the retailers to demand more from their suppliers in terms of inventory management, quick response, more frequent deliveries, and so on. As retailers develop their own private label collections, they also change the competitive dynamics of the textile and apparel supply chain, since they become competitors, rather than customers, of traditional apparel manufacturers and designers. Finally, retailers are pushing globalization in a direct way both as importers and by demanding lower prices from manufacturers, which in turn forces them to go overseas. Because they themselves do not have production experience, however, the retailers in buyer-driven chains are dependent upon the suppliers in their global sourcing networks. In Asia, a number of these manufacturers are integrating forward from specification contracting to developing and selling their own brands. In North America, U.S. textile companies are forming production clusters with local apparel firms in Mexico to assure themselves of a customer base. Thus, growing concentration at the retail end of the apparel commodity chain is generating networks of collaborators as well as competitors in the upstream segments of the chain.

How does the control structure of commodity chains affect industrial upgrading in the producing regions for these chains? First, our comparison of apparel imports to the United States and the EU reveals distinct regional patterns of sourcing. While both the United States and the EU source heavily out of Asia, they each have nearby sourcing bases as well: Mexico, Central America, and the Caribbean for the United States, and

Eastern and Central Europe and North Africa for the EU. More importantly, these different regional supply bases for apparel are organized in terms of different kinds of networks. The Asian sourcing is done on the basis of direct imports and specification contracting, while both the Caribbean Basin and Mediterranean Basin sourcing patterns utilize forms of international subcontracting, whereby U.S. and EU textiles are sent to nearby low-wage countries for assembly into garments. The controlling agents in these two networks are different; they are retailers and designers in the Asian trade, and textile and apparel manufacturers for outward processing trade. The possibilities for integrated local industrial development are greater in the specification contracting pattern where Asian manufacturers have developed an important form of social capital in the guise of the multifaceted and dense networks utilized to offer "full-package" supply. In the outward processing or production sharing pattern, the production networks are much thinner in the supplying countries. One of the most interesting responses to emerge is Mexico's attempt to emulate the full-package supply of the East Asian NIEs by constructing networks involving U.S. textile firms, Mexican apparel companies, and U.S. retailers.

U.S. companies have facilitated the upgrading of their Asian suppliers by making sophisticated products in the region that will be sold in the U.S. market. In the case of the footwear industry, a typical buyer-driven chain, Chinese leadership actually is premised on continuing control by Taiwanese manufacturers, who transferred low-value-added jobs to China but retained the key manufacturing and servicing functions in Taiwan. This same pattern prevails in apparel, with Hong Kong firms playing a leading role. Over time, we would expect China to internalize many of these responsibilities, but the buyer-driven industries already are shifting to lower-wage nations in South Asia and socialist economies like Vietnam in Southeast Asia. Thus, China's own development dynamic may follow the path of the East Asian NIEs, whereby it moves to more high-value-added producer-driven chains while simultaneously sustaining a competitive position in the midstream and upstream segments of buyer-driven chains.

Notes

1. See World Bank, *The East Asian Miracle* (New York: Oxford University Press, 1993).
2. Gary Gereffi, "The Organization of Buyer-Driven Global Commodity Chains: How U.S. Retailers Shape Overseas Production Networks," in *Commodity Chains and Global Capitalism*, ed. Gary Gereffi and Michael Korzeniewicz (Westport, Conn.: Praeger, 1994).

3. Richard Child Hill, "Comparing Transnational Production Systems: The Automobile Industry in the USA and Japan," *International Journal of Urban and Regional Research* 13, no. 3 (1989): 466.

4. Richard Florida and Martin Kenney, "Transplanted Organizations: The Transfer of Japanese Industrial Organization to the United States," *American Sociological Review* 56, no. 3 (1991): 381–398.

5. Richard F. Doner, *Driving a Bargain: Automobile Industrialization and Japanese Firms in Southeast Asia* (Berkeley, Calif.: University of California Press, 1991).

6. Jeffrey Henderson, *The Globalisation of High Technology Production: Society, Space and Semiconductors in the Restructuring of the Modern World* (New York: Routledge, 1989); and Michael Borrus, "Left for Dead: Asian Production Networks and the Revival of U.S. Electronics," in *The China Circle: Economics and Electronics in the PRC, Taiwan, and Hong Kong*, ed. B. Naughton (Washington, D.C.: Brookings Institution Press, 1997).

7. Kitty G. Dickerson, *Textiles and Apparel in the Global Economy*, 2nd ed. (Englewood Cliffs, N.J.: Prentice Hall, 1995), p. 452.

8. Trevor A. Finnie, "Profile of Levi Strauss," *Textile Outlook International* 67 (September 1996): 22.

9. This is the same group of companies I refer to as designers or branded marketers (e.g., Liz Claiborne, Donna Karan, Calvin Klein, Ralph Lauren).

10. These figures do not include the production-sharing activities of U.S. apparel firms in Mexico and in the Caribbean Basin, which also have been expanding very rapidly. As we will see below, Asian imports of finished apparel items and Mexican/Caribbean Basin imports based on production sharing rely on very different kinds of sourcing networks, which generate greater backward linkages and industrial development in Asia than in the Caribbean. See Jackie Jones, "Forces Behind Restructuring in U.S. Apparel Retailing and Its Effect on the U.S. Apparel Industry," *Industry, Trade, and Technology Review* (March 1995): 25–26.

11. Michael Scheffer, *The Changing Map of European Textiles: Production and Sourcing Strategies of Textile and Clothing Firms* (Brussels: L'Observatoire Européen du Textile et de l'Habillement, 1994), pp. 11–12.

12. Quick response (QR) systems use computers to speed the flow of goods, services, and information among segments of the apparel pipeline, linking apparel producers with textile suppliers and retailers. See Jones, "Forces Behind Restructuring," p. 26.

13. L'Observatoire Européen du Textile et de l'Habillement, *The EU Textile and Clothing Industry 1993/94* (Brussels: OETH, 1995), pp. 11–13.

14. Japan Textile News, "Japan's Distribution and Retail Industry," *JTN Quarterly* 2, no. 2 (1996): 14–30.

15. Dickerson, *Textiles and Apparel in the Global Economy*, p. 472.

16. Bennett Harrison, *Lean and Mean* (New York: Basic Books, 1994).

17. See Gary Gereffi, "Global Production Systems and Third World Development," in *Global Change, Regional Response: The New International Context of Development*, ed. B. Stallings (New York: Cambridge University Press, 1995); and Gary Gereffi, "Global Shifts, Regional Response: Can North

America Meet the Full-package Challenge?" *Bobbin* 39, no. 3 (November 1997): 16–31.

18. Michael Selwyn, "Radical Departures," *Asian Business* (August 1993), pp. 22–25.

19. Ibid., p. 24.

20. "What's in a Name? After Years of Building a Brand, Daewoo's Back to the OEM Game," *Asiaweek*, May 12, 1995, p. 56.

21. Ibid., p. 57.

22. Gereffi, "The Organization of Buyer-Driven Commodity Chains."

23. Sri Ram Khanna, "Structural Changes in Asian Textiles and Clothing Industries: The Second Migration of Production," *Textile Outlook International* 49 (September 1993): 19.

24. Jozef De Coster, "Hong Kong and China: The Joining of Two Giants in Textiles and Clothing," *Textile Outlook International* 68 (1996): 65.

25. Khanna, "Structural Changes in Asian Textiles," p. 19.

26. Jozef De Coster, "Productivity: A Key Strategy of the Hong Kong Textile and Clothing Industry," *Textile Outlook International* 68 (1996): 96.

27. Suzanne Berger and Richard K. Lester, *Made By Hong Kong* (New York: Oxford University Press, 1997), p. 9.

28. Richard P. Appelbaum and Gary Gereffi, "Power and Profits in the Apparel Commodity Chain," in *Global Production: The Apparel Industry in the Pacific Rim*, ed. E. Bonacich et al. (Philadelphia, Pa.: Temple University Press, 1994).

29. Khanna, "Structural Changes in Asian Textiles," pp. 29–30.

30. Gary Gereffi and Mei-Lin Pan, "The Globalization of Taiwan's Garment Industry," in *Global Production: The Apparel Industry in the Pacific Rim*, ed. E. Bonacich et al. (Philadelphia, Pa.: Temple University Press, 1994), p. 130, supplemented by more recent data from the Taiwan Textile Federation.

31. Gary Gereffi, "Commodity Chains and Regional Divisions of Labor in East Asia," *Journal of Asian Business* 12, no. 1 (1996): 94.

32. The data in this section are drawn from the excellent study by You-tien Hsing, "Traders, Managers, and Flexibility of Enterprise Networks: Tawianese Fashion Shoe Industry in Southern China" (paper prepared for the conference on Economic Governance and Flexible Production in East Asia, October 4–6, 1996, Hsinchu, Taiwan).

33. United States International Trade Commission, *Production Sharing: Use of U.S. Components and Materials in Foreign Assembly Operations, 1992–1995,* USITC Publication 3032 (Washington, D.C.: USITC, 1997), pp. 3–4.

34. International Labor Organization, *Globalization of the Footwear, Textiles and Clothing Industries* (Geneva: ILO, 1996), p. 53.

35. Raphael Kaplinsky, "Export Processing Zones in the Dominican Republic: Transforming Manufactures into Commodities," *World Development* 21, no. 11 (1993): 1855–1856.

36. United Nations Conference on Trade and Development, *World Investment Report 1994: Transnational Corporations, Employment and the Workplace* (Geneva: UNCTAD, 1994), p. 90.

37. Inter-American Development Bank, *Economic and Social Progress in Latin America* (Washington, D.C.: IDB, 1990), p. 28.

38. International Labor Organization, *Recent Developments in the Clothing Industry*, Report I (Geneva: ILO, 1995), pp. 35–36.

39. Wal-Mart announced on June 3, 1997, that it will pay $1.2 billion for a controlling stake in Cifra. This will increase the number of Wal-Mart outlets in Mexico from 145 to 373 stores, making Mexico the U.S. retail leader's largest foreign market (Mary Beth Sheridan, "Wal-Mart to Buy Mexico's No. 1 Retailer," *Los Angeles Times*, June 4, 1997).

40. When foreign production or sourcing does not involve the temporary export of fabrics, then importation occurs under a regime of "direct imports."

41. Scheffer, *The Changing Map of European Textiles*, p. 4.

42. L'Observatoire Européen du Textile et de l'Habillement, *The EU Textile and Clothing Sector 1995* (Brussels: OETH, 1996), pp. 51–52.

43. Dickerson, *Textiles and Apparel in the Global Economy*, p. 188.

44. Scheffer, *The Changing Map of European Textiles*, p. 17.

PART TWO

South and East Asia

ㅇㅣㅓ ㅇㅣㄱ
Fㅓㅣ Fㅇ군

4

Globalization, Economic Integration, National States, and Regional Response in Southeast and East Asia

Sam Ock Park

Cross-border cooperation and economic integration have become a distinctive trend at various levels of the global space economy. The EU and NAFTA present examples of cross-border economic cooperation at a macroregional level. In Pacific Asia, a comparable process of economic integration or regionalization has not emerged yet. Instead, subregional projects of economic integration have been organized as part of a complex trend of integration and disintegration among the nations of Pacific Asia.[1]

Until the recent financial crisis took away the magic, Southeast and East Asia had been dynamic regions within the global economy for quite some time. Within the last decade, subregional integration has been accelerating through cross-border economic cooperation and an increase in the shares of intraregional trade and intraregional FDI.[2] Several factors, such as the collapse of communism in the Soviet Union, the rise of the Chinese reform and open door policy, the effect of protectionist policies by North America and the EU, and the industrial restructuring of the Asian NIEs, have contributed to a new momentum for economic cooperation in the region.

Still, conflicts and uncertainties for regional integration remain as a result of cultural differences, historical factors, political conflicts, and differences in levels of economic development. The economies in Southeast and East Asia show a diversity of industrial organizations, industrial cultures, and urban systems. The trend is to go beyond coexistence and aim at regional integration. The regional spatial economy is being

Figure 4.1   Southeast and East Asia

reorganized, due to subregional cooperation and the interaction between growth areas.

In this chapter I will analyze these trends toward economic integration in Southeast and East Asia and the responses at the subregional level against the background of developments in the areas of international trade and FDI in the region.

Recent Trends of Trade and Foreign Direct Investments in the Pacific Asia

Significant changes in the organization of economic space as a result of growing economic internationalization have presented themselves in

Pacific Asia since the mid-1980s. Trade volumes and direct investments had increased significantly as a result of the dynamics of industrialization. The evolving trade structure reflected the growing complementarity among the countries of the region. Intraregional trade was served by the end of the Cold War, the open-door policy of China, and the geopolitical realignment after the collapse of the Soviet Union.[3] In addition, Pacific Asia's share in world trade increased significantly.[4] Recent data on merchandise exports in Asia emphasize this increase of intraregional trade. The share of intraregional exports within Asia amounted to close to 50 percent of total Asian merchandise exports in 1997.

In Pacific Asia, Taiwan, Hong Kong, Malaysia, the Republic of Korea, Singapore, and Thailand are primarily responsible for the increase in trade volumes between Asia and the rest of the world. Within this international trade, North America is the dominant destination for most of the Southeast and East Asian exports, although this role is declining for countries like Japan, Korea, Hong Kong, Singapore, and Indonesia. China and Malaysia have been able to increase their exports to the United States.

Trade discrimination in the region as a result of ASEAN (Association of South East Asian Nations) and also EEC (European Economic Community) trade policies have contributed to the growth of intraregional trade and will continue to do so. In addition, the bilateral trade flows between China, Hong Kong, Taiwan, and South Korea are accounting for a major part of the increase in intraregional trade.[5] These changes in trade structures and the growing interdependence within the region have created a need for intraregional economic cooperation.[6]

Pacific Asia has received impressive volumes of FDI. Among these, intraregional FDI is increasing. Japan used to be the leading source of FDI in Pacific Asia. However, the Asian NIEs are increasingly important investors in the region, especially for the FDI in China and Southeast Asia, where they are replacing the traditionally dominant role of the United States. The share of Asian NIEs as sources for intraregional FDI in Malaysia, Thailand, Philippines, and Indonesia has been increasing since the late 1980s.In China the share is more than 50 percent and may have increased again in the mid-1990s with Korean FDI in the country.

The complementary nature of the stages of development in the various economies in Pacific Asia has been a significant factor stimulating FDI in the region. With the decline of the labor-intensive industry in the upper-middle income economies, these production facilities are transferred to the economies that follow closely behind. The needs in these two different types of economies match each other well and have given rise to an ever increasing intraregional FDI in the region.[7] Geographical proximity and cultural ties are additional significant factors contributing to the growth of intraregional FDI in the Pacific Rim.[8] Hong Kong and Taiwan have taken a dominant role in the FDI in South China. The major area for the investments is the neighboring. cross-border region in Guangdong and Fujian provinces.[9] Korea has significantly increased its FDI in neighboring areas in the Bohai region and the northeastern provinces in China. These account for more than three-quarters of Korea's FDI into China (see Table 4.1) with Shandong Province, which is the nearest to Korea, as the most important destination. These close ties between neighboring countries are related not only to geographical proximity, but also to historical and cultural relations. It should be noted also that more balanced FDI flows in several bilateral relations are emerging as a result of growing Taiwanese, Korean, and Singaporean investments into Japan and Malaysian investment into Taiwan and Singapore.[10]

Regionalization in Pacific Asia

The movement toward regional economic cooperation in the world has been active for quite some time already. Between 1947 and 1995, a total of 121 regional agreements were established. Since January 1, 1995, when the new era of the WTO started, an additional twelve regional agreements have been concluded. It seems that this trend toward regionalization is functioning as an intermediate stage in a process

Table 4.1   Korea's FDI in China by Regions (to February 1996)

	Total number of FDIs	Percentage of FDIs	Investment in million US $	%
Bohai region	1372	47.7	1440.1	54.1
Shandong	812	28.2	829.9	31.2
.Beijing	181	6.3	243.3	9.1
Tianjin	296	10.3	312.7	11.8
Hubei	83	2.9	54.5	2.1
Northeast region	1064	37.0	516.1	19.4
Jilin	295	10.3	102.9	3.9
Heilongjiang	153	5.3	104.1	3.9
Liaoning	616	21.4	309.1	11.6
Southeast region	315	10.9	584.3	21.9
Other regions	125	4.4	121.4	4.6
Total	2876	100.0	2662.3	100.0

Source: Bank of Korea, 1997.

toward globalization. Except for the EC, past regional agreements have involved developing countries. The more recent ones, however, include not only developing countries but also advanced economies. In addition, cooperation between neighboring trading blocs is increasing. Examples are the Mediterranean agreements and the relationship between the EU and Eastern Europe. There are several reasons for this new trend.[11] First of all, the complementarity in factor endowments is greater between the advanced and developing economies than among developing economies only. Second, a free trade agreement between an advanced economy and adjacent developing economies will create employment in the latter, facilitate access to the market for technology transfer, help in debt reduction, and stimulate FDI from the member advanced economies into the developing economies. In addition, the agreement may help to limit illegal migration between the developing and the developed economies.

The share of intraregional trade in the major regions has been increasing—from 52.8 percent to 69.9 percent in Western Europe, 31.5 percent to 33.0 percent in North America, and 41.1 percent to 49.7 percent in Asia between 1958 and 1990.[12] Among these three major regional blocs, Europe and North America have become well organized. The ASEAN bloc APEC (Asian Pacific Economic Cooperation), which was formed in 1989, has remained a rather loose consultative organization and is still in the formation stage. Creating a strong and tightly organized regional bloc like the EU or NAFTA, however, may prove to be a difficult enterprise in Pacific Asia. The region lacks the favorable conditions for regional integration that presented themselves in Europe.[13] Even though intraregional trade has been steadily increasing in recent years, the export-led economies of Japan and the Asian NIEs are still heavily dependent on the North American market and the markets of the other advanced economies. The increasing number of economic ties between countries in Pacific Asia have not been motivated by political considerations, but have resulted from the exigencies of economic development.[14]

Regionalism in the Pacific Asia is market oriented and has been driven by complementarities in factor endowments, stages of industrialization, and levels of technical development.[15] Initially, intraregional cooperation in these areas began through capital investments from Japan in the 1970s and 1980s and was later followed by investments made by the Asian NIEs. This cooperation does not represent a region-wide arrangement covering Pacific Asia, but is organized at a subregional level based on economic motivations. This process of subregionalism is closely related to the industrial restructuring of the Southeast and East Asian NIEs.

Industrial Restructuring and
Subregionalization in Asian NIEs

After having experienced remarkable growth during the last three decades, the Asian NIEs are currently undergoing industrial restructuring. Because of this common pattern, most Western literature has been dealing with the Asian NIEs as a homogeneous group, ignoring the considerable differences between them. Generally, the Asian NIEs have been moving from a labor-intensive to an assembly-intensive industrial structure. They are also shifting toward more complex technologies. The decline in the share of the labor-intensive industry in the ASEAN countries, though, is not shared by China.

The major triggers of the industrial restructuring in the Asian NIEs, as Gordon Clark and Won Bae Kim have pointed out, are the rapid increase in wage levels and labor shortages in production jobs.[16] From the 1960s through the 1980s, the role of the state was critical in bringing about industrial change.[17] While the state is still an important player in the process of industrial restructuring in the Asian NIEs, firms and their strategies have become more important actors in the pursuit of industrial competitiveness. Confronted with the erosion of competitive advantage, especially in the labor-intensive industries, firms have responded, singularly or in combination, by introducing new technologies, changing location and industrial organization, and developing local labor markets.[18] Research on industrial restructuring in Hong Kong, Pusan, Seoul, and Singapore has shown the importance of dynamic strategies among firms in the process of industrial restructuring.[19] Flexible employment based on part-time or temporary workers, in addition to the employment of foreign workers, has been adopted as a major strategy to counteract the problems of high wage levels and labor shortages in the manufacturing sectors of Hong Kong, Singapore, and Metropolitan Seoul. Subcontracting has been adopted by most firms in the major cities of the Asian NIEs as a competitive strategy meant to lower labor costs. Thus, subcontracting is directly related to a labor strategy.[20] In addition, overseas investments in plants or factories are being considered as a major locational strategy by many firms in the labor-intensive industries. Lower wage costs, easier market access, and the availability of land for industrial activity are major factors motivating overseas investment by firms. Many companies in the Asian NIEs are investing heavily in the introduction of new technologies as a long-term strategy, above all to increase productivity and, further, to improve quality and reduce costs.[21] In comparison, labor and organization strategies are seen more as short-term adjustment strategies, responding to the problems of high wages and labor shortages in the Asian NIEs.

The important role that FDI and technological development are playing in the process of industrial restructuring in the Asian NIEs reveals subregionalization in Pacific Asia to be a direct result of industrial restructuring. The loss of comparative advantage and the need to maintain competitiveness have forced the Asian NIEs to invest heavily in Southeast Asia and China in order to combine the capital and technical know-how with the low cost, resource, and other incentives of the host country.22 In this way the Asian NIEs have contributed to the increase of intraregional trade, direct investment, interindustry cooperation, and the subregional division of labor within Pacific Asia.

Subregionalization in Southeast and East Asia

Two trends have appeared in the evolution of new industrial spaces in Pacific Asia: the establishment of free economic zones and subregionalization by economic integration with neighboring countries. Free economic zones have been successfully developed in Southeast Asia during the last two decades. In recent years, several zones have been proposed in the Northeast Asia region. They are the Greater Vladisvostok Free Economic Zone, the Hunchun Economic Zone, the Rajin-Sonbong Free Economic Zone, the Suifenhe Economic Zone, the Amur River Free Trade Zone, and the Manzhouli Economic Zone.[23] Most of these will function at the miniregional or metropolitan level.

The trend toward subregionalization through the formation of subregional economic groupings between neighboring economies, however, is a more important phenomenon in Pacific Asia.[24] These subregional economic groupings have emerged as a result of the industrial restructuring and adjustment of the Asian NIEs.[25] The regional economies in Southeast and East Asia have become complementary to each other through a new regional division of labor.

The Asian Development Bank does regard subregionalization, or the formation of growth triangles or subregional economic zones, as a unique Asian solution to the operational problems of regional integration and cooperation among countries at different levels of economic development and with different social and economic systems.[26] The subregional economic groupings are more export oriented than the trading blocs and are a means of maintaining competitiveness in exports. Economic complementarity and geographical proximity among the members are primary conditions for the successful development of these subregional economic groupings. Geographical proximity will reduce transaction costs and will create the opportunity to take advantage of cultural and linguistic affinities. It appears that the trend toward subregionalization is an almost natural result of East Asian traditional business relations, operating through personal contact rather than through bureaucratic practices.[27]

The most developed and at the same time the clearest examples of subregionalization are represented by the Southern China Economic Area comprising Hong Kong, Taiwan, and Guangdong and Fujian Provinces in China; and the growth triangle of Singapore, Malaysia, and Indonesia. In recent years, the city-states of Hong Kong and Singapore have been aggressively pursuing economic integration with neighboring economies, resulting in the formation of subregional economic groupings. These have developed into cross-border regions with substantial recent manufacturing growth in the territories adjacent or in close proximity to longer established nuclei of export-oriented industrial production.[28] This subregionalization reflects the increasing tendencies toward economic integration across national boundaries.

In the Southern China Economic Area, massive FDIs from Hong Kong and Taiwan have fuelled economic growth in the region.[29] Hong Kong, for example, accounts for more than 50 percent of the FDI in Shenzhen.[30] The Chinese "open door" policy and the subsequent liberalization of economic policies, major differentials in production costs—especially labor costs—a shared cultural heritage, and geographical proximity were the major factors contributing in the growth of FDI. The special regime granted to Guangdong and Fujian Provinces by the central government also contributed to the expansion of investments to the inland areas of Guangdong and the neighboring provinces.[31] In this Southern China Economic Area, Hong Kong's investments are directed toward Guangdong Province and the Shenzhen Special Economic Zone, due to their geographical proximity, while Taiwanese investments are concentrated in the southeast coastal province of Fujian due to kinship ties, a common language, and geographical proximity.

Hong Kong has poured investments, technology, marketing know-how, business services, special skills, and management expertise into southern China, especially into Guangdong Province. The future of this enterprise will depend on how the integration of Hong Kong into China proceeds. Economic expansion and integration with Hong Kong's immediate hinterland is expected to generate bargaining power with Beijing.[32] This expansion by Hong Kong firms is also the result of a competitive strategy at the firm level as part of the process of industrial restructuring. Within this growth triangle, Guangdong and Shenzhen provide cheap labor, raw materials, and easy access to the markets of southern China, while capital, technology, and management skills are being provided by Hong Kong. Taiwan's investments cover a broader area and include ASEAN countries as well as southern China. A shared social and cultural background and the existence of traditional business ties are important factors stimulating Taiwanese investments. Subregional economic integration based on Taiwan's investments has been directed above all toward production and market cooperation.[33]

The SIJORI (Singapore-Johor-Riau) Growth Triangle, including Singapore, the Malaysian state of Johor, and the Indonesian Riau Islands (Batam and Bintan), was formed by government-led initiatives. The Johor-Singapore link was driven initially by market forces. However, the suggestion of the formation of a "triangle of growth" by then Deputy Prime Minister of Singapore, Goh Chok Dong, in 1989 gave impetus to the development of this subregional economic grouping.[34] Growing pressures in Singapore resulting from rapid increases in wage rates and land prices, in addition to existing complementarities resulting from the differences in factor endowments among the three areas of the triangle, triggered economic cooperation. FDI to Johor and Riau, especially from Singapore, has increased rapidly since the late 1980s.[35] Singapore's share of the FDI in Batam is almost 50 percent.[36] The rapid industrial growth of Johor and Riau's transformation into an industrial center and tourist destination in recent years are surely a result of subregional economic cooperation. As Singapore's industry is heavily dependent on foreign investment, including investment from many transnational corporations, it is expected to participate in the growth triangle through the advanced technology provided by transnational corporations.[37] Actually, the growth triangle is trying to attract foreign investment through Johor's and Batam's cheap labor and the availability of land, in combination with Singapore's efficient infrastructure and technical expertise.

Next to these two already-established processes of subregionalization, another in Southeast Asia and three more in Northeast Asia can be noted.

1. growth triangle is developing between southern Thailand, northwestern Malaysia, and western Sumatra; Malaysia has proposed to jointly develop infrastructure, natural resources, and industries.
2. The Tumen River Delta Area project involves China, eastern Russia, and South and North Korea; a plan for the Tumen River Basin Economic Zone (TRBEZ) is being developed by UNDP. This TRBEZ has great potential for subregional economic cooperation due to the significant complementarity in natural resources and labor between China, Russia, and North Korea, in addition to South Korean and Japanese capital and technology. However, a large number of institutional and economic issues should be resolved before the project can proceed.[38]
3. The Yellow Sea Economic Zone involves northern China, South and North Korea, and Japan. This Economic Zone has not proceeded far beyond the proposal stage. It offers a considerable

complementarity through economic links between China, South Korea, and Japan.
4. The Japan Sea (East Sea) Economic Zone involves Japan, eastern Russia, northeastern China, and South and North Korea.[39] This project also has not left the drawing board yet.

A Northeast Asian trade bloc, which would combine the latter three subregional economic groupings, has been suggested by academics and businessmen, with politics—as usual—lagging behind. A significant increase of FDI and trade flows in this area in recent years, however, has indicated irreversible trends toward subregionalization in the area.

Industrial Networking: Localization and Globalization

During the last two decades, in addition to the growth triangles of cross-border regionalization and trade blocs comprising several countries, several growth centers based on special economic zones or industrial districts have appeared as another distinctive feature of industrialization in Pacific Asia. These growth centers include the organization of specialized industrial complexes and technology parks and high-tech industrial districts, and they are the result of the complex interaction between state policies at the national, regional, and local levels, networking through interfirm and intrafirm relations that emerge through the industrial production process, and the globalizing tendencies that influence firms' industrial restructuring strategy.

The importance of industrial networking through a variety of interfirm relations has grown in the global economy. The major forms of interfirm relations are arm's length transactions between firms, equity investments by one firm in another, joint ventures between independent firms, technology licensing, interfirm alliances for the purpose of pooling strategic assets, and supplier and other networks among firms.[40] Research has shown that the importance of interfirm relations and the emergence of new industrial spaces are related to flexible specialization.[41] Recent studies in Italy contend that flexible specialization based on the cooperative interfirm relations among small and medium-sized enterprises has been competing successfully with the mass production of large enterprises.[42] In Pacific Asia, however, diverse production systems coexist and various forms of interfirm relations are important not only among the small firms, but also between small and large firms and among the large firms.[43] Originally, interfirm relations were not as significant in Pacific Asia (with the exception of Japan) as in the developed economies. The intrafirm relations of large enterprises were more important, due to the branch plant investments of large firms. In recent years, however, the importance of interfirm relations has grown as part of industrial restructuring strategies at the company level. In order to remain competitive in a situation of rapid increasing labor costs, firms are readjusting their production organization by emphasizing industrial networks. The increase in subcontracting activities since the late 1980s in Asian NIEs is one of the results of such restructuring strategy.[44]

Both localizing and globalizing tendencies have stimulated the growing importance of interfirm relations. In Pacific Asia and also in the United States, new industrial districts are mainly satellite-type creations consisting of branch plants, or they form part of hub-and-spoke type complexes dominated by one or a few large firms.[45] Initially, local interfirm relations were negligible in the new satellite industrial districts. However, in the process of developing the new industrial districts, local interfirm relations have become significant with the increase in cooperation among firms in the local area and with the development of local subcontracting activities designed to reduce transaction costs, transportation costs, and sunk costs. Interfirm relations are also extended to the international level and tie in with the globalizing tendencies in industrial activity. The growing importance of interfirm cooperation and the significance of local and global networks in industrial districts can be found in the case of Korea.[46]

In the new industrial districts of the Asian NIEs, firms are trying to increase competitiveness through an expansion of interfirm relations at the local and global levels.[47] In the new industrial districts of Korea, localization has progressed in recent years through interfirm cooperation between large firms and their small and medium-sized suppliers, cooperation with customers, and with local competitors—leading to spin-offs and cooperation with local trade associations, universities, and government institutions.[48] Interfirm relations at the international level are not as strong as at the local level. Global networks in production, R&D, and marketing in the industrial districts of Korea have been increasingly important, however. Strategic alliances, FDI, contracting out production beyond the national boundaries, and cooperation with foreign suppliers and customers are all adding to the importance of global networks in industry.

In China and the ASEAN countries, localization through the development of interfirm relations is not well developed yet. In Singapore, for example, intrafirm ties in the form of production chains predominate regionally and globally, and local interfirm ties are not well developed.[49] These local interfirm relations are also relatively insignificant in most of the new industrial districts in the developing areas of Pacific Asia. However, in recent years a trend toward localization of industry through improving interfirm relations can be noted. Parallel to globalization, we see the development of localization. Among Korean subsidiaries in Indonesia, for example, firms tend to experience an increasing level of localization over time in out-sourcing, recruiting management, and raising capital.[50] The growing importance of these local networks can be regarded as the result of the restructuring strategy among firms and the industrial policy by the host country.

Industrial networking through the development of interfirm and intrafirm relations on a local as well as a global level has been supported by the development of information technology. The Multimedia Super Corridor in Malaysia presents a good example of industrial networking through the application of information technology directed at regional development. The core of the Multimedia Super Corridor will be the new administrative capital of Malaysia, to be designed as a high-tech, hard-wired information hub with a telecommunication infrastructure.[51] Complexes of software industry, producer services, and high-tech industries, which have developed in the Asian NIEs and in some of the ASEAN countries in recent years, are also using this formula of interfirm industrial networking coupled to the development of a telecom infrastructure.

Conclusion

In this chapter I have examined regional responses in Southeast and East Asia to the trends of globalization and economic integration. The significant increase in international trade and FDI within Pacific Asia and the emergence of cross-border subregional economic groupings or growth triangles are causing distinctive changes in the spatial organization of economic activities in the region. To these trends we have to add the effects of interfirm relations; though not a decisive factor determining the localization of industry, they have proven to be a factor of influence in the organization of industrial spaces in Southeast and East Asia in recent years. Industrial restructuring in the Asian NIEs has generated momentum for significant political change. However, subregional economic integration in the region is being driven by firms' restructuring strategies, rather than by political motivations. Cultural ties and geographical proximity have become important considerations in the definition of these strategies and have contributed to the growing importance of subregionalization and localization in Southeast and East Asia.

The return of Hong Kong to China in 1997 and the joining of Mayanmar, Laos, and Cambodia to ASEAN in the same year will obviously also have a significant impact on these trends. As part of the development toward subregionalization, subnational players like the Guangdong, Fujian, or Shandong Provinces of China may enter into direct negotiations with multilateral agencies and other nongovernment actors, bypassing the state.[52]

The rapid industrial growth and subregional economic integration in Pacific Asia have generated serious environmental pollution and degradation, problems of branch plant economy, and increasing interregional disparities. A cooperative networking strategy working at the intrafirm, interfirm, and interinstitutional levels and coordination between governments at the local, subregional, national, and regional levels will be needed to meet head on the problems threatening the sustainability of development in Pacific Asia.[53] Cooperative networking will facilitate the localization of industry, saving in transaction, transportation, and sunk costs at the local level. It will stimulate subregionalization with an adequate exploitation of resources, the improvement of labor skills, the development of appropriate, environmentally sound technologies, and the transfer of new technologies, financing, and skills development for adapting these technologies.

Cooperative networking is undoubtedly supported on all levels in Pacific Asia. However, the formation of a single economic bloc like the EU will not be an easy task in a region marked by distinct cultural, socioeconomic, and political differences and a geographical structure that poses physical barriers against integration. Given these difficulties, cooperative networking strategies should focus on the development of coordination functions at the early stage. The political leadership in Pacific Asia should promote cooperative networking, in particular in the areas of technology development and the protection of the environment. At this initial stage, the organization of a regional forum could facilitate intraregional communication and cooperation in these areas and serve to define policies that will contribute to the improvement of the quality of life and help to create the conditions for sustainable development in Southeast and East Asia.

The recent financial crisis in Korea and Southeast Asia is showing us the importance of economic regionalization for this type of sustainable development. The foreign exchange crisis in Korea and Southeast Asia is a direct result of the globalization of financial systems. However, the severity of the economic problems appears to vary with the degree of economic regionalization each individual economy has been subjected to. Among the four Asian Tigers (Singapore, Hong Kong, Taiwan, and Korea), only in Korea has the financial crisis deepened, leading to the financial tutelage of the IMF. At the same time, Korea is the only economy among the four that has not reached the stage of regional economic integration or economic regionalization that has developed in the Greater South China, including Hong Kong, Taiwan, and Guangdong and Fujian Provinces or in the SIJORI Growth Triangle. Economic regionalization has been crucial in the process of industrial restructuring, in the formation of external economies, and in the continuation of economic growth in Hong Kong and Taiwan. South Korea has been investing in Shandong Province in China, but economic cooperation with North Korea would have been much more effective. The present crisis will slow down the process of economic (sub)regionalization, which, might otherwise have been a major factor in softening the impact of the crisis.

A considerable amount of industrial and spatial restructuring will take place in the region. In Korea, the chaebols will be restructured, including downsizing, financial reorganization, mergers, and even liquidations. The consequences of these processes will differ among regions, according to existing differences in industrial structure, innovation potential, labor market, infrastructure, and the importance of industrial networks. It appears that in Korea bankruptcies resulting from the crisis and industrial restructuring are less common in the capital region. Peripheral regions are more severely affected. In the short term, export industries may be able to increase exports to the United States and Europe as a result of the devaluation of the currency, a phenomenon that may present itself also in the other South and Southeast Asian countries affected by the crisis. In the long term, there will be no solution for the large firms other than to radically restructure their production systems, labor relations, firm organization, and spatial structure in an attempt to regain their competitive advantages.

Notes

1. Gillian Cook, M. A. Doel, and R. Li, *Fragmented Asia: Regional Integration and National Disintegration in Pacific Asia* (Aldershot, England: Avebury, 1996).
2. ESCAP, *Regional Forum for Sustainable Industrial Development and Restructuring in Asia and the Pacific* (New York: United Nations, 1994).
3. Ross Garnaut and Peter Drysdale, eds., *Asia Pacific Regionalism* (Pymble, NSW, Australia: Harper Educational, 1994).
4. Claes Alvstam, "Integration Through Trade and Direct Investment: Asian Pacific patterns," in *The Asian Pacific Rim and Globalization*, ed. Richard Le Heron and Sam Ock Park (Aldershot, England: Avebury, 1995), pp.107–128; Leo van Grunsven, Shuang-Yann Wong, and Won Bae Kim, "State, Investment and Territory: Regional Economic Zones and Emerging Industrial Landscapes," in Le Heron and Ock Park *The Asian Pacific Rim and Globalization*, pp. 151–184; Garnaut and Drysdale, *Asia Pacific Regionalism*, p. 120.
5. Alvstam, "Integration through Trade."
6. Seung-Hoon Lee, "The Regional Forum for Industrial and Technological Restructuring in Asia and the Pacific," *A Report to ESCAP* (mimeo, 1996).

7. Ibid.

8. Katharyne Mitchell, "Flexible Circulation in the Pacific Rim: Capitalism in Cultural Context," *Economic Geography*, no. 71 (Winter 1995): 364–382.

9. Philippe Lasserre and Hellmut Schutte, *Strategies for Asia Pacific* (South Melbourne, Australia: Macmillan, 1995); Pochih Chen, "Foreign Investments in the Southern China Growth Triangle," in *Growth Triangles in Asia, A New Approach to Regional Economic Cooperation*, ed. Myo Thant, Min Tang, and Hiroshi Kakazu (Hong Kong: Oxford University Press, 1994) pp. 73–92.

10. Alvstam, "Integration through Trade."

11. Seung-Hoon Lee, "The Regional Forum."

12. Kym Anderson and Harald Norheim, "History, Geography, and Regional Economic Integration," in *Regional Integration and Global Trading System*, ed. Kym Anderson and Richard Blackhurst (New York: Harvester Wheatsheaf, 1993).

13. Cook, Doel, and Li, *Fragmented Asia*.

14. Ibid.

15. Seung-Hoon Lee, "The Regional Forum."

16. Gordon Clark and Won Bae Kim, eds. *Asian NIEs and the Global Economy* (Baltimore and London: Johns Hopkins University Press, 1995).

17. Ann R. Markusen and Sam Ock Park, "The State as Industrial Locator and District Builder: The Case of Changwon, South Korea," *Economic Geography*, no. 69 (1993): 157–181; Byung Nak Song, *The Rise of Korean Economy* (New York: Oxford University Press, 1990).

18. Sam Ock Park, "Seoul, Korea: City and Suburbs," in *Asian NIEs and the Global Economy*, ed. Gordon Clark and Won Bae Kim (Baltimore and London: Johns Hopkins University Press, 1995), pp. 143–167.

19. Clark and Won Bae Kim, *Asian NIEs and the Global Economy*.

20. Sam Ock Park, "Seoul, Korea: City and Suburbs," pp. 143–167.

21. Clark and Won Bae Kim, *Asian NIEs and the Global Economy*.

22. Cook, Doel, and Li, *Fragmented Asia*, p. 148.

23. Shoichi Kobayashi, "Free Economic Zones in the Northeast Asia Region," in *Regional Economic Cooperation in Northeast Asia, Proceedings of the Vladivostok Conference*, ed. Won Bae Kim et al. (Northeast Asian Economic Forum, 1992), pp. 117–132.

24. Van Grunsven, Shuang-Yann Wong, and Won Bae Kim, "State Investment and Territory."

25. Fu-Kuo Liu, "Industrial Development and the Impetus to Regional Integration in Pacific Asia," in Cook, Doel, and Li, *Fragmented Asia*, pp. 137–168.

26. Myo Thant, Min Tang, and Hiroshi Kakazu, eds.; *Growth Triangles in Asia, A New Approach to Regional Economic Cooperation* (Hong Kong: Oxford University Press, 1994).

27. Steven Burton, "Growing by Leaps-and-Triangles," *Time*, January 17, 1994, pp. 24.

28. Van Grunsven, Shuang-Yann Wong, and Won Bae Kim, "State, Investment and Territory."

29. Pochih Chen, "Foreign Investments in the Southern China Growth Triangle," p. 80; Edward K. Y. Chen and Ann Ho, "Southern China Growth Triangle: An Overview," in Myo Thant, Min Tang, and Hiroshi Kakazu, *Growth Triangles in Asia, A New Approach to Regional Economic Cooperation*, pp. 29–72.

30. Myo Thant, Min Tang, and Hiroshi Kakazu, *New Approach to Regional Economic Cooperation*.

31. Wang Jun, "Expansion of the Southern China Growth Triangle," in Myo Thant, Min Tang, and Hiroshi Kakazu, *Growth Triangles in Asia*, pp. 151–174.

32. Clark and Won Bae Kim, *Asian NIEs and the Global Economy*.

33. Fu-Kuo Liu, "Industrial Development," pp. 137–168.

34. Sree Kumer, "Johor-Singapore-Riau Growth Triangle: A Model of Subregional Cooperation," in Myo Thant, Min Tang, and Hiroshi Kakazu, *Growth Triangles in Asia*, pp. 175–217; Garnaut and Drysdale, eds., *Asia Pacific Regionalism*.

35. Ibid.

36. Myo Thant, Min Tang, and Hiroshi Kakazu, *Growth Triangles in Asia*.

37. Fu-Kuo Liu, "Industrial Development," pp. 137–168.

38. Hiroshi Kakazu, "Northeast Asian Regional Economic Cooperation," in Myo Thant, Min Tang, and Hiroshi Kakazu eds., *Growth Triangles in Asia*, pp. 243–276.

39. Siow Yue Chia and Tsao Yuan Lee, "Subregional Economic Zones in Southeast Asia," in *Pacific Dynamism and the International Economic System*, ed. C. Fred Bergsten and Marcus Noland (Washington, D.C.: Institute for International Economics, 1993) pp. 225–269.

40. ESCAP, *Regional Forum*.

41. Michael Piore and Charles F. Sabel, *The Second Industrial Divide* (New York: Basic Books, 1984); Alan Scott, *New Industrial Spaces - Flexible Production Organization and Regional Development in North America and Western Europe* (London: Pion, 1988).

42. Edward Goodman and John Bamford, *Small Firms and Industrial Districts in Italy* (London and New York: Routledge, 1989).

43. Sam Ock Park, "Network and Embeddedness in the Dynamic Types of New Industrial Districts," *Progress in Human Geography*, no. 20 (Winter 1996): 476–493.; Sam Ock Park and Ann Markusen, "The State as Industrial Location," pp. 157–181.

44. Clark and Won Bae Kim, *Asian NIEs and the Global Economy*.

45. Ann R. Markusen, "Sticky Places in Slippery Space: A Typology of Industrial Districts," *Economic Geography*, no. 72 (Autumn 1996): 293–313; Ann R. Markusen and Sam Ock Park, "The State as Industrial Location"; Sam Ock Park, "Network and Embeddedness."

46. Sam Ock Park, "Localization and Global Networks of High Technology Industries in Korea," *The Journal of Korean Planners Association*, no. 31 (Spring 1996): 27–42 (in Korean with English summary).

47. Ibid.; Kong Ching Ho, "Interfirm Linkages in Singapore's Electronics Industry" (paper presented at the International Conference on Interfirm Linkages, Industrial Restructuring, and Regional Development, Pusan National University, Pusan, Korea, May 19–20, 1995).

48. Sam Ock Park, "Location and Global Networks," pp. 29–42.

49. Kong Ching Ho, "Interfirm Linkages."

50. Mannsoo Shin, "Localization of Korean Subsidiaries in Southeast Asia: In the Case of Indonesia" (paper presented at the 3rd Pacific and Asia Conference on Korean Studies, Sydney, Australia, July 1–4, 1996).

51. Kenneth E. Corey, "Digital Tigers: Information Technology and Public Policy in Singapore, Malaysia, and Thailand" (paper presented at the annual conference of the Western Regional Science Association, Waikoloa, Hawaii, February 24–27, 1997).

52. Cho-Oon Khong, "Pacific Asia as a Region: A View from Business," in Cook, Doel and Li, *Fragmented Asia*, pp. 167–180.

53. Sam Ock Park, "Rethinking the Pacific Rim" (paper presented at the Pacific Rim Symposium of the 28th International Geographical Congress, The Hague, Netherlands, August 4–10, 1996).

5

Business Strategy, State Intervention, and Regionalization in East Asia

Tak-Wing Ngo

A central issue in the globalization debate concerns state-capital relations. Some suggest that the regulatory capacity of national states is radically weakened by the process of globalization, resulting in the emergence of a "borderless world" dominated by "footloose" transnationals.[1] Others argue that instead of being weakened in their regulatory capacity, states indeed actively adjust their economies to globalization by regulating for deregulation. In doing so, the state is helping to impose a global market discipline on the domestic economy.[2] A middle ground position emphasizes that states can no longer direct investment decisions, they can only negotiate such decisions with private capital. At the same time, transnational capital also has to seek alliance with national states to enhance its capacity to compete in the world market.[3]

This chapter looks at how state-capital relations in East Asia shape and are shaped by global economic restructuring. East Asia is an interesting case because states in the region are commonly seen as strong and capable of directing economic adjustment or even "governing the market."[4] Yet the recent literature has also described the region as undergoing a "market-induced" economic integration driven not by the state but by private capital responding to global restructuring.[5] This contentious understanding offers a good place to start an inquiry into state-capital relations in the process of globalization.

In order to limit the scope of analysis, I focus on the cases of Taiwan, Hong Kong, and mainland China during the 1980s and the early 1990s. These three are seen as all having strong states while pursuing different strategies of intervention: dirigiste capitalism, laissez-faire capitalism, and market socialism. Despite such differences, enterprises have increasingly "regionalized" their investment in all three economies. The growing integration of the three economies leads observers to speak of the formation of a "Greater China."[6] By re-examining the process of regional integration, this chapter argues that such a process can be attributed to neither market induction nor state regulation alone. Rather, it is the result of interaction between the state and capital as active agents in their pursuit of both political and economic goals. Thus, states and capital are not just passive recipients or vehicles of global capitalist logic. Their actions contribute to and shape the very process of globalization in the region.

Quasi-Multinationals and Regionalization

Before examining state-capital relations that shape the process of globalization in the region, let us first look at the global economic circumstances that created the pressure of restructuring in the domestic economy. Let us begin with Taiwan and Hong Kong. These two export-oriented economies have traditionally relied heavily on the global market. For three decades after the Second World War, when trade protection in the Western markets was relatively low, Taiwan and Hong Kong produced labor-intensive, low-value manufactured export goods for the European and U.S. markets. Dominated by small enterprises, they succeeded in exploiting market niches by relying on international commercial subcontracting. Under such a subcontracting arrangement, all export sales of products were ordered in advance, and marketing was arranged by the buyer.[7] The colonial legacy enabled producers in both places to rely on Japanese and British commercial networks for overseas orders. At the same time, manufacturers managed to keep labor and production costs low by various forms of internal subcontracting and informal work arrangements involving casual labor.[8]

This kind of labor-intensive production for export encountered difficulties in the late 1970s, when the increase in labor and production costs was matched by protectionism in the European and the U.S. markets. At the same time, local producers faced intensified competition in the world market because of accelerating technological change, increasing capital mobility, internationalization of production, and reduction of product lifetimes.

In response to these changes, business enterprises in Taiwan and Hong Kong demanded that their governments improve the investment environment and assist in industrial upgrading. Their "voice" calling for government action was, however, supplanted by the emergence of an "economic exit" that allowed for the relocation of production and investment to a low-cost region.[9] This happened when mainland China opened its economy to foreign trade and investment in 1978. The huge China market became at the same time an outlet for products, a source of cheap labor, and a place for investment.

The regionalization of production and investment turned business enterprises in Taiwan and Hong Kong into a kind of quasi-multinational, since they were not recognized as foreign investors by the Chinese government. Taiwanese and Hong Kong enterprises in mainland China were officially categorized as "special domestic capital"—"special" because they could enjoy the same privileges, such as tax reduction and foreign exchange retention, as foreign capital.

Taking this advantage, Hong Kong's enterprises were among the first to invest in mainland China. As soon as China set up the Special Economic Zones in the Pearl River Delta, Hong Kong manufacturers started to relocate their production units on a large scale. The relocation mainly involved outward processing. Hong Kong investors supplied machinery, materials, and design to factories in mainland China. The latter provided plant and labor and carried out assembly or processing jobs. Some of the products were re-exported through Hong Kong, in which case the Hong Kong factories were responsible for marketing. Following the lead of Hong Kong enterprises, the first Taiwanese investor set up his mainland factory in 1983. Since then Taiwanese investment had been growing steadily, especially when mainland China announced regulations to attract Taiwanese investors in 1988. After the Taiwanese government officially approved the first Taiwan-financed joint venture in 1991, Taiwanese investors started to come in large numbers into mainland China. Like their Hong Kong counterparts, Taiwanese investors concentrated on export processing and in the relocation of sunset industries to mainland China.[10] In both cases, investment in mainland China continued to grow. The majority of the giant enterprise groups in Taiwan and Hong Kong had already set up their plants on the mainland. Their investment plans became longer, and many of them formed joint ventures with mainland partners. Investment was no longer confined to Fujian and Guangdong— the two provinces located near Taiwan and Hong Kong—but expanded to other provinces as well.

The Political Implications of Regionalization

The picture described above highlights the macroeconomic outcome of adjustment. Stopping at this point leads some observers to emphasize so-called *market-induced* regionalization, seeing it as an economic process and overlooking its political dimension, in which governmental and business actors negotiate and manipulate the course of change. Such negotiation and manipulation takes place because the growing economic interdependence of mainland China, Taiwan, and Hong Kong has important political implications for the sensitive relationships among the ruling regimes.

Let us briefly review such relationships and the political implications of regionalization. From the outset, mainland China and Taiwan have been governed by rival regimes who are technically still at war with each other. Direct trade, mail, transportation, and the movement of people between the two places have been stopped for decades. Tension across the Taiwan Strait eased somewhat in the 1980s, but it built up again in the early 1990s when Beijing condemned Taiwan's push for independence. Political hostility reached a peak in 1995 and 1996, when Beijing launched test missiles and conducted military exercises in the East China Sea in condemnation of the Taipei government's push for international recognition. Under such circumstances, industrial relocation and the outflow of capital into mainland China aroused anxiety in Taiwan. Public opinion there expressed worry that this might lead to de-industrialization, make Taiwan dependent on the mainland, and ultimately threaten the security of Taiwan.[11]

The development of close economic ties also has political implications for the relationship between Hong Kong and mainland China. Since the beginning of the Sino-British negotiation over the future of Hong Kong in 1982, public debate in Hong Kong was overwhelmingly concerned with how to maintain the autonomy of the territory in the countdown to the handover and after. Economic integration raised the question of whether such a development would strengthen or reduce Hong Kong's capacity in bargaining for political autonomy. The use of economic leverage aroused much controversy when Hong Kong came into direct confrontation with Beijing in 1989, when people from all walks of life denounced the ruling regime in Beijing for cracking down on the pro-democracy movement.

Trade and investment between Taiwan and Hong Kong themselves were kept informal and unofficial, because the colonial government of Hong Kong did not recognize the regime in Taiwan. The tremendous increase in indirect trade between Taiwan and mainland China via Hong Kong also aroused fears that Taiwan's economic independence would suffer when Hong Kong became a Chinese territory after July 1, 1997.

The political implications of economic integration were fully understood by the mainland Chinese government, who saw investment by quasi-multinationals from Taiwan and Hong Kong as not only an economic activity but also an instrument in its "united front tactics" aiming toward unification. The tactic of wooing business owners by offering them investment privileges is described by some as the "business encirclement of politics."[12] In the case of Taiwan, it involved using trade and investment across the strait as a bridge of communication, an instrument of cross-strait economic influence, and a means of persuading the Taiwanese government to come to the negotiation table. In the case of Hong Kong, it was a strategy of obtaining the support of the Hong Kong business class during the transition and avoiding capital flight after the handover. To encourage cross-border investment, the Hong Kong Xinhua Agency—the de facto mouthpiece of the Beijing government in Hong Kong—even organized business trips for Hong Kong investors to mainland China and for mainland enterprises to Hong Kong.[13]

In sum, investment decisions in the Greater China region had political meaning because of specific historical and geopolitical circumstances. In deciding whether to regionalize their investment, private capitalists were not making only an economic decision but also a decision with a political impact. This gave them the power of leverage in dealing with their governments, the power to exchange political concessions for economic gains. In more general terms, regionalization in this context involved a process in which the state tried to shape capital investment for political ends while capital tried to influence state intervention for economic ends.

Shaping Capital Investment
Versus Influencing State Intervention

In their active pursuit of political and economic goals, both the state and capital tried to influence the course of regionalization by exploiting the political implications associated with the process. Because of security considerations, the Taipei government's initial policy toward mainland trade and investment was one of prohibition. However, this policy was rendered ineffective by those quasi-multinationals who conducted indirect trade and investment on the mainland via Hong Kong. Under pressure from the business sector, Taipei subsequently agreed that the government would not interfere with indirect export to the mainland and even allowed the indirect import of specified mainland raw materials into Taiwan. Since the late 1980s, the range of materials allowed to be exported and imported across the strait has steadily broadened.

To put further pressure on the government, big business enterprises declared an investment strike in Taiwan. These enterprises, whose mainland investments were under more stringent restrictions than those of the small enterprises, threatened to halt future investment plans in Taiwan unless the government agreed to liberalize the economy, improve the investment climate, and readjust its economy policy toward mainland investment.[14] This move exerted enormous pressure on the government.

It not only added to the anxiety about the political consequences of capital flight to the mainland but also created a consensus on the need for government assistance in industrial restructuring and in offering investment inducements to business.

Eventually, the government worked out a new plan that aimed at developing Taiwan into a so-called Asia-Pacific Operation Centre. In this plan, the economic restructuring process is designed to complement Taiwan's division of labor in the Greater China region: Taiwan is to become a high-tech, R&D center linking advanced Western technology to mainland China and a transshipment center linking mainland production to the Asia-Pacific region. The plan represents the concession made by the Taiwanese government to the business demand that obstacles to capital regionalization be removed, in exchange for the business community's concession that the government be allowed to guide the course of regionalization.

Under this plan, Taipei changed its mainland policy from prohibiting Taiwanese investment to a policy of "governmental guidance." It allowed low-tech, labor-intensive industries to relocate to mainland China, while restricting investment projects above a certain scale. Taiwanese financial institutions were allowed to establish indirect operations on the mainland to finance industrial projects. A government-backed unofficial organization, the Strait Exchange Foundation, was set up to deal with the mainland authorities concerning cross-strait trade and investment.

While allowing the relocation of labor-intensive industries to mainland China, the government also actively promoted industrial upgrading through state-sponsored R&D in the development, acquisition, and diffusion of new technologies. It removed virtually all sectoral restrictions on FDI in Taiwan in an attempt to attract overseas investment to boost the technological capacity of Taiwanese industries. It also required high-tech enterprises that wished to regionalize production into mainland China to make corresponding investments in Taiwan. In addition, tax reduction, land usage, preferential loans, and other privileges were offered to domestic enterprises in the high-tech sector to expand their investment in Taiwan.

In order to reduce over-reliance on the mainland economy, the Taiwanese government also encouraged investment diversification into other regions, particularly Southeast Asia. And by improving the infrastructural facilities for air and sea transit, the government planned to turn Taiwan into a regional distribution and transshipment center that served not only Greater China but also the rest of the East Asian region.

In general, the plan succeeded in promoting the relocation of labor-intensive industries into mainland China and in restructuring the manufacturing sector to more high-tech production. But the policy of restricting the scale of Taiwanese investment in the mainland had limited success. To circumvent the restriction, some enterprises set up large-scale projects in mainland China through their overseas subsidiaries.[15] Taipei could do little in these instances beyond negotiating with or persuading these enterprises to restrain their activities.

In the case of Hong Kong, the concern over the territory's future under Chinese rule contributed to a government-business consensus on the need to integrate the Hong Kong economy with that of mainland China. This consensus arose from the belief that fostering close ties with the mainland economy would ensure that Beijing would do nothing to harm Hong Kong, because it was in its own best interests to allow the territory to flourish and prosper. Local political and business elites believed that Hong Kong could survive only by proving its value as the economic dynamo of China in terms of capital, information, management knowhow, accounting and legal expertise, and so on.

This "golden goose" theory, as one observer describes it,[16] led the Hong Kong government to launch aggressive plans to turn Hong Kong into an entrepôt, business, and financial center for China. Under the so-called Port and Airport Development Strategy and related projects, huge investments were made in construction—including a new airport, container terminals, a convention center, and cross-border highways—in order to strengthen Hong Kong's service sector and its link to the Chinese economy. At the same time, industrial relocation to mainland China was facilitated by government-sponsored retraining programs that helped industrial workers to enter the service sector.

Adapting and Structuring Local Practices

For the quasi-multinationals from Taiwan and Hong Kong, overcoming the political obstacles and shaping government intervention in their domestic setting constituted only one side of the story. To regionalize their investment into mainland China, they had to face yet another problem: operating in a socialist system. This problem was, of course, not unique for Taiwan and Hong Kong enterprises; it was one that confronted all multinational enterprises that wanted to invest in China.

Global capital, as Stuart Hall points out, is far from overarching or all-absorbing in its pursuit of global accumulation, but actually works in and through particularity and locality.[17] In this regard, the success of the quasi-multinationals from Taiwan and Hong Kong in penetrating the socialist market of mainland China provides a good example of the capacity of globalized capital: on the one hand, their adaptation to local circumstances stands out and on the other hand, we note their ability to transform local markets in the pursuit of accumulation. I will highlight three aspects of this capacity here.

First, contrary to the assumption that globalized production cuts across cultural and ethnic boundaries, Taiwan and Hong Kong enterprises were attracted to the mainland market because they possessed one special competitive advantage over other well-established multinational corporations: social and cultural ties. It is obvious that sharing the same language and customary practices will facilitate business transactions, enterprise management, and labor relations. But the advantage goes further than that. These quasi-multinationals, especially the smaller ones, tended to start their business with relatives or friends in the Guangdong and Fujian Provinces. This enabled them to gain immediate familiarity with the local environment, get rapid access to local resources, and hence minimize risk and delay.[18]

In another example of adaptation to local circumstances, most of the investors from Taiwan and Hong Kong followed a strategy of investment less frequently taken by foreign multinationals. This strategy involved the activation of social/personal connections in negotiations with the government and the manipulation of project scale in response to different levels of authority. This represents an adaptation/exploitation of the power structure in a socialist system under reform.

Under the reform, local authorities enjoyed various degrees of autonomy in dealing with "foreign investments." Investment projects below a certain scale were approved by the county authorities; above that scale they had to be approved by municipal governments, provincial governments, or in the case of major projects, the central government. In other words, the larger the project, the higher the level of authority to deal with, the more departments to contact, the more bureaucratic procedures and rules to follow, and the longer the delay. For quasi-multinationals dependent on flexible production and quick response to world market changes, reducing bureaucratic delay was essential. One strategy to avoid bureaucratic blockage was to divide a large investment plan into a number of independent smaller projects. In this way an investor could avoid dealing with the higher authorities, and delays in one particular project would not jeopardize the whole investment.

One study gives the example of a shoe manufacturer who divided his production into six different establishments, locating them in different neighboring districts. Each individual establishment had an investment of less than US$1 million and employed fewer than six hundred workers. This meant that he had to negotiate only with the county authorities, thus saving time and avoiding complications.[19] Some investors even avoided the more well-developed Special Economic Zones and relocated their factories to more remote counties and villages in order to circumvent stringent regulations, on the one hand, and to make use of the cheaper land rent, lower electricity and water charges, lower taxes, and better raw material supplies, on the other hand.

For other quasi-multinationals, especially the big investors, the hierarchical state and party structure did not necessarily mean blockage and delay, provided one knew the pivotal point for maneuver. This involved obtaining high-level party/leadership blessing or patronage and then making use of such relationships in overcoming bureaucratic delay in various levels of government. Two eye-catching examples are the widely reported cases of Hong Kong tycoon Li Ka-shing and Taiwan magnate Wang Yung-ching. Li managed to realize a controversial property development project in the capital city, Beijing, because he secured the participation of the sons and daughters of party elders Deng Xiaoping and Wang Zhen in the project. Wang had the blessing of Deng Xiaoping, Premier Li Peng, and Party General Secretary Jiang Zemin for his petrochemical plant in Fujian. Li Peng was reported to have overseen the project personally.[20] The result was that the Fujian provincial authorities wasted no time in improving infrastructural facilities in Haicang for the project. Even when Wang abandoned his plan in 1993, the Fujian government continued to make it clear that the site in Haicang was still reserved for Wang's project.[21]

And lastly, quasi-multinationals also exploited the internal contradiction within the mainland system to increase their bargaining power. Having more autonomy under market reform, local authorities were keen to attract overseas investments into their own locality. The competition for Taiwanese and Hong Kong investment thus gave the quasi-multinationals some degree of leverage vis-à-vis local governments in bargaining for special privileges. In addition to offering the above-mentioned privileges of cheaper land prices, lower electricity and water charges, and so on, local authorities also drew up attractive investment policies to compete for Taiwanese and Hong Kong investment. Hong Kong and Taiwan investment zones were established in a number of counties in Guangdong and Fujian. The Shenzhen and Xiamen Special Economic Zones even received autonomous legislative power to enact laws to protect the interests of overseas Chinese investors. Other provinces also offered favorable policies with the establishment of Taiwan investment zones, industry-specific districts (such as the Taiwan Electronics Street in Shanghai, the Taiwan Products Exhibition Street in Fuzhou, and Hong Kong Streets in a number of municipalities), and some even allocated sites to be developed exclusively by Taiwanese and Hong Kong investors.

The most extreme cases of such maneuvers even resulted in the change of provincial development plans. For instance, Taiwanese investments in

Xiamen had been concentrated in labor-intensive sectors and in the chemical industry. This conflicted with the Socio-economic Development Plan of the Xiamen authorities to make the high-tech electronics industry the development priority. In the wake of competition to attract incoming overseas investments, the Xiamen authorities eventually abandoned their original plan and declared petrochemicals to be their new development emphasis.[22]

In general, the ultimate bargaining power of globalized capital is the decision to make or withhold investments. Although governments can affect business decisions through development plans and economic intervention, they can never control investment decisions. Even in mainland China, the power of these quasi-foreign investors to withhold capital or move capital elsewhere has forced local governments to enter into bargaining relations with them.[23]

Escaping Local Practices

The instances described above represent the strategies taken by Taiwan and Hong Kong quasi-multinationals in adapting to local practices when expanding their investment to a different politico-economic system. An equally intriguing case is the regionalization of mainland Chinese enterprises in order to escape the constraints of their socialist system. The economic reform carried out so far in mainland China still allowed party bureaucrats to interfere with the business activities of enterprises, especially those enterprises under state or collective ownership and control. One way for these enterprises to circumvent bureaucratic interference and ideological constraints was to move their management headquarters to Hong Kong or to diversify their investment through Hong Kong.

Most of the mainland enterprises that regionalized their investment into and through Hong Kong were under the direct control of either the central government, the provincial and municipal governments, or the county and district level authorities. Officially there were more than eighteen hundred such enterprises on the eve of Hong Kong's handover. Many well-established enterprises have been listed in the Hong Kong stock market and became the so-called red-chip companies. One report estimated that the total capital assets of these red-chip companies exceeded US$42.5 billion in 1996.[24] These companies invested in a broad range of activities and businesses, including banking, trading, manufacturing, property development, shipping, construction, energy, communications, hotels, and supermarkets.

An eye-catching example of these enterprises is the New China Hong Kong Group, set up in 1993. The Group began with start-up capital of US$65 million from fifty-four shareholders. These shareholders included companies directly under the control of Chinese central government ministries (such as the State Council, Ministry of Finance, Ministry of Foreign Economic Relations and Trade, Ministry of Transport, State Commission of Science and Technology); companies belonging to the municipal and provincial governments of Beijing, Liaoning, Sichuan, and Jilin; and registered companies in Hong Kong that belonged to or were affiliated with state enterprises (such as Capital Iron and Steel, Bank of China, and China Resources). Also included among the shareholders were major business tycoons in Hong Kong, including Li Ka-shing, Tsui Tsin-tong, Stanley Ho, James Tien, the Hysan Lee family, and the Lam Pak-yan family. The Group's initial investment also contained capital from Taiwan, Singapore, Indonesia, and Thailand. Its main investments included infrastructural development, real estate, telecommunications, and the manufacturing industry in mainland China.[25]

In fact, setting up companies in Hong Kong and then using the Hong Kong companies to invest back into mainland China was a strategy used by many mainland enterprises. In such a way, they enjoyed a higher degree of autonomy in mobilizing their capital and making investment decisions, and they benefitted from privileges granted to the "special domestic capital" from Hong Kong. Although the Chinese government had strict procedures controlling the establishment of companies outside mainland China, it is reported that more than five thousand "underground" enterprises existed in Hong Kong by the mid-1990s, set up by various authorities and state/collective enterprises through informal channels and means.[26]

In addition to the obvious economic advantages, there were political reasons for the approval of such a strategy by the mainland government. The idea of the mainland authorities was to strengthen the share and influence of mainland capital in the Hong Kong economy in order to increase Beijing's leverage over Hong Kong. The authorities even hoped that companies like the New China Hong Kong Group would pull the Hong Kong tycoons together to form a pro-Beijing bourgeois class.[27] The increasing presence of mainland capital in Hong Kong was also welcomed by politicians and businessmen in the territory. This is no mere coincidence, because such a presence, in addition to creating more opportunities for business, would strengthen the "golden goose" status of Hong Kong and thereby enhance the territory's chance of survival after the handover.

The Emerging Regional Division of Labor

The outcome of the process described above was an emerging regional division of labor that, far from being merely "market-induced," was shaped by business strategy and state intervention in the pursuit of political as well as economic goals. In this division of labor, Hong Kong acted as an entrepôt and a center of commercial and financial services; Taiwan turned increasingly to R&D and high-tech production; and mainland China provided cheap land and labor for manufacturing. In this complementarity, a complex triangular network of production and export ran through all three.

During this process, Hong Kong underwent the most drastic changes in less than fifteen years. As manufacturers moved their production plants across the border, Hong Kong transformed from a manufacturing center to a commercial center. The manufacturing industry's contribution to GDP declined each year: 20.9 percent in 1992, 18.5 percent in 1993, and 16.9 percent in 1994. At the same time, the service sector's contribution to the economy increased every year, amounting to 79 percent, 81 percent, and 83 percent of the GDP in the years 1992, 1993, and 1994 respectively. More than four million workers in Guangdong were employed by or on behalf of Hong Kong enterprises in the mid-1990s, representing more than ten times the size of Hong Kong's own manufacturing workforce. The relocation of production units to China changed the nature of the Hong Kong "factories," which now concentrated more and more on marketing, product design, quality control, purchase of raw materials, inventory control, management and technical supervision, and financial arrangements. These activities were similar to those performed by the traditional British trading houses under the international commercial subcontracting arrangement. In essence, these factories-turned-multinationals became a new generation of trading houses, which differed from the traditional ones by virtue of their manufacturing experience.[28]

In the case of Taiwan, the relocation of low-valued manufacturing to mainland China boosted industrial upgrading on the island. The percentage of exports in traditional labor-intensive products such as garments dropped from 48 percent in 1982 to 33.5 percent in 1991. During the same period, the proportion of high-tech export products, such as electronics and sophisticated machine tools, increased from 29.2 percent to 43.7 percent.

Paralleling the course of economic restructuring, the volume of trade and investment throughout the three economies grew tremendously. Mainland China became Hong Kong's largest trading partner in 1985. China's share in Hong Kong's global trade jumped from 9.3 percent in 1978 to 34.8 percent in 1995. Hong Kong became mainland China's largest export market, taking 24.2 percent of China's total exports by value in 1995. Between 1978 and 1995, imports from mainland China to Hong

Kong increased at an average rate of 26 percent. Hong Kong has remained mainland China's largest direct "foreign" investor, accounting for about 60 percent of the national total. Over 75 percent of Hong Kong's offshore investment in the mid-1990s went to mainland China. At the same time, mainland China also became the largest investor in Hong Kong, overtaking Britain, the United States, and Japan. Between Taiwan and mainland China, indirect trade via Hong Kong grew from US$78 million in 1979 to US$9.1 billion in 1994, an increase of nearly 116-fold. Taiwan's export to the mainland alone increased more than 400-fold, from US$21 million in 1979 to US$8.5 billion in 1994. By the end of 1992, Taiwan had become the second largest investor in mainland China. Similarly, trade between Taiwan and Hong Kong grew significantly. Hong Kong became the largest market for Taiwan's exports by 1993, taking in 21.7 percent of Taiwan's total exports.

Besides trilateral trade, new export drives were created by the emerging division of labor among the three. Investments from Hong Kong and Taiwan, involving mostly export-oriented processing/assembly projects, contributed to mainland China's export growth. This growth was aided by the long-existing network of overseas marketing and subcontracting arrangements that Taiwan and Hong Kong had established over the decades. In addition, outward processing in mainland China constituted a source of "indirect export" for Hong Kong and Taiwan. Whereas mainland China's trade with the developed countries was mostly interindustry trade, its trade with Hong Kong and Taiwan included substantial intraindustry trade—a high proportion of which was in fact intrafirm trade.[29] By supplying essential components, semi-finished products, intermediate inputs, and so on to mainland China for final assembly and export to the Western markets, Taiwanese and Hong Kong enterprises were able to export their products indirectly to markets that had already set up trade barriers against them. One study suggested that between 1989 and the first half of 1992, some 71 to 77 percent of Hong Kong's exports to mainland China were destined for outward processing. It estimated that the finished manufactures accounted, on average, for 68 percent of Hong Kong's total exports to the United States during the same period.[30] A survey in the early 1990s estimated that Taiwanese enterprises in mainland China obtained, on average, 54 percent of their raw material and intermediate inputs from Taiwan.[31] Another survey finds that nearly 70 percent of Taiwanese manufactures in mainland China were exported, 20 percent were consumed locally, and only 10 percent were imported back to Taiwan.[32]

The growing economic integration among mainland China, Taiwan, and Hong Kong leads some observers to suggest that a new economic actor—the Greater China—is emerging.[33] While the idea of a singular economic actor capable of acting in concert is still too far-fetched, given the sensitive political relationships among its members, it is true that their common economic interests in the global economy have become more pronounced. This has important implications for the Asian region as well as the rest of the world because of the collective strength of these three economies. Together they accounted in the mid-1990s for the world's third largest GDP, the third largest trading turnover, and the largest foreign exchange reserves. Their trilateral economic relationship has already contributed to an increased volume of intraregional trade in Asia. Whereas the value of trade among Japan, the four NIEs, ASEAN, and China was worth US$106 billion in comparison to their US$132 billion trade with the United States in 1983, by 1993 the volume of intraregional trade had outgrown the interregional trade. Intraregional trade increased by 3.9 times to US$420 billion, exceeding the US$363 billion trade with the United States. The region absorbed more than 47.7 percent of the exports from the ten East Asian economies in 1993, while the United States took only 32.4 percent.[34] Such a trend will certainly affect the structure of the global economy and is thus an important aspect of globalization. A fuller exploration of the implications, however, is beyond the scope of this paper.

Conclusion

The foregoing discussion of the three East Asian cases shows that globalization is not a process external to domestic polity and economy that destines national states to a universal trajectory of accumulation. Rather it is a process involving policy choices, consensus building, and political compromise. In other words, it is a process shaped by active agency. At the risk of oversimplification, this discussion has highlighted the agency role played by states and capital in shaping the development of a regional economy while reflecting global and domestic, economic and political concerns.

This case study also suggests that the agency role of states and capital does not conform to the romanticized polarized views of strong states governing the market and mobile transnationals defying national barriers. Rather, agency is manifest in the bargaining, manipulation, and even personal exchange between governmental and business actors to influence the course of development. In this way, actors accommodate global market pressure by facilitating the development of a specific regional pattern of globalization, while at the same time fulfilling their political ends through such a pattern.

Notes

1. Kenichi Ohmae, *The Borderless World* (New York: Harper Collins, 1990); Kenichi Ohmae, *The End of the Nation State: The Rise of Regional Economies* (New York: Free Press, 1995).
2. Ankie Hoogvelt, *Globalisation and the Postcolonial World: The New Political Economy of Development* (London: Macmillan, 1997).
3. John Stopford and Susan Strange with John S. Henley, *Rival States, Rival Firms: Competition for World Market Shares* (Cambridge: Cambridge University Press, 1991).
4. Gordon White, ed., *Developmental States in East Asia* (London: Macmillan, 1988); Robert Wade, *Governing the Market: Economic Theory and the Role of Government in East Asian Industrialization* (Princeton: Princeton University Press, 1990); Richard P. Appelbaum and Jeffrey Henderson, eds., *States and Development in the Asian Pacific Rim* (Newbury Park: Sage, 1992).
5. See, for instance, Richard Stubbs, "The Political Economy of the Asia-Pacific Region," in *Political Economy and the Changing Global Order*, ed. Richard Stubbs and Geoffrey R. D. Underhill (London: Macmillan, 1994), pp. 366–377.
6. See the discussion in Harry Harding, "The Concept of 'Greater China': Themes, Variations and Reservations," in *Greater China: The Next Superpower?* ed. David Shambaugh (Oxford: Oxford University Press, 1995), pp. 8–34.
7. Michael Sharpston, "International Sub-contracting," *Oxford Economic Papers* 27, no. 1 (March 1975): 94–131. Gereffi calls these "buyer-driven commodity chains." See Chapter 3 in this volume and Gary Gereffi, "The Organisation of Buyer-Driven Global Commodity Chains: How U.S. Retailers Shape Overseas Production Networks," in *Commodity Chains and Global Capitalism*, ed. Gary Gereffi and Miguel Korzeniewicz (Westport, Conn.: Praeger, 1994), pp. 95–122.
8. G. S. Shieh, *"Boss" Island: The Subcontracting Network and Micro-Entrepreneurship in Taiwan's Development* (New York: Peter Lang, 1992); Victor Fung-shuen Sit and Siu-lun Wong, *Small and Medium Industries in an Export-Oriented Economy: The Case of Hong Kong* (Hong Kong: Centre of Asian Studies, University of Hong Kong, 1989).
9. Albert O. Hirschman, *Exit, Voice, and Loyalty: Responses to Decline in Firms, Organizations, and States* (Cambridge, Mass.: Harvard University Press, 1970).
10. Qi Luo and Christopher Howe, "Direct Investment and Economic Integration in the Asia Pacific: The Case of Taiwanese Investment in Xiamen," *China Quarterly*, no. 136 (December 1993), pp. 753–756.
11. Wang Tu-fa, "Taiwan yu Zhongguo jingmao jiaoliu dui Taiwan jingji fazhan de yingxiang" (The Effect of Taiwan-China Economic and Trade Exchange on Taiwan's Economic Development) (manuscript, 1995); Wei Hua, "An Investigation into the Current Cross-Strait Economic and Trade Situation," *Zhonggong Yanjiu* 26, no. 8 (August 1992): 45.

12. Tak-Wing Ngo, "Business Encirclement of Politics: Government-Business Relations across the Taiwan Strait," *China Information* 10, no. 2 (Autumn 1995): 1–18.
13. Xu Jiatun, *Xu Jiatun Xianggang Huiyilu* (Xu Jiatun's Memoir of Hong Kong) (Hong Kong: United Press, 1993), ch. 9.
14. Jenn-hwan Wang, "The State, Capital, and Taiwan's Political Transition," *Taiwan: A Radical Quarterly in Social Studies* 14 (March 1993): 147.
15. One example is the Formosa Plastics Group's investment in electric power and paper-making in Fujian and Hainan. See the report in *Yazhou Zhoukan*, April 21–27, 1997, pp. 21–26.
16. Ian Scott, "Political Transformation in Hong Kong: From Colony to Colony," in *The Hong Kong-Guangdong Link: Partnership in Flux*, ed. Reginald Yin-Wang Kwok and Alvin Y. So (New York: M. E. Sharpe, 1995), pp. 189–223.
17. Stuart Hall, "Old and New Identities, Old and New Ethnicities," in *Culture, Globalization and the World-System: Contemporary Conditions for the Representation of Identity*, ed. Anthony D. King (London: Macmillan, 1991), p. 29.
18. See the study by Josephine Smart and Alan Smart, "Personal Relations and Divergent Economies: A Case Study of Hong Kong Investment in South China," *International Journal of Urban and Regional Research* 1, no. 2 (1991): 216–233.
19. You-tien Hsing, "A New Pattern of Foreign Direct Investment: Taiwanese Guerilla Investors and Local Chinese Bureaucrats in the Pearl River Delta," *Taiwan: A Radical Quarterly in Social Studies*, no. 23 (July 1996): 174–176.
20. *International Herald Tribune*, December 19, 1990.
21. *Lianhebao*, January 14 and 15, 1993.
22. Luo and Howe, "Direct Investment and Economic Integration," p. 758.
23. This applies not only to Taiwan and Hong Kong investors, but to foreign investors as well. See Margaret M. Pearson, *Joint Ventures in the People's Republic of China: The Control of Foreign Direct Investment under Socialism* (Princeton: Princeton University Press, 1991).
24. *Yazhou Zhoukan*, September 8, 1996, p. 53.
25. *Far Eastern Economic Review*, May 27, 1993, pp. 62–67.
26. *Yazhou Zhoukan*, September 8, 1996, p. 60.
27. Xu, *Xu Jiatun's Memoir*, ch. 9.
28. Sit and Wong, *Small and Medium Industries*, p. 229.
29. Yun-wing Sung, "Economic Integration of Hong Kong and Guangdong in the 1990s," in Reginald Yin-Wang Kwok and Alvin Y. So, *The Hong Kong-Guangdong Link: Partnership in Flux*, p. 226.
30. Robert F. Ash and Y. Y. Kueh, "Economic Integration within Greater China: Trade and Investment Flow Between China, Hong Kong and Taiwan," *China Quarterly*, no. 136 (December 1993): 727–728.
31. *Far Eastern Economic Review*, March 5, 1992, p. 54.
32. Quoted in Hsing, "A New Pattern of Foreign Direct Investment," p. 174.

33. Michael Yahuda, *Hong Kong: China's Challenge* (London: Routledge, 1996), p. 29.

34. Yun-han Chu, "The East Asian NICs: A State-led Path to the Developed World," in *Global Change, Regional Response: The New International Context of Development*, ed. Barbara Stallings (Cambridge: Cambridge University Press, 1995), p. 230.

6

Globalizing Vietnam: The Nation State in the Region

Stephanie Fahey

Vietnam, like the other countries in Southeast Asia, has been subjected to both global economic pressures to stabilize, liberalize, privatize, and decentralize and international political pressures to actualize political pluralism and democratization. These pressures have not been unproductive. The Vietnamese state is acutely aware that its continued legitimacy is dependent on its ability to reproduce economic growth, which in the present context will mean engagement with global capitalism through liberalized trade and investment and through membership in various regional organizations such as ASEAN, APEC, and the WTO. It is clear from protests in Indonesia against the former Suharto government that an economic crisis fuels latent political discontent.

Nevertheless, the Vietnamese state is attempting to engage with the global economy on its own terms: to increase foreign investment but also to maintain state ownership in strategic sectors, to maintain overall control of the economy, and to resist at all cost the pressures for pluralism and the emergence of a self-determining civil society, which is a development threatening the southern part of the country. In the view of the Vietnamese leaders, the state is best prepared to accommodate the casualties of global engagement and rapid economic growth, such as the increasing inequality in income distribution, increasing disparities between rural and urban standards of living, the deteriorating position of women in decision making and income earning, and the growing income disparity and ideological tension between the generations.

In Vietnam, as in many parts of Asia, the impact of globalization is not confined to the economic and political spheres, but has pervaded all corners of Vietnamese society—much to the preoccupation of the state. In the face of these influences, Vietnamese leaders are asserting the integrity of Vietnam's own cultural identity. They appear to fear deeply the erosion of Vietnamese morality by the infusion of foreign cultural mores. At the same time, however, they resist a return to Confucian principles and fundamentalist Buddhism. It appears that Vietnam is experiencing simultaneously the impact of cultural globalization and the impact of official pressures toward indigenization. These often conflicting processes are producing social tensions across class and generational divides—tensions that have become the object of deep concern among Vietnamese leaders in recent years.

Since the end of the Vietnam War, Vietnam has been exposed to great external pressures by foreign investors and trading partners, multilateral agencies (e.g., the World Bank, the IMF, the Asian Development Bank (ADB), and the UN Development Program), and bilateral aid agencies. As Vietnam becomes reintegrated into the global economy through membership in ASEAN and as a future participant in the ASEAN Free Trade Area (AFTA) and possibly in APEC and the WTO, these tensions will increase and the central economic and political control by the Vietnamese Communist Party (VCP) will face more serious challenges.

Socioeconomic Transition in Vietnam

Vietnam is on a roller-coaster ride of transition from a planned to a market economy. Vietnamese planners have neither past experience nor clear cut conceptual frameworks on which to base this shift. Experiences in other former communist regimes give little direction. The political and economic legacies vary enormously.[1] This has fuelled various debates about the nature of the transition and the direction Vietnam is heading both economically and politically.[2] Those from the Right argue that the fundamental flaws of socialism are responsible for catapulting countries like Vietnam, China, and the former Soviet bloc countries into unrestrained capitalism.[3] Some are concerned about the dangers of partial reform and the possibility of development stagnating in the "twilight zone" of transition.[4] Those from the Left argue that transition in socialist economies is a reaction to the same pressures experienced by other developing countries—both socialist and capitalist—to liberalize, marketize, privatize, and internationalize as dictated by global capital and international market forces. In this respect, Vietnam is not unique in becoming inexorably reintegrated into a single, all-encompassing global economy.[5]

In fact, the Vietnamese process of transition has been rather gradual and began with microeconomic changes followed by macroeconomic reforms. The political reforms were few and limited in scope.[6] The intention of Vietnamese policy makers is not to create room for the development of a free-market system following capitalist recipes, but to maintain a socialist command economy with public ownership of the means of production and under leadership by the VCP.

The pressure for reform in Vietnam initially emanated from the grass roots. Sectors within the peasantry and workers in state owned enterprises (SOEs) had become increasingly dissatisfied with the inefficiencies of collectivism. They began experimenting with alternative ways of organizing their work, experiments that initially were tolerated by the Party and later were formalized by decree. However, the motives that were given for this policy included the need for efficiency through the decentralization of decisions in favor of enterprises and small family business, with the explicit objective of continuing on the road toward socialism.

These internal pressures for change were complemented by the external pressures to open the economy for international trade and investment. Vietnam's entry into the global economy, however, met with complications. Following its entry into Cambodia in 1979, Vietnam had been subjected to a U.S. trade embargo that hampered the inflow of foreign capital and technology. In addition, the embargo effectively impeded borrowing from multilateral agencies such as the World Bank, the IMF, and the ADB, it limited Official Development Assistance (ODA) from the West, and it prevented trade and technology transfer from the other major western economies. When the embargo was lifted and lending was resumed in the early 1990s, Vietnamese planners were determined to engage in the world economy on their own terms and to negotiate their own path of economic growth and national development, in defiance of the reform dictates presented by the western development cooperation community.

Since the end of the Vietnam-American War, the Vietnamese government has experimented with various economic strategies. The initial strategy—with fiscal and technical support from both China and the Soviet bloc—was to pursue socialist policies, to eliminate the bourgeoisie as a power factor in economy and society, and to organize the peasantry and handicraft producers into cooperatives. Factories were brought under direct control of the ministries. These allocated the necessary inputs and set the production targets. Retail stores were integrated into the state commercial network. Industry was heavily subsidized by the state and the cities were favored over the countryside in infrastructural investment. Agriculture was under- resourced. As a consequence, by mid-1978, the collectivization of agriculture in the south had floundered and the collection of food by the state had stagnated in the north. Bad weather conditions and aid cuts added to an emergency situation, with food shortages in several parts of the country. It was at this time that the need for substantial reform became evident.

The rice shortages and the problem of providing industry with the necessary inputs led to reforms in some agricultural cooperatives and industrial enterprises. These involved spontaneous private productive activities not covered by the plan economy. The state later formalized these activities, issuing an important resolution in August 1979 that encouraged trade relations, commodity relations, and the development of small family businesses. However, all inputs were to be provided through state channels, which caused problems of coordination, red tape, and delay, making it difficult for these sectors to flourish. Nevertheless, this initiative revealed an awareness and an appreciation of market criteria.

The experiment with productive activities outside the plan was later formalized through the introduction of two reforms. These included the so-called Three Plan System, which legalized market activities by SOEs alongside the activities included in the state plan, and the measure permitting the development of an output contract system next to the existing cooperative system. This measure led to a mushrooming of private activities, provoking a call for stricter control on the private staples trade in 1982 by *Nhan Dan*, the Party's newspaper.[7] In subsequent years, politics regularly intervened in the reform process.

In the first half of the 1980s, the state sector continued to be heavily subsidized. The private sector and the free markets were meant to play a subordinate role. The growth of industrial production in the non-state sector was hampered by low capital investment and low productivity.[8] This sector accounted for over 70 percent of industrial employment, but produced only 40 percent of total industrial output. By 1985 the reforms had proven to be inadequate. In particular, the agricultural sector was again having problems.

In 1986, the Sixth Party Congress was compelled to lift further restrictions on the functioning of the private sector, and two years later major policy reforms in the areas of FDI and land reform were announced. The Vietnamese leadership could not continue to ignore the demonstration effect of its neighbors' outstanding economic success.[9] A number of other factors as well almost forced Vietnam onto the road of reform. The extensive smuggling along its porous borders was undermining the functioning of the command economy. In 1989, Vietnam lost aid from and preferential trade agreements with the USSR, and Soviet-provided inputs, on which the economy had become so dependent, had to be replaced with inputs produced elsewhere. At the 1990 meeting of the Council for Mutual Economic Assistance (CMEA), several countries declined to commit support to Vietnam's 1990–1995 Five Year Plan. Vietnam lost trading partners, contracts were cancelled, and imports were restricted and had to be paid for in hard currency. For Vietnam, the only remaining alternative was to liberalize its economy further in order to secure support from

Bretton Woods organizations. The assistance of these institutions, however, is conditional. A certain degree of structural adjustment and "room" for market mechanisms are preconditions for receiving assistance.

The post-1989 reforms are characterized by commercialization: resources are to be bought and sold through the market rather than through administrative means. The subsidies to the state sector through the provision of inputs to SOEs were eliminated. The existence of a two-price system (official price and market price) was ended. This meant a most significant change in favor of the market mechanism. The reforms, however, failed to create an economic dynamism. Between 1989 and 1992, priority allocation of credit and subsidized interest rates to SOEs led to an increasing dominance of the state over the private sector. The contribution to gross domestic industrial product (GDP) by the state sector increased from 57 percent in 1989 to 64 percent in 1995. In 1994, the private sector employed 80 percent of industrial labor, but only produced 36 percent of total industrial output; moreover, labor productivity in the private sector was only 20 percent of that in the SOEs, highlighting the latter's relative capital intensity.[10] The state has kept its control of foreign trade involving the major export commodities such as rice, oil, and marine products and closely watches foreign investments through joint ventures with SOEs.

In practice since 1989 and formalized in the Constitution since 1992, government policy has permitted non-socialist components of the economy, including the self-employed and private sectors, mainly because of their capacity to employ the increasing number of jobless people. Although the private sector is permitted legally, few in the domestic sphere have access to necessary resources, such as capital, land, technology, know-how, and access to export networks. In this respect, private enterprise can offer little competition to the SOE sector in manufacturing. Although bank loans to the private sector are technically possible, the requirement of the ever-elusive collateral will frustrate this possibility in practice. A limited number of private entrepreneurs have managed to accumulate private domestic investment capital through land speculation, illegal activities (e.g., smuggling and trade in gold and precious stones), the mobilization of hidden savings, and remittances from abroad. Also, the management of some SOEs has channeled capital into privately owned, parallel businesses. But these activities are conducted surreptitiously and require the protection of politically powerful personal networks.

In the 1990s, the reforms continued in the areas of interest rates, foreign capital investment, growth of the private sector and private enterprise legislation, rationalization of the SOE sector, de facto privatization of state assets, the liberalization of the land law, banking reforms, wage reform, administrative reform, and the promulgation of a new labor code. The Eighth Party Congress, held in 1996, restated the objective of modernization through industrialization even though the fastest rate of growth was registered in the service and construction sectors. The new industrialization policy emphasized the production of machinery and electronics as a priority objective. In addition to light industry associated with the food and forestry sectors, the government planned to expand manufacturing under SOE leadership by 13–15 percent, so that by 2000 manufacturing would contribute 30 percent of GDP. The official growth rate of the economy has averaged about 8 percent since the late 1980s. International trade has increased tenfold. However, in 1996 Vietnam still had a negative trade balance.[11] Its major exports are crude oil, unprocessed agricultural products (rice and fish), minerals (coal and tin) and textiles/clothing. The main imports are higher-value-added products (e.g., iron and steel, petroleum products, fertilizers, wheat flour, and televisions). Committed FDI in Vietnam increased from a total of US$366 million in 1988 to US$26 billion in 1996.[12] From these commitments only 40 percent has been realized in the 1990s. The national current account deficit increased to 11.3 percent in 1996 but was reduced to 8.6 percent the next year. The long-term financial plan of development in Vietnam was reorganized during 1997–1998. Foreign investment and international trade have come under increasing pressure due to diminishing returns, the shortage of regional investment capital, and diminished purchasing power in the wake of the Asian meltdown. The new Vietnamese leadership, appointed in early 1998, are manifesting support for the liberalization of international trade and investment and the development of the domestic private sector. The Asian crisis may even speed up this reformist trend.

Global Pressures on Vietnam's Economy

During the 1950s and 1960s the pressure for global trade was immense and multinational companies proliferated. But in those years Vietnam was in the grip of regional Cold War struggles. The country was at war and any surplus was channeled toward the war effort. Non–war related international trade and investment in Vietnam were virtually absent. When it did enter the global economy, the country was a late starter.

After the Vietnam-American War, the country's international economic engagement was primarily with the CMEA countries. The economy was heavily dependent on foreign aid and subsidized trade relations. Its trade policy was a simple one: Vietnam imported what it needed and exported whatever was in excess in the domestic economy, ignoring notions of comparative advantage, international division of labor, specialization, etc. Technical and structural change in the Vietnamese economy were slow in coming.[13]

The collapse of the CMEA forced Vietnam to build economic relations with non-communist countries. This move was impeded somewhat by the U.S. trade embargo, although Vietnam managed to negotiate behind this barrier with other western countries. Vietnam facilitated international economic engagement initially through the establishment of diplomatic relations with the intention of creating international confidence. Even without a fundamental political shift, Vietnam's diplomatic relations with non-communist countries increased at an unprecedented rate from 23 in 1989 to 161 in 1996. During the early mid-1990s, Vietnam also normalized relations with the two superpowers—China and United States—who had been its long-standing antagonists. In September 1993, the United States lifted restrictions on lending by the World Bank, the ADB, and the IMF and allowed U.S. firms to tender for their projects. By February 1994, the U.S. administration lifted the trade embargo, which had been enacted under the 1917 Trading with the Enemy Act. Vietnam's incorporation into the global economy was supported in the mid-1980s through ODA and FDI from western countries, including France, the Netherlands, the United Kingdom, Canada, Sweden, and Australia. During the 1990s, these sources were replaced by regional interests in both trade and investment.

Globalization and Regionalization in the Asia Pacific Region

In the 1980s, internationalizing and globalizing tendencies began to have a strong impact in the Asia Pacific region. New information technologies and deregulation facilitated the globalization of financial flows and supply and demand. The flow of capital and technology transfers and the demand on the U.S., European, and Japanese markets was feeding the growth of the "Asian Tigers." China and the ASEAN countries followed. This growth process was explosive until the recent global currency crisis—which first became evident in Thailand and then spread throughout the region—created the need for re-adjustment of these economies.

The processes of globalization are accompanied by an increasing tendency toward regionalization.[14] The sources of FDI in Vietnam also reflects the increasing impact of this trend. In January 1997, the top foreign investors in order of importance were Taiwan, Hong Kong, Japan, Singapore, and South Korea, followed by the United States. Former significant investors, like Australia, France, the United Kingdom, and the Netherlands had slipped in prominence. The present dominant investment trend is regional, emanating from China and mainly directed toward industry and real estate. These investments are increasingly organized through EPZs to protect factories from inflated costs associated with the domestic economy and the predations of its agencies.[15]

Regionalism is even more apparent in production and sourcing. In the mid-1970s, only 33 percent of trade from the Asia Pacific region was within the region. This figure had increased to 40 percent by the mid-1990s. Much of this regional trade involves bilateral flows between Japan and other countries rather than among all countries.

The future development of Vietnam within the context of the Asia Pacific region is intimately linked to this role of Japan. In 1994, over 30 percent (US$1.08 billion) of Vietnam's exports went to Japan, whereas only 11 percent (US$511 million) of imports came from that country. Singapore, Taiwan, and South Korea are the more important—and cheaper—providers of Vietnam's imports. As a regional supplier of raw materials, Vietnam is one of the few countries to run a trade surplus with Japan. In the area of FDI, since 1991 and especially after the lifting of the U.S. trade embargo in 1994, Japan has risen rapidly in prominence from ninth to third top foreign investor in Vietnam. Also, Japan is Vietnam's leading aid provider, although much of the aid is tied to construction projects executed by Japanese companies. Vietnam's reliance on Japan is not unusual within the region and undoubtedly the global Japanese organization and distribution of plants, distribution networks, and research centers will influence the Vietnamese inclination to emulate international business practice.[16]

During the 1990s, Vietnam's volume of trade with ASEAN countries increased at a rate of 27 percent per year. This trade now comprises one-third of Vietnam's total foreign trade. Vietnam's export to ASEAN countries includes products like crude oil, rice, beans, rubber, sea products, steel products, timber, corn, cashew nuts, coal, tin, tanned leather, handicraft wares, tea, vegetables, and fruit. Vietnam imports raw materials, intermediate products, and industrial goods.[17] Foreign direct investment from ASEAN countries also increased rapidly and comprised 16 percent of total FDI in 1995, with major investment coming from Singapore, Malaysia, and Thailand in areas such as machinery assembly, construction, hotels, and tourism. Investment in general manufacturing and in high-tech areas has remained limited. Singapore is Vietnam's second most important economic partner after Japan, receiving 15 percent of Vietnam's exports and supplying 22 percent of its imports (1994). It also ranks fourth on Vietnam's list of top foreign investors.

One of the most important steps taken by Vietnam in recent times is its membership in ASEAN and its commitment to participate in the AFTA.[18] In July 1995, Vietnam became the seventh member of ASEAN and will now be joined by Burma, Cambodia, and Laos. Vietnamese leaders consider their membership as a signal to the international community indicating the seriousness of their intentions to transform the economy, to accept the market mechanism in allocating resources, and to further openness. Vietnam aspires to membership in the WTO and membership in APEC. Through ASEAN membership, the Vietnamese leaders have stated, they will be "implementing administrative reform, improving the judiciary and the legal system, promoting regional cooperation, increasing our capability to compete internationally, and pursuing a policy of peaceful dialogue, independence, and sovereignty."[19]

A major rationale for the establishment of AFTA was to enlarge the regional market and to attract FDI. In recent years, FDI inflows to the ASEAN countries have dropped significantly. With the Asian financial crisis, FDI in the region has decreased further. The major mechanism for the implementation of AFTA is the Common Effective Preferential Tariff (CEPT), which includes acceptance of consistency in trade-related structures and procedures, the reduction of tariff barriers to a rate between zero and five percent, the liberalization of foreign exchange and payment regimes, and the establishment of a structure of consultation with partners on other issues. Vietnam is due to conform fully by 2006, whereas other members have the more immediate deadline of 2003.

Compliance with AFTA exposes the Vietnamese economy to the pressures of regional competition. Vietnam will be able to maintain control over the infrastructure and the energy sectors (telecommunications, electricity, oil, and transport). However, there is concern is that Vietnam's infant industries may be jeopardized as cheap manufactured products from ASEAN countries flood the market—a situation exacerbated by the Vietnamese preference for imported commodities. The level of technology in Vietnam is low and although the labor costs are among the lowest in the region, the labor component in most branches of industry continues to decline, which erodes Vietnam's comparative advantage. Furthermore, Vietnam's participation in AFTA also means a loss of revenue from export and import taxes. These currently account for about 23–25 percent of total government income. About 5 percent of this tax income is generated by trade with ASEAN member countries.[20]

The porousness of Vietnam's borders also remains a big problem. Taxes are paid by foreign companies and successful SOEs. Local traders who engage in regional trade regularly evade payment and flood the Vietnamese market with cheap, illegally imported commodities from ASEAN countries and China. Some control over the trade can be implemented by limiting the number of import-export licenses managed by the state corporations. Realistically, Vietnam is unlikely to allow its economic growth to be jeopardized through its membership of ASEAN.

In addition to the consequences of membership in ASEAN for its regional economic relations, there are important political considerations: ASEAN was initially defined as a regional alliance supporting U.S. interests, and Vietnam's membership has affected China's influence over Vietnam, making Vietnam less threatening and thus a more viable economic partner to the United States.[21]

The Impact of The Asian Financial Crisis

Unlike those of its neighbors, Vietnam's capital inflows comprise principally FDI and overseas development assistance rather than short-term portfolio investment. Consequently, the impact of the Asian financial crisis has been somewhat muted in Vietnam. Nevertheless, the progressive devaluation of the Japanese yen and the Taiwan won against the U.S. dollar has created a negative impact in Vietnam as import values and international loans are usually calculated in U.S. dollars. In addition, regional FDI and trade declined dramatically in 1998.

Fortunately, Vietnam's banking sector is highly regulated and has limited global integration. It has been insulated from the financial crisis to a large extent. Until the economic reform of the 1990s, the banking system consisted of only the State Bank. There were no commercial banks. The State Bank would extend credit to the SOEs, whereas small businesses and the self-employed would operate in the cash economy. With inflation running high, there was no incentive for domestic deposits, and private borrowing was limited to credit circles organized among friends and relatives. In 1988, the commercial functions of the State Bank were transferred to government owned, specialized banks and by mid-1990, legislation was passed to develop a market-oriented banking system. Foreign banks are now permitted to operate but they are still not allowed to mobilize domestic savings.[22] All movement of capital in and out of the country has to be officially authorized, and in 1994 all foreign currency deposits above a certain amount were obliged to transfer to the State Bank. The use of foreign currency in local transactions was made illegal. The measure, however, was not strongly enforced. In February 1998, all foreign currency deposits, large and small, had to be transferred to the State Bank in a desperate government attempt to procure hard currency and to keep the national current account in check.

Capital controls have been eroded, partly as a result of the opening up of international trade. For example, in 1996 domestic currency loans were scarce so the interest rate increased, exceeding the rate on loans in U.S. dollars. This increased the incentive for enterprises to borrow in U.S. dollars in the form of deferred letters of credit, which were guaranteed by state-owned commercial banks. Rather than investing in productive inputs, some SOEs channeled borrowed funds toward real estate investments while others engaged in speculative international trade. When demand declined, letters of credit became bad debts. The State Bank baled out the commercial banks and recaptured control over letters of credit.

During the first wave of the Asian financial crisis, the Vietnamese dong was effectively devalued by 15 percent. In October 1997, the government's intervention band on the exchange rate widened from 5 percent to 10 percent, leading to another devaluation of 5.3 percent in February 1998. The inflow of foreign capital remained small. In addition, the government imposed a ceiling on domestic interest rates. It strictly controlled foreign borrowing, which provided little incentive for the inflow of capital. Nevertheless, it is not clear whether the Vietnamese planners will continue to pursue such a high level of financial regulation in their future long-term economic management. New initiatives, including the establishment of a stock market, are regularly discussed, reflecting the impact of increased international integration. It remains to be seen whether the demand for foreign capital and the international pressures for increased liberalization will force the Vietnamese government to change its course.

The Globalization of Vietnamese Culture

Vietnam is not closeted against the pressures that result from an increasing integration into international economic and cultural networks or against the impact these pressures have on the leadership's power to control sociopolitical change. The complexities of cultural change run deep in a country that was once split between north and south and that was occupied by Chinese, French, Japanese, and American forces. Vietnam is located at the crossroads of world civilizations and the convergence point of complicated international relations and acute political struggles. The country has a long history of exposure to foreign cultural influences, observed in foreign practices such as drinking coffee, eating baguettes, and snacking on creme caramel; in the built environment, which strongly reflects the influence of Chinese, Soviet, and French architecture; and in the language, which takes much of its root stock from Chinese and its alphabet from the Roman script.[23] This mixture of tradition and modernity is leading to a growing cultural heterogeneity: cyclos and air-conditioned taxis, traditional medicine and modern pharmaceuticals, traditional female Vietnamese dress (*au dai*) and western cosmetics. Today, Vietnamese often jest about their preference for foreign goods and their selective but rapid adoption of western fashion and technology (e.g., mobile phones, microwaves, and taxis). The desire for knowledge about the world outside Vietnam is satisfied through TV, radio, newspapers, travelers' tales, and stories from relatives overseas.

Much of what can be observed as foreign cultural influence, however, is only superficial, the trappings of culture. At the heart of Vietnamese culture remains a strong sense of morality that does not change as easily as summer fashion. Spiritual development is considered most important, and Vietnamese cultural ideals are to enhance the moral standards of the population, to promote high ideals, moral integrity, better education, and a strong sense of discipline and to resist what the Vietnamese leaders perceive to be the corrosive influence of decadent thought, which results from Vietnam's increased openness to the international community. "Social evils" such as drug use, HIV infection, prostitution, pornography, consumerism, marriage breakdown, and youth homelessness are mentioned in this context and attributed to globalization.[24] More specifically, Vietnamese reflect on the loss of moral compass for the younger generation as the directives of the Party seem to have lost relevance in directing their future. Particularly in the cities, the generation gap is deepening as the young quickly absorb the new technologies, the English language, and other capabilities that enable them to occupy the new positions within the market economy.

The Role of the State

Within the VCP there is no unanimity of opinion as to the pace and direction of reform, apart from the position that the Party must stay in power and resist any pressure for pluralism. It is clear that the Party's legitimacy is based on the success of the economic strategy, resulting in sustained economic growth behind a thin veil of socialist rhetoric. The mobilizing basis of the present reform process appears to replace class consciousness with a new economic nationalism.[25] The growth of the Vietnamese economy during the 1990s is certainly impressive, with rates of between 6 percent and 9.5 percent.[26]

Nevertheless, the goals of sustained economic growth and the maintenance of a single party state present certain contradictions. The most obvious presents itself between engagement in the financial commodity and technology markets of the global economy and resistance to the globalizing pressures for deregulation, privatization, and pluralism. Moreover, in order to maintain its position, the Party must have access to financial resources, must control the emergence of a private sector that may demand further deregulation, and must control the social, cultural, and political influences from abroad that may apply pressure for pluralism. The Party's financial resources include the taxation of joint ventures and SOEs, income generated by SOEs, international development assistance, and domestic and foreign loans. This necessitates the maintenance of state control over infrastructure and high income–generating investments (e.g., oil, energy, transport, etc.) in the face of pressure from foreign companies and lending agencies who recommend a state retreat from the economy.

The Vietnamese government plans to create larger, more centralized and rationalized state corporations. The approximately one hundred and fifty state companies and enterprise unions will be restructured and combined, resulting in the organization of one hundred state corporations in which Vietnamese industrial and financial capital will be concentrated. The formation of state corporations effectively restricts the number of import licenses held by major companies and will give the government more control over imports in the approach to Vietnam's full participation in AFTA in 2006.

The Party's attitude toward the development of domestic private enterprise is ambivalent, even though such development is constitutionally supported. The registration of these businesses is controlled by the state and the right to operate may be taken away at any point. This ambivalence was also reflected in the 1996 decision to equitize SOEs through the distribution of stock among employees. However, only small and medium-sized SOEs can participate and any individual share in excess of 10 percent of the enterprise capital or six months salary is prohibited.

Since the early 1990s, foreign investors have been clambering over each other to invest in what they perceive to be the last frontier in Asia. Australian and South Korean investors raced toward Vietnam to outrun their competitors in the United States and Japan. Taiwanese investors are using their long-standing linkages with Vietnam through the Chinese-Vietnamese minority. Multilateral funding of major projects in infrastructure, energy, mining, and other economic sectors has been divided among various countries and investors. No one has been allowed to gain a position which in any way could threaten the country's economic sovereignty.

Although Vietnam is known for its faithful execution of the IMF's formula for structural adjustment, there are many examples of the state's resistance to the policy recommendations of multilateral lending agencies. It intends to maintain control and ownership of infrastructure such as energy, telecommunications, transport, ports, and the energy and mining sectors. This counters the World Bank recommendations that the state allow foreign capital investment in these areas and retreat from its own activities in the economy, concentrating instead on social services such as education and health. The Vietnamese government has refused loans from both multilateral agencies and foreign governments when they are perceived to threaten national sovereignty. However, its position with regard to foreign investment is not always consistent. Encouragement of foreign investment through English language newspapers such as the *Vietnam Investment Review,* through attempts to curb corruption, to improve infrastructure, and to strengthen normative legislation has alternated with decrees that undermine foreign investment, such as the recent move to limit foreign company advertising.

The Vietnamese state has increasing difficulties finding a balance between the exigencies of global economic engagement and its desire to maintain control of foreign cultural and political influences in Vietnam. The dilemma is reflected in the state's schizophrenic response to technology use (e.g., faxes and the Internet), the media, advertising, and international conferences. The Party feels compelled to exert control, particularly over external social, cultural, and political influences, by actions such as limiting access to the Internet, refusing registration of foreign tour operators (even though they have tacit permission to operate), restricting the number of international conferences, occasionally restricting overseas travel of potential dissidents, and implementing campaigns against English language advertising. Regularly, the government wages campaigns against "social evils" as manifest in foreign language advertising, pornography, prostitution, drug abuse, and gambling—all "noxious" western influences that ride on the back of reform *(doi moi)*. The crackdown on "social evils" is an example of the campaign style of management used by the state in Vietnam. Because it does not have the capacity to implement the bevy of restrictions designed to maintain the state's social and economic control, such campaigns are launched periodically. When the campaign concludes, slowly everything returns to normal.

In December 1997, Vietnam opened a gateway to the Internet, but it is clear that the government is still ambivalent about the decision. Several Web pages are forbidden for fear of influence from overseas Vietnamese using the Web as a weapon to attack the ruling Communist Party. Internet access is offered through the post office as the major service provider, but it is expensive and lacks technical support. The regulations prohibit receiving or sending information that, broadly interpreted, reveals state secrets, propagates reactionary ideas, or attacks the country, the Party, or national cultural values.

As Vietnam becomes increasingly integrated into the regional and global economy (for example, as international businesses demand fewer limitations on their access to the Internet), it is anticipated that the implementation of these restrictions will become problematic. However, it is clear that Vietnam's reintegration into the global economy is not passive. Vietnam has a long history of resistance to external pressures and continually has attempted to manipulate international powers. It appears that Vietnam has successfully fuelled what I have referred to elsewhere as "Vietnam fever."[27] On the one hand, Vietnam portrays the image of national poverty, attracting unprecedented volumes of ODA, and on the other hand, the state projects the image of a burgeoning economy.[28]

Conclusion

Through its engagement with global capital, Vietnam has become increasingly exposed to the globalizing pressures of liberalization, privatization, decentralization, and pluralism. But its engagement is on its own terms: maintenance of state ownership of the economy and resistance to the emergence of a self-determining civil society. It is clear that the VCP's future rests with its ability to reproduce economic growth. What is not so clear but is equally axiomatic is that economic growth is premised on the survival of the Party. Because of the integral role played by the Party in the economy, if the VCP collapses so will the economy.

Although the transition process in Vietnam is marked by gradualism and has been initiated from the grass roots, external pressures have cemented the reforms. Although Vietnam's regional economic engagement with Japan and the ASEAN countries is seen as essential for economic growth, this engagement poses a threat to Vietnam's sovereignty economically, politically, and culturally. However, Vietnam is not a passive player; it has defined structures and legislation in order to resist these external pressures. So far the state has been successful in keeping privatization and pluralism at bay. However, significant changes are occurring across the generational divide which may eventually undermine the state's strategy of political control, cultural purity, and economic self-determination.

The VCP is attempting to develop market socialism, but the country is not insulated from the pressures from world economic processes that impact on developing countries irrespective of their style of socialism or capitalism. The balance between the effects of the globalization processes in financial institutions, trade networks, marketing, and so on and the efforts to strengthen the national identity in economics, politics, and culture is very delicate. The government is currently promoting policies to resist further international, social, and political influences. For the time being, Vietnam may remain a very idiosyncratic case of managing the forces of globalization.

Notes

1. Zhu Ying and Stephanie Fahey, "Impact of Economic Reform on Labour Relations in China and Vietnam," *Communist Economies and Economic Transformation*, forthcoming.
2. Stephanie Fahey, "Vietnam and the 'Third Way': The Nature of Socio-Economic Transition," *Tijdschrift voor Economische en Sociale Geografie* 88, no. 5 (1997): 469–480; Adam Fforde, *Statistical Appendix* (Canberra: ADUKI Pty Ltd., 1997); Adam Fforde, *Vietnam: Economic Commentary and Analysis* (Canberra: ADUKI Pty Ltd., 1997).

3. Donald Dapice, "Vietnam at the Starting Point: Just Another East Asian Economy?" in *The Challenge of Reform in Indochina*, ed. Bo Ljunggren (Cambridge: Harvard Institute of International Development, 1993), pp. 167–182; Dick Perkins, "Reforming the Economic Systems of Vietnam and Laos" in Ljunggren, *The Challenge of Reform in Indochina*, pp. 1–18.
4. Dapice, "Vietnam at the Starting Point."
5. See Barry Gills and Simon Quadir, introduction to *Regimes in Crisis: The Post-Soviet Era and its Implications for Development* (New Delhi: Sage Publications, 1994), pp. 1–3.
6. Charles White, "Recent Debates in Vietnamese Development Policy," in *Revolutionary Socialist Development in the Third World*, ed. Graham White, Ron Murray, and Charles White (Brighton: Harvester, 1983), pp. 234–274; John Werner, "Socialist Development: the Political Economy of Agrarian Reform in Vietnam," *Bulletin of Concerned Asian Scholars* 16, no. 2 (1984): 48–55; Paul Ronnas, *Employment Generation Through Private Entrepreneurship in Vietnam*, (New Delhi: ILO, 1992); Richard Mallon, "Restructuring Socialist Enterprise: Vietnam" in *Revitalising Socialist Enterprise: A Race Against Time*, ed. Jonathan Heath (London and New York: Routledge, 1993); John Utting, "Social Origins of Economic Reform in Post-Revolutionary Third World Societies" in Gills and Quadir, *Regimes in Crisis*, pp. 149–171; Adam Fforde and Stefan de Vylder, *From Plan to Market: The Economic Transition in Vietnam* (Boulder, Colo: Westview Press, 1988).
7. Fjorde and De Vylder, *From Plan to Market*, p. 132.
8. Ibid., p. 108.
9. William Turley, introduction to *Reinventing Vietnamese Socialism: Doi Moi in Comparative Perspective*, ed. William Turley and Marc Seldon (Boulder, Colo.: Westview Press, 1993), pp. 6–7.
10. *Statistical Yearbook, 1989–1995* (Hanoi: General Statistical Office, 1989–1995).
11. *Statistical Yearbook, 1993, 1996* (Hanoi: General Statistical Office, 1993, 1996).
12. Fforde, *Vietnam: Economic Commentary and Analysis*, p. 67.
13. Charles Gates and Thanh-Dan Truong, "Development Strategy and Trade and Investment Policies for Structural Change" in *Vietnam in a Changing World*, ed. Inger Norlund et al. (Surrey: Curzon Press, 1995), pp. 85–108.
14. Fforde, *Vietnam: Economic Commentary and Analysis*, p. 48.
15. Brian Duffield, ed., *Vietnam and Japan. Japanese Investment and Aid Strategies in Vietnam: Implications for Development Directions* (Victoria, B.C.: University Centre for Asia-Pacific Initiatives, 1995).
16. Vu Tuan Anh, "Impacts of Joining AFTA on Vietnam's Economy," *Vietnam's Socio-Economic Development* 5 (1996): 56.
17. Thanh-Dan Truong and Charles Gates, "Vietnam and ASEAN—Economic Reform, Openness and Transformation: An Overview," in *Vietnam in ASEAN: Economic Reform, Openness and Transformation*, ed. Charles Gates and Thanh-Dan Truong, special issue of *ASEAN Economic Bulletin* 13, no. 2 (1996): 159–168.

18. Allen Goodman, "Vietnam and ASEAN: Who Would Have Thought it Possible?" *Asian Survey* 36, no. 6 (1996): 598–599.

19. Vu Tuan Anh, "Impacts of Joining AFTA on Vietnam's Economy," *Vietnam's Socio-Economic Development* 5 (1996): 64.

20. Goodman, "Vietnam and ASEAN," p. 592.

21. World Bank, *Vietnam: Refining Reform for Growth* (Washington, D.C.: World Bank, 1997).

22. Stephanie Fahey, "Vietnam's Women in the Renovation Era," in *Gender and Power in Affluent Asia*, ed. Kuo Sen and Maila Stivens (London: Routledge, 1998), pp. 222–249.

23. Pham Xuan Nam, "Cultural Factors in Socio-Economic Development Planning in Vietnam" in *Methodologies for Incorporating Cultural Factors into Development Projects and Planning*, ed. Pham Xuan Nam (Hanoi: Social Science Publishing House, 1995), pp. 153–175.

24. Gerald Greenfield, "The Development of Capitalism in Vietnam," *The Socialist Register 1994* (London: Merlin Press, 1994), pp. 203–234.

25. Fforde, *Vietnam: Economic Commentary and Analysis*, p. 14.

26. See *Vietnam Living Standards Survey, 1992–1993* (Hanoi: State Planning Committee and General Statistical Office, 1994), p. 5.

27. Stephanie Fahey, "The End of 'Vietnam Fever," *Overseas Trading* 3 (1996): 26–27.

28. At the Paris donor conference in 1993, a total of US$18 billion of ODA was committed. See Stephanie Fahey, "Vietnam: Pivotal Year?" in *Southeast Asian Affairs* (Singapore: Institute for Southeast Asian Studies, 1994), pp. 337–350.

7

Global Forces, State Responses, and Industrial Development in Singapore and Malaysia

Leo van Grunsven and August van Westen

Singapore and Malaysia were among the first countries in Southeast Asia to seize the opportunities presented by the internationalization of production. They created an attractive investment climate for foreign investors in search of low-cost production locations. Thus, they became industrial nations through insertion in the globalizing production systems engineered by foreign TNCs (transnational corporations).[1] At the end of the 1970s, however, their industrialization paths began to diverge. After a decade of rapid export-oriented industrialization, Singapore changed its strategy and moved toward more advanced industries and more rewarding segments in cross-border commodity chains.[2] Toward the end of the 1980s, the new strategy began to show results. Singapore has become an international business center with a diversified economy.

Malaysia has been equally affected by globalization. However, here the pace and source of industrial development, rather than its characteristics, have changed. From the mid-1980s on, export-oriented industrialization in Malaysia has been shaped by the regionalization of assembly work by Japanese TNCs. Similar firms from other Asian countries followed Malaysia's lead. As a result, Singapore and Malaysia developed complementary roles. Malaysia became a production platform for low- to middle-value-added final products and components for international markets, especially in electronics and electric consumer goods. Singapore, on the other hand, managed to develop the higher-value-added manufacturing and service industries within the regional economy. In recent years, Malaysia and Singapore have embarked on new economic strategies in response to changing conditions at the global, regional, and local levels.

In this chapter we will analyze these processes, focusing on state and firm responses to changes in external and domestic conditions. At the end of the chapter we will briefly consider the effects of the Asian financial crisis of 1997–1998 on the regional strategies of industrial development.

Singapore Under Globalization

Since its independence in 1965, Singapore's economic development has been characterized by continuously high growth rates, a structural transformation of its economy, a prominent role for international capital, and a strong state influence on the economy. Economic growth was impressive indeed. The GDP over the period 1965–1980 increased at an average annual rate of 9.1 percent. In the mid-1980s, growth slowed down, but it rapidly resumed in the following years at a rate of 9 or 10 percent annually.[3] As a result, Singaporeans now enjoy income levels far superior to those of surrounding countries.

In terms of economic structure, Singapore was transformed from an entrepôt economy to a low-tech manufacturing and trade economy in the 1960s and 1970s, and to an economy based on high-tech manufacturing and financial and business services in subsequent decades (see Table 7.1).

The transition from low- to high-tech manufacturing has passed through several phases marked by changes in state development strategy and subsequent responses by international capital (see Table 7.2). After the divorce from Malaysia, the Singaporean state adopted a development strategy centered on export-oriented industrialization, to be financed by capital from the core economies searching for lower-cost production sites. To this end, the state did create a suitable infrastructure and guaranteed a low-cost business environment though a strong control of labor. Foreign capital reacted positively and poured massive investment into the city-state. In the early 1980s, foreign-controlled companies accounted for close to 70 percent of cumulative investment in manufacturing.[4] Singapore rapidly developed into a dynamic offshore production and export base. Most manufacturing activities during the 1960s and 1970s were in the labor-intensive, low-value-added production segments. At the time, this development helped to solve the existing unemployment problem.

Changing Local Conditions and State Responses

By the end of the 1970s, Singapore had a tight labor market in spite of its high labor-force participation rate. The immigration of foreign workers was not favored, which meant that a change toward less labor-intensive

Table 7.1 Distribution of Singaporean GDP by Sector of Origin, Selected Years (percentages)

Year	Manufacturing	Utilities	Construction	Commerce	Transport & Communications	Financial Business Services	Other Services
1965	15.2	2.2	6.5	27.2	11.5	16.6	17.6
1970	20.2	2.6	6.9	27.4	10.7	16.6	12.9
1975	23.3	1.8	7.9	24.8	10.8	18.2	11.1
1980	28.1	2.1	6.2	20.8	13.5	19.0	8.8
1985	22.0	1.9	10.0	15.9	12.6	25.6	11.0
1990	27.2	1.8	5.2	17.9	12.2	25.0	10.3
1995	24.9	1.5	6.7	18.6	11.1	26.9	10.0

Source: Singapore Department of Statistics, 1995.

Table 7.2   Economic Planning and Development in Sinagpore

1959–1965	**Economic diversification**
	Industrialization through importsubstitution, based on domestic capital within the Federation of Malaysia
1965–1979	**Integration in the new international division of labor through the EOI strategy**
	Export-oriented industrialization; offshore production base for international capital, with emphasis on low-value-added, labor-intensive production activities
1980–1985	**Second industrial revolution**
	• start of industrial restructuring
	• shift toward higher-value-added industrial activites
	• more capital- and skill-intensive
1985	**Economic recession**
1986–1990	**Total business center strategy**
	More services and nonproduction activities in the value chain of foreign industrial enterprises; financial and business center
1990	**Total business center and core of an economic triangle**
1991	**Strategic economic plan**
	Deepening of industrial restructuring; emphasis on:
	• building of industry clusters in high-value-added-manufacturing
	• nonproduction corporate activities, i.e., R&D, operational headquarters
	• attracting globalizing services and export of services
	• relocation of low-value-added, labor-intensive production
1995	**"External Wing"**
	• internationalization of the economy; besides receiver of FDI also investor abroad
	• developed country status

activities was indicated. In 1980, the state introduced a strategy of industrial restructuring, the "Second Industrial Revolution." The objective was to restructure the manufacturing sector in favor of higher-value-added activities and to achieve growth through increases in productivity, rather than through the addition of ever more (labor) resources. To this end, wages were adjusted, education and training was strongly supported, automation, mechanization, and computerization was encouraged, and policies of selective investment promotion with an emphasis on R&D were implemented. The government set up the Singapore Science Park, which was designed to provide a focal point for the high-quality infrastructure essential for industrial R&D and to create an environment conducive to interaction between industry, academic, and research groups.[5]

Initially, the response to this strategy from international capital was not very positive. The steep increase in labor and other business costs had led to a rapid erosion of international competitiveness and a stagnation of FDI, eventually resulting in a deep recession in 1985. Measures were taken to restore international competitiveness. The exhaustion of the low-level export manufacturing model, increasing protectionism in export markets, the loss of GSP (Generalized System of Preferences) trading preferences, and the appreciation of the local currency compelled Singapore to promote the development of high-value-added manufacturing and services—particularly financial and business services—and nonproduction activities in the value chain of foreign enterprises operating in the Asian region (e.g., R&D, logistics, management).[6] The low-value-added and labor-intensive production would have to be relocated out of Singapore. This strategy was to be served by the creation of a cross-border economic growth triangle, in which Singapore would be the core of an integrated export-oriented economic complex that would incorporate neighboring regions in Malaysia and Indonesia.[7]

The Strategic Economic Plan, published in 1991, reiterated this general strategy and outlined the instruments to achieve it.[8] The state would again assume a guiding role and provide the institutional and infrastructural framework. The plan concluded that two decades of economic development under globalization had left Singapore with a weakly integrated production structure. The changing procurement strategies of TNCs presented new opportunities to develop a wider range of activities in the production chain, especially those related to higher-value-added, skill- and technology-intensive activities, either downstream or upstream from current manufacturing operations. In addition, nonproduction activities, particularly those developed by R&D and operational headquarters, as well as by other establishments of globalizing services, were to be promoted.[9] The relocation of production out of Singapore was planned to contribute to the creation of an "external wing" of the local economy, making Singapore a foreign investor in its own right, especially in Southeast Asia.[10] The major programs involved in the Strategic Economic Plan are listed in Table 7.3.

Singapore's new strategy met with success. The international business community was ready to invest substantially in the Asia-Pacific region and Singapore offered competitive conditions. What was motivating international capital to commit large investment to the region?

By 1990, many TNCs in the core economies had begun to modify their global and regional strategies in response to changing conditions in their home economies and changing models of corporate organization. Moreover, the Asia-Pacific region had emerged as an important market in its own right. Existing trading preferences in addition to several

Table 7.3   Programs Linked to the Singapore Strategic Economic Plan

Strategic Program	*Objectives*
Manufacturing 2000	To sustain the GDP share of manufacturing at more than 25 percent and the employment share at 20 percent in the medium to long term. M2000 will seek to upgrade capabilities across the entire value chain of each industry cluster including product and process development, production, manufacturing engineering, and strategic marketing.
International Business Hub 2000	To enhance Singapore's position as a business services gateway to the region. Singapore will add value and assist the flow of goods, people, capital, technology, information, and ideas by providing highly skilled services. These services include internationally tradeable and high-value-added activities that complement the M2000 program.
	The four key-clusters are Regional Headquarters (including those serving as a base for business expansion into the region), Logistics (total capability hub), Communications and Information (broadcasters/programmers; advanced telecommunications applications; satellite communication; data-hubs and call centers; multimedia content development), and Lifestyle services (publishing and electronic media; film/television/music; health care and education).
Regionalization 2000	To build an external economy that is closely linked to and enhances the domestic economy by participating in Asian growth. This program seeks to form a network of strategic zones in key markets with emphasis on building good linkages between regional projects and domestic clusters.
	Key elements are the Singapore/Johor/Riau Growth Triangle; flagship regional industrial parks as gateways to regional economies for local companies and multinational corporations; facilitating regional investment out of Singapore through the Co-Investment program.
Promising Local Enterprises 2000	To strengthen the role of local enterprises in key clusters and to groom a group of promising local enterprises (PLEs) into MNCs and industry leaders of tomorrow. The PLE program target is to nurture 100 local enterprises with sales of more than S$100 million in the next ten years.
	Key elements are promoting strategic business management and planning; expanding the Local Industry Upgrading Programme; increasing the pool of Venture Capital Funds.
Co-investment 2000	To build on and extend the relationships with leading companies through co-investment partnerships in projects of significance and thereby reduce risks for partners.
	Key elements are supporting the cluster development plan by addressing critical gaps in the industry clusters and enhancing core capabilities.

Source: Singapore, Economic Development Board, 1991. On-line posting, available from <www.sedb.com.sg>.

exchange rate modifications (especially the rise of the yen and the "Tiger" currencies) enhanced the attractiveness of the region as an investment destination.

Many TNCs moved toward more comprehensive and regionally focused operations, including a widening and deepening of their operations in Southeast and East Asia.[11] TNCs from the core economies transferred not only a wider range of product lines to the region, comprising technologically complex operations, but also established more nonproduction activities. Many specialized firms in specific segments of commodity chains (e.g., distribution) have also opened shop in Southeast Asia, often in Singapore.

Within the region, firms have transferred labor-intensive production activities to lower-cost locations in order to remain competitive in increasingly crowded markets.[12] This strategy tallies with the evolution of new ways of organizing production, through which multiple plants and service units are linked in extensive networks. Increasingly, functions such as management, logistics, marketing, and research are being separated from production and located in the most favorable business environment. Singapore has become a major location for the regional management and control centers, or "operational headquarters," of large firms.[13] Production has become embedded in networks, through which different sections of the production chain are assigned to different establishments. These networks operate on different geographical scales, from the local to the macroregional. Their form and composition seems to be in constant flux, responding to changes in corporate strategy, local conditions, market access considerations, and government policies, and resulting in ever-changing geographies of industrial activity. On the one hand, the application of Japanese organizational models (for example, "just-in-time" delivery) has stressed the importance of proximity in procurement networks. Major TNCs operate large final assembly plants, around which they organize extensive localized supply networks. While local firms do participate in such networks, many of the production units specializing in specific operations or steps in the production chain are in fact transplants from dependent supply firms from the home country of the TNC, or *flagship firm*. On the other hand, the imperatives of comparative geographical advantage have induced firms to create "supralocal" supply networks. In this strategy, firms respond to differences among countries and regions in factor endowment and working conditions and assign steps in the production chain or specialist activities to different locations according to their particular advantage.[14]

Singapore has gone through two major processes of adjustment within this regional context. These involved the in situ reorganization of production and a geographical reorganization of economic activity in the region.[15] Industrial restructuring encourages regionalization of the economy.[16] The existing industrial complex has grown beyond the national boundaries into adjoining territories, bringing into reality the SIJORI growth triangle, which consists of Singapore, the neighboring Malaysian State of Johor, and Indonesia's Riau archipelago, particularly Batam Island. SIJORI is one of the best known examples of a cross-border industrial zone in Pacific Asia.[17]

The *twinning* concept underlying SIJORI can be perceived as an attempt by Singapore to enhance its international competitive position by incorporating the resources of adjacent territories and creating a *microregional* division of labor. Faced with the need to restructure Singapore's maturing economy, the state intervened and helped firms to adjust by moving out selected types of production to neighboring jurisdictions that are functionally integrated into Singapore's industrial complex. At the same time, the SIJORI triangle offered a timely policy response to the emergence of more spatially clustered industrial procurement networks, in which separate suppliers and support industries are functionally organized around a flagship assembly plant. However, in the course of time the economic raison d'être of the trinational industrial zone—an international division of labor separating high-wage from low-wage activities within a relatively small area—may disappear. Rapid growth and subsequent labor shortages in Johor are already challenging its resource-complementarity with Singapore.[18]

Within Singapore, the adjustment process has resulted in a technological upgrading of production processes—including process automation—the replacement of some product lines with other, higher-value-added products, and a more flexible labor strategy, designed to increase labor productivity and the return on capital investment. Routine assembly and other simple production jobs have been relocated out of Singapore, leaving little of such manufacturing activity in the island state. The adjustment processes have produced a diversified production structure through the introduction of R&D, procurement, distribution, and logistics functions, as well as the management functions of the headquarters established in the region. These strategies are not limited to the TNCs. Increasingly the large and medium-sized local enterprises have followed suit and have upgraded their operations.

Singapore and Globalization: The Current Pattern

In the course of the restructuring of its economy, Singapore's position within the global economy has changed. Its global and regional roles have moved to a higher plane, in line with the "niche" position envisaged by the Singaporean state. Manufacturing has changed in line with the "upgrading" strategy. Unlike Hong Kong, Singapore has been selected as a production base by technology-driven industries, leaving a significant manufacturing segment in its economy. The placement of major R&D activities in Singapore by a large number of firms has made Singapore into a major regional center for knowledge-based activity. Over the past ten years many TNCs have also set up regional headquarters in Singapore. The Economic Development Board has bestowed operational headquarters (OHQ) status on some seventy-five offices, where corporate management activities for the region—such as organization, coordination, control, sourcing, distribution, and logistics—are concentrated. In addition to these official OHQs, some three hundred more foreign companies have established regional offices in Singapore. More recently, Singapore seems to be emerging as a media hub for global communications and information services industries, like broadcasting. The sizeable cluster of financial and business services, ranging from banks and insurance companies to all sorts of activities linked to the stock and international monetary exchange, have made Singapore into the prime financial center in Southeast Asia.

At the same time, the "External Wing" of the Singaporean economy has grown rapidly. At the end of 1993, Singapore-based companies in the private nonfinancial sector had invested some $50 billion Singaporean dollars (S$) abroad.[19] By the end of 1996, total foreign investment in the target countries in the region had reached S$35 billion.[20] A little over half of the investment outflows originated from foreign companies based in Singapore, suggesting that Singapore's traditional entrepôt role had broadened to that of an international investment center. A large share of Singaporean capital moving abroad is in the financial and business services. Manufacturing still accounts for a quarter of total investment. In this sector, state-linked companies developing high-profile industrial parks in countries such as China, Vietnam, Indonesia, and India play an important role. Thus, industrial complexes in the region are linked to the Singaporean economy and reinforce its regionalization.[21]

Malaysia's Industrialization
in Global Perspective

With independence, Malaysia inherited a fairly well-organized and competitive economy, based on exports of primary commodities such as rubber and tin. Manufacturing played a very limited role there at the time, being largely concentrated in Singapore, which was no longer a part of Malaysia after 1965. Since then, Malaysia has pursued an active policy of industrial development, passing through four successive phases (see

Table 7.4). In 1996, the country embarked on a new strategy aimed at "climbing the technology ladder." A year later, that strategy was hit by the Asian currency crisis.

The development of manufacturing industry in Malaysia gained momentum at the end of the 1960s, when tensions between the Malay majority and the ethnic Chinese who had dominated business since the colonial era prompted the government to embark upon a new development strategy. Until then, a decade of import substitution industrialization (ISI) had produced inefficient factories that yielded handsome profits to predominantly foreign owners at the expense of Malaysian taxpayers and consumers.[22] The New Economic Policy (NEP) of 1970 was designed to reduce poverty and sever the link between ethnic affiliation and occupation. It had two important consequences for industrial development. First, it implied a more activist role for government, creating a

Table 7.4   Phases of Industrialization Policy in Malaysia

1958–1968	Import substitution industrialization (ISI-1):
	• Industrialization through domestic and foreign capital, using policies such as a protected domestic market, also tax incentives, infrastructure and subsidies
	• International orientation: partial isolation attempted
1969–1980	Export-oriented industrialization on a selective basis (EOI-1):
	• Industrialization through FDI, offering cheap export production platform for low-end production/assembly operations
	• International orientation: selective liberalization, limited to FDI and export industry
1981–1985	Heavy import substitution industrialization (ISI-2):
	• State corporations, often with foriegn partners and foriegn borrowing
	• International orientation: renewed portectionism in ISI sectors, but continued dependence on external technology and capital
1986–1995	Export-oriented industrialization and liberalization (EOI-2):
	• Integration in production section of East Asian TNCs
	• International orientation: gradual liberalization, increasing regional integration
1996–	Continued EOI-2, with technology push and cluster approach:
	• International orientation: simultaneous pressures toward regional integration and increasing international competition for FDI and technology
	• Restructing and selective financial closure following the Asain crisis (1997,1998)

Source: Elaboration of data from Kwome Sundaram Jomo, ed., *Industrialising Malaysia: Policy, Performance, Prospects,* (London: Routledge, 1993) and *Second Industrial Master Plan* (Kuala Lumpur: Ministry of International Trade and Industry , 1996).

Malaysian version of the developmental state. Second, the NEP rein-forced a shift toward an export-oriented industrialization (EOI) strategy, following the example of Singapore. Gradually, a range of policy mea-sures were put into place that made Malaysia an attractive production platform for TNCs seeking to cut production costs, especially labor and taxes, while producing for international markets.[23] Malaysia was one of the first countries to pursue the strategy of selective opening to the global economy while retaining restrictions with regard to its domestic indus-tries. At the same time, it was among the most successful. Manufacturing exports increased by 20–30 percent per annum throughout the 1970s. Low-wage employment in the Export Production Zones (EPZs) soared.

The northern port of Penang, home of much of this export manufac-turing, emerged as the second area of economic importance, next to the Klang Valley area of Kuala Lumpur. Johor is the third major industrial area of the country, due, obviously, to its proximity to Singapore. In all three areas high-tech industrial estates are being realized.

However successful, export manufacturing remained limited to a nar-row range of activities, among which the assembly and testing of elec-tronic components were paramount.[24] Linkages between the export sec-tor and local firms remained insignificant. In the early 1980s attempts by the state to overcome these weaknesses by emulating South Korea's heavy and chemical industrialization (HCI) policy of the previous decade met with only partial success. Massive public sector investment in uncompetitive heavy industry—iron and steel, cement, engineering, and the famous "National Car Project," much of it concentrated in the Klang Valley area—led to a rapid accumulation of debt and undermined the country's competitive position.[25]

A sharp recession in 1985–1987 led to the definition of the UNIDO (UN Industrial Development Organization)-inspired first Industrial Master Plan (IMP-1, 1986–1995). It proclaimed a resumption of export-oriented industrialization based on foreign capital. To this end, the Malaysian state implemented what are basically neoliberal economic policies. Trade bar-riers were reduced and many of the public and semipublic corporations created under the NEP since 1970 were privatized. Malaysia's renewed EOI strategy met with huge success, supported by a favorable interna-tional economic climate. In the first place, the appreciation of the yen fol-lowing the 1985 Plaza Agreement *(endaka)* and the resulting restructuring of Japanese manufacturing triggered a massive relocation of lower-level production capacity to low-cost locations such as Malaysia. By the early 1990s similar developments in the Tiger economies of South Korea, Tai-wan, and Hong Kong allowed them to overtake Japan as the major source of industrial investment in Malaysia. The presence on Malaysia's doorstep of Singapore, long a major source of FDI, enabled the southern state of Johor to emerge as a third manufacturing region in Malaysia, as production activities were relocated across the causeway due to cost pressures.[26] In the second place, the gradual maturing throughout the 1980s of the semiconductor industry, the country's leading export sector, worked to Malaysia's advantage. In this industry, a more integrated and localized industrial pattern has emerged through the years.

At the end of IMP-1 in 1995, Malaysia had achieved the objectives it had defined a decade before. Many plan targets had actually been surpassed by a wide margin. Exports of manufacturing goods, for instance, had expanded by an average of 28.6 percent per year over the decade, instead of the targeted 9.8 percent.[27] In little over a generation, a thorough transformation of the economy had been accomplished (see Table 7.5). Manufacturing had become the leading sector of the economy, accounting for 25.9 percent of employment and 79.6 percent of exports in 1995.[28] The key to success was reaching out and grabbing opportunities in global markets. Malaysia's industrial performance over the last decade was thus based on a globalization strategy, making effective use of foreign capital, technology, and markets by offering a competitive manufacturing base for TNC transplants.

In spite of Malaysia's undeniable success, further progress will hinge on solving some major issues. More immediately, the country needs to tackle the consequences of the financial crises of 1977–1998 and the weakness in its economic institutional framework underlying the crises. Beyond that, Malaysia's challenges involve changing the industrial structure while meeting the challenge of competitive pressures internally and externally.

Malaysia's Industrial Structure

The second Industrial Master Plan, 1996–2005 (IMP-2) implicitly identifies three key issues that need to be resolved if Malaysia's industrial development path is to be sustainable in an economic sense. First, the industrial structure is too *narrow* and too *shallow*. It is narrow in that it is based on a fairly small number of industries, each of which specializes in a limited range of activities. The industrial structure is shallow in that these industries rely heavily on imported inputs, capital, and technology. The linkages between the key export sector and the domestic and resource-based industries are limited. Differences in the sources of investment, management, and technology as well as different policy frameworks and market orientations have kept these three subsectors of manufacturing apart and operating according to a different entrepreneurial logic. The most notable exception is emerging within electronics and electrical goods industries—semiconductors, air conditioners,

Table 7.5 Distribution of Malaysian GDP by Sector of Origin, selected years (percentages)

Year	Agriculture	Mining	Manufacturing	Construction	Services	RM million (1978 prices)
1970	30.9	14.2	14.8	4.1	38.2	21,587
1980	23.5	10.4	20.2	1.9	44.0	44,511
1990	18.6	9.6	26.7	3.5	41.6	79,103
1995	13.5	7.4	33.1	4.5	44.3	155,780

Source: Elaboration of data from Kwome Sundaram Jomo, ed., *Industrialising Malaysia: Policy, Performance, Prospects* (London: Routledge, 1993) and *Second Industrial Master Plan* (Kuala Lumpur: Ministry of International Trade and Industry, 1996).

portable telephones, VCRs, and televisions. These industries have experienced significant localization effects with the rise of integrated networks of suppliers and assemblers within Malaysia. The heavy investment over time by foreign investors, the gradual build up of specialized skills, and the rise of Southeast Asia as a major market for electronics components have equipped Malaysia with competitive advantages in these activities beyond those of a mere low-cost production platform.[29] Thus—in these industries, at least—the local embeddedness long eluding Malaysian policy makers started to emerge, once the foreign TNCs could make savings by subcontracting the production of parts and components to cheaper local suppliers while reducing inventories in favor of "just-in-time" delivery strategies.[30] Several Asian investors had domestic suppliers relocate production capacity to Malaysia or widened the range of their own activities locally. Similarly, the GSP trade programs enacted by several importing nations—which grant lower entry tariffs to imports when a minimum level of value added is realized in a developing country—favored local sourcing of inputs in export industries. While this contributed to a more integrated production structure encompassing a larger section of the commodity chain, it is limited to a few export industries.

Second, locally owned firms have not been able to secure leading market positions. The very success of export-oriented industrialization has produced an economy that revolves around foreign TNCs. Economy-wide, the share of noncitizens in equity ownership may have declined, from 63 percent in 1970 to 25 percent in 1990,[31] in line with the NEP policy of increasing Malaysia's stake in business, or creating a *Bumiputera* Commercial and Industrial Community (BCIC), as it is called. Ownership of plantations and other local firms was partly transferred to *Bumiputera* individuals and trust agencies. But aggregate ownership figures do not accurately reflect the role of foreign players within the economy. Foreign capital accounts for much of the highest-performing industry in Malaysia, especially in the open and competitive export sector. Foreign firms continue to have a key role in technology and finance. The *Bumiputera* partner is sometimes no more than a front man for foreign owners. With few exceptions (palm oil, for example), Malaysian-owned firms lack the ability to produce technology independently and have difficulty in accessing international markets, especially since Malaysian brand names are not familiar to consumers elsewhere.[32] As a result, Malaysian corporations have not really attained the status of full-fledged competitive players in the world market.

Third, the resource base for further industrial growth is meeting its limits. Malaysia's spectacular progress over the last decade was based on mobilizing ever new resources for industrial use. Labor, for instance, was transferred from low-productivity activities in agriculture, petty trade, and domestic work to factories, and capital scarcity has been offset by massive foreign investment. However, attracting foreign capital is a fiercely competitive undertaking, the odds of which Malaysia can control only in part. The labor market is a case in point. The very success of EOI growth allowed the expansion of manufacturing employment at an average annual rate of 8.9 percent in the decade 1986–1995. Prior to the 1997 currency crisis, this growth had produced a tight labor market, which forced the restructuring of the traditional commodity sector, rubber, and also nibbled at the country's advantages as a low-cost manufacturing base. More important, rapid industrialization caused a shortage of skilled workers—technicians, managers, and professionals—and risked putting a brake on the upgrading of Malaysian industry toward more advanced activities. Meanwhile, the country's ample natural resource endowment, long a source for public sector spending, is being depleted and polluted at an alarming rate. Beyond the supply of these resources, congestion of infrastructure and service delivery require ever more expensive solutions and may eventually undermine Malaysia's competitiveness in the industries it currently relies on.

Basically, this issue is one of productivity, as Krugman has argued.[33] According to official estimates, manufacturing growth in 1995 was the result of labor inputs (17 percent), capital investment (61 percent), and TFP, or total factor productivity (22 percent).[34] Hence, almost four-fifths of sectoral growth was due to adding more resources, and just over a fifth to productivity gains—making better use of available capital, labor, and materials. Future growth will have to rely more on increasing productivity. In view of the limited technological ability of local enterprise discussed above, this is likely to be a greater challenge than the path of growth followed so far.

Malaysia's Changing Competitive Position

The need for change in Malaysia's economic structure is closely related to the changing competitive position of the Malaysian economy, both in terms of domestic factor endowment and its competitiveness within the Asia-Pacific region. Within the domestic economy, a tight labor market and rising cost levels compel the economy to move to less labor-intensive activities. These pressures have been momentarily eased by the recession and the depreciation of the currency, the ringgit, but they are not less urgent. On the positive side, massive investment over the years has provided Peninsular Malaysia—especially the industrial corridor along the western lowlands—with infrastructure and support services approaching the standards of the less advanced OECD (Organization for Economic

Cooperation and Development) countries. Rising skill levels have prepared the country for more sophisticated industries than standard assembly-type production work. Moreover, Malaysia's domestic market has grown, although this growth was interrupted by the Asian crisis. Its own consumer market has expanded. A corporate sector has emerged in need of substantial supplies of intermediary inputs and support services, especially in the electronics and electrical consumer goods industries. Malaysia's domestic economy, in sum, is losing the cost advantages of a low-skilled labor supply but gaining stature in infrastructure, services, and in the size of its domestic market.

From a regional perspective, Malaysia's competitive position is also testing new waters. For a long time, Malaysia was primarily linked with western markets and had few ties to the Asia-Pacific region apart from Singapore. This changed dramatically with the second EOI drive in the mid-1980s. Investment from Japan and the NICs rapidly integrated Malaysia into an Asia-Pacific regional division of labor. It became a workshop supplied with machinery and other inputs from Japan and the NICs to produce final products for the North American and European market.[35] In recent years, a more complicated pattern has emerged, reflecting TNC efforts to make use of the comparative advantages of different ASEAN countries through a vertical division of labor. Japanese firms in particular, keen on cutting costs, set up supply networks linking low-cost, labor-intensive production in China, Indonesia, and Vietnam with medium-tech operations in Malaysia and Thailand, as well as with more advanced activities in Singapore and, increasingly, Malaysia. Final products are not only shipped to western markets, but also serve Japan and markets in the region. As a result, intra-regional trade has been expanding rapidly. The intraindustry and intrafirm trade has become increasingly significant.[36]

Out of this changing regional context new pressures arise for Malaysia. The opening up of new destinations for international capital in search of cheap production locations has put pressure on Malaysia's FDI-based growth strategy. Also, some domestic industries are facing external pressures, arising from trade and investment liberalization at the global (i.e., WTO) and regional (i.e., AFTA—the emerging ASEAN Free Trade Area, and, in the long run, APEC) levels. Moreover, in addition to recovering from the 1997–1998 financial crisis, Malaysia has to prepare for the future loss of GSP privileges, while its strongest industries—semiconductors and electrical consumer goods—are suffering price losses in international markets. Thus, both domestic and international competitive pressures are forcing Malaysia to restructure and to move up into more advanced and more rewarding activities. Such industrial upgrading programs will develop huge financing needs that will very likely be beyond local capability. Once again, the need for attracting foreign capital is indicated.

Malaysia's responses to changes in its competitive position are forged by government and individual enterprises, often in close coordination. In spite of a strong market orientation, the Malaysian state takes a leading role in defining the course of the economy, as has been the case with many so-called developmental states in East Asia.

Domestic Responses to Changing Competitive Pressure

The ultimate developmental objective of the Malaysian state (what it calls *Vision 2020*) is to have a fully matured industrial economy by the year 2020. The strategy, as elaborated in IMP-2, revolves around the concept of "cluster-based industrial development." This attempt to redress the narrow and shallow production structure seeks to create functionally integrated industrial complexes that include manufacturing establishments, suppliers, and business support services, as well as the "economic foundations," such as public sector institutional framework, human resources, infrastructure, technology, and other elements of the business environment. The defining characteristic of such clusters is "high connectivity,"[37] which will allow for synergetic effects along the entire spectrum of the value chain. Malaysian policy identifies three types of industrial clusters: "internationally linked" clusters, which are meant to foster local embeddedness in TNC-dominated export industries; "resource-based" clusters, which are based on the exploitation of natural resources; and the interesting category of "policy-driven clusters," built around strategic industries promoted by the state in order to fill crucial technological gaps in the country's industrial profile. These include the transportation equipment industry (especially automotive), machinery and equipment, and industrial materials industries (e.g., ceramics and metals). Efforts to create industrial clusters have been widened to include business support services ("the next engine of growth") as well as manufacturing per se. Manufacturing as a whole was expected to contribute 36.6 percent of GDP in 1998. It will have reached a level rarely exceeded in the development trajectories of other countries. The cluster approach and the concern for Malaysian-owned businesses have renewed the interest in the small and medium-sized industries (SMIs), which have long been neglected by Malaysian policy makers and foreign firms alike.

The guiding principle in the cluster approach is the so-called *Manufacturing++* strategy. The first "plus" in this approach is designed to overcome the heavy concentration by foreign investors on low- to medium-tech assembly and component production; diversification should take place by "moving along the value chain" toward upstream activities, such as product design and R&D, and downstream activities, such as distribution and marketing. Such activities at the start and the tail end of the value chain generally result in higher-value-added per worker. In addition to this two-sided move along the value chain, Manufacturing++ simultaneously aims to upgrade the value chain as a whole, that is, to create more advanced industries with higher-value-added along the entire chain. The second "plus" refers to the need for product differentiation to achieve higher returns and productivity increases, or "moving to productivity-driven growth," as it is defined by Michael Porter, the guru of competition management who has inspired Malaysia and Singapore.[38]

The aggressive push to upgrade Malaysia's industrial structure has once again reinforced the need to attract foreign suppliers of technology and capital. Various high-profile projects have been initiated to lure prominent firms, especially in information technology, and have succeeded. Interestingly, this aggressive push ahead is moving Malaysia from a strategy emphasizing complementarity with Singapore—with Malaysian cost advantages on one side of the causeway and Singapore's skills and infrastructure on the other side—toward one of direct competition. Following the introduction of IMP-2, press reports are reflecting increasing competition between the two countries.[39]

Responses at the Regional Level

The IMP-2, curiously enough, does not plan developments in a regional economic context, despite the increasing importance of intraregional trade and investment. Yet, like Singapore, Malaysia actively pursues an internationalization policy and encourages Malaysian firms to venture abroad, gain access to foreign markets, acquire foreign technology, and secure access to natural resources.

Independent from government policy, corporate responses to the changing competitive position of Malaysia are changing the economic map of the region. Malaysian firms have started to transfer simple, labor-intensive production capacity to countries such as Indonesia, China, and Vietnam because the cost structure in Malaysia can no longer sustain international competition.[40] Other companies are seeking access abroad to natural resources that are being depleted in Malaysia. Wood, rubber, and palm oil production is being shifted to Indonesia and Thailand. An important role in this internationalization process is being shifted to the large ethnic Chinese business community, which is spreading its assets over several countries, including China. These corporate responses tally with the government's objective of gaining access to international markets and technology without having to rely on foreign TNCs. The internationalization of Malaysian companies, however, is likely to suffer from the devaluation of the ringgit.

Malaysia's economic future will depend to an important extent on the pattern of regional economic integration pursued within ASEAN. AFTA has been designed to facilitate intraregional trade in parts and components for export-oriented industries and to strengthen the competitive position of Southeast Asia in attracting foreign investment. Malaysia and, even more so, Singapore are the most ardent supporters of closer regional integration and are ahead of schedule in cutting tariffs for trade within the AFTA region. Both countries stand to benefit from regional trade liberalization. In both Malaysia and Singapore, intraindustry trade accounted for over 60 percent of growth in intra-ASEAN trade between 1986 and 1991.[41] This phenomenon suggests that in this case, the lowering of trade barriers will cause only limited adjustment problems. Other ASEAN countries, however, do not share this position and may well resent having to bear such costs. Yet even Malaysia is trying to reduce the costs of integration and has voiced objections to the entry of AFTA partners into strategic product markets. In 1994, it erected new barriers to protect its petrochemicals industry. Without protection, Malaysia's prestigious national car program would almost certainly collapse. Malaysian ambivalence toward AFTA is further highlighted in the IMP-2 statement: "[A] third round of import substitution strategy may be necessary to further encourage the manufacture of intermediate and investment goods."[42] Thus, the ultimate scope and scale of AFTA remains to be seen, although the direction is clear and the momentum is undeniable.

Singapore, Malaysia, and the Asian Financial Crisis

The Asian financial crisis has caused a sudden change in context for the development process in Singapore and Malaysia. It raises the question of whether and to what extent the state development strategies can be upheld and successfully implemented under substantially more adverse conditions. In the meantime, the implications of the economic turmoil as well as the government responses have become clear.

First of all, Singapore has not experienced the kind or scope of problems faced by some of its fellow NICs (South Korea and Hong Kong in particular) and some of the other ASEAN countries (Thailand, Indonesia, and Malaysia). Its currency has been temporarily depreciated and the stock market has shown more volatility as a result of the changes in the regional economic situation. However, the magnitude of it all has been nowhere near that experienced by other countries. Although the proportion of faulty loans of both local and foreign banks and finance companies has not been fully disclosed, the situation appears to be free from dramatic developments. Singapore's financial sector has remained relatively stable and robust. Singapore's authorities have learned major lessons from the 1985 recession, developed additional control mechanisms, and forced institutions in the financial sector to abide by strict rules that minimize the risk of bad loans. The reforms deemed necessary in the financial sector elsewhere in Asia, including regulation, accountability and transparency, have already been addressed. The relatively good shape of Singapore's financial sector vis-à-vis that of other countries or centers of finance in the region may contribute to international confidence in this area and support its competitive position as a major regional center for financial services. Nevertheless, in quantitative terms, the regional situation will undoubtedly hamper further growth in the financial services sector over the next few years.

A significant slowdown of growth in the short-term applies to the other sectors of the Singaporean economy as well, because of their close links to the regional economies through trade and investment. Regional import demand for raw materials, consumption, and capital goods has dropped. For the Singapore economy, this has resulted in a sharp fall in external demand, affecting growth in the commerce, transportation, logistics, and communications sectors. Domestic consumption has shown a downward trend, depressing—inter alia—the real estate market. Public sector infrastructure projects, which the state does not find difficult to finance, will help to maintain growth in the construction sector.

Singapore's manufacturing operations in the areas of industrial upgrading, regionalization, and the growth of nonproduction higher-value-added activities may react differently. First, Singapore has already gone a long way in the upgrading process and it is unlikely that the regional economic crisis will wipe out much of what has been achieved already. On the contrary, the upgrading that has been realized over the past decade—reflected in significantly higher levels of efficiency and productivity—serves to maintain competitiveness of high-end manufacturing in its major export markets: the United States and the EU. However, due to the weakening of the regional currencies against the Singapore dollar, the relative competitiveness of Singapore for the lower-end of production and service activities will the further affected. This will continue to force these activities within the Singaporean economy carried out by larger TNCs to relocate elsewhere. The new regional circumstances are producing significant changes in labor and procurement costs. The outcomes will vary significantly among individual firms and industries. Changes may be expected to occur in industrial sourcing patterns. The procurement of supplies within Southeast Asia may be enhanced in a number of industries, where costs can be reduced by tapping lower-cost suppliers within the region. Other industries, depending on production arrangements and local market prospects, may actually reduce procurement within the region. Singapore may experience a slowdown in the establishment and expansion of regional offices of large international companies and nonproduction corporate functions. Because of contracting demand, the crisis is slowing down the regionalization of those Singaporean firms that operate on the regional markets. The name of the game in Singapore has been a continuous (re)-assessment of its competitiveness and of its response to changes in domestic and external dynamics. Shortly before the crisis, a Committee on Singapore's Competitiveness (CSC) had been installed with the task to project the country's competitiveness for the next fifteen years and propose adequate strategies of action. Once the crisis had made itself felt, the Committee's task was broadened to deal with this situation and to indicate possible ways of recovery. It was understood that structural reforms would be necessary to create a leaner and more competitive economy. The Committee proposed a package of measures, aimed at reducing business costs while maintaining access of companies to working capital.[43] The measures were speedily implemented by the government. For the long term, proposals were formulated toward capabilities building, market diversification and investment promotion and, in general, toward a deepening of the earlier adopted strategies.

Malaysia is affected much more seriously by financial woes. Its government makes much of the fact that it has not had to apply for outside assistance (as have Thailand, Indonesia, and South Korea), but this cannot conceal the weakness of the country's financial and monetary position. The national currency lost some 30 percent of its value in dollar terms in 1997. As a result, public and private foreign debt has ballooned when expressed in local currency. Malaysia's banks are heavily burdened with bad debts, much of it in loans for speculative investment in little-productive assets, especially real estate. The real position of the financial system is not entirely clear, especially since the authorities are cushioning the impact for political reasons. While focusing publicity as much as possible on the role of foreign speculators in undermining the ringgit, the Government has quickly taken steps to merge ailing financial institutions with larger banks in order to keep the financial sector afloat without loss to deposit holders. This policy, however, implies increased risk exposure for the healthier institutions and risked to delay the restoration of investor confidence and hence, the stabilization of financial markets.

The country's political leadership split along generational lines in mid-1998 on the issue of the strategy that would be necessary to overcome the economic woes. The old guard, rallying around long-standing

Prime Minister Mahathir, chose to defend the Malaysian model of a developmental state, with its extensive and intimate connections between public and private sectors and with a leading role by the state. This strategy called for a partial abandonment of the policies pursued in the preceeding dozen years of rapid export-driven growth. In contrast, Anwar Ibrahim, Mahathir's deputy and the man groomed to become his successor, pushed for a strategy more akin to the policies favoured by the IMF, i.e., an orthodox approach to financial and monetary stabilization within the framework of international market forces. This approach would involve a restructuring of Malaysia's financial and economic institutions along more western lines. This dispute on economic policy led to a political confrontation between Anwar's "reformasi" movement on the one hand and Mahathir's aging political establishment on the other, a struggle deftly won by the wily old Prime Minister. The National Economic Recovery Plan of August 1998 announced strong public sector action to stabilize markets and revitalize the sectors of the economy affected by the crisis. Rather than following the prescriptions of the multilateral financial agencies, Malaysia's policies aim at maintaining the supply of credit to firms to avoid the economic distress that would be the result of a credit crunch. Currency controls were defined to protect the domestic economy from external pressures—a daring step in an economy relying so extensively on foreign investments. However, in subsequent months, the policy has proven fairly successful in stabilizing the economy and rekindling growth.

Trouble in the financial system obviously affects the rest of the economy. In the first place, the government is no longer in a position to undertake the massive investment in infrastructure and facilities envisaged for the high-tech push of IMP-2. Parts of the ambitious public sector investment program have been postponed in order to ensure financial credibility. This includes the plans for a second international airport near Penang, costly construction projects in Kuala Lumpur, the contested giant Bakun hydroelectric scheme in Sarawak, and Putrajaya, parts of the planned "paperless capital" for twenty-first-century Malaysia. But other projects, such as the high-profile Multimedia Super Corridor, a centerpiece of the technology push strategy, remain on schedule.

In the first year of the crisis, domestic companies, never on the leading edge in upgrading Malaysia's economic structure, experienced difficulty in committing new investments in view of higher capital costs and a drop in domestic demand. The basic ISI industries have suffered an especially serious setback. The prestigious national car projects are a clear example of this. But not only large enterprises faced difficulties; many SMIs in their local supplier networks were in dire straits, just when official policy aims at beefing up their role in creating genuine Malaysian industrial clusters. These problems have in part been relieved as a result of the currency controls by government.

Meanwhile, the export sector is not affected by a drop in demand; these companies can reap the benefit of enhanced competitiveness in the wake of the lower national currency and a controlled exchange rate. Indeed, for the time being Malaysia is likely to attempt to export itself out of trouble. The country's international trade balance has recently produced a surplus, though still due more to a cut in imports than to increasing exports. So far, there are few signs that investment in the expansion of production is picking up again. When it does, it will more likely entail, at least initially, a horizontal expansion of the economy, adding to production and export capacity in existing industries rather than making much progress in scaling the technology ladder in the direction of more advanced industries. While Malaysia's manufacturing sector is basically sound and competitive—certainly its export sector is—it may find that is not as easy to increase exports as expected after a considerable currency depreciation. Many of its immediate competitors in the Asia-Pacific region have experienced worse depreciations, while major destinations of Malaysian exports, like Japan and South Korea, would appear to be in no position to boost their imports of Malaysian products. The inflow of foreign investment, such a key element of Malaysia's economic strategy, suffered from financial instability and the ensuing crunch in consumer credit. Since the imposition of currency controls, foreign investors are reluctant to commit themselves to increased FDI or portfolio investments. Firms intent on long-term strategic investment will not be deterred, given the low prices at which Malaysian assets can now be acquired and considering the export position, but many other investors wait and see.

In spite of present gloom, Malaysia's long-term prospects appear to be less affected. One of the strategies envisaged in IMP-2 may actually benefit from the turmoil. The localization of supplies and, hence, the emergence of more integrated clusters of activity may actually be encouraged by lower local prices—that is, in industries where local sources can produce at competitive price and quality. Once Malaysia manages to reorganize its financial system and restore investor confidence, there is no reason for the country not to return to rapid progress. What may complicate the restructuring of the financial system is the close connection between the financial system and political interests. Initially, some signs pointed to a willingness among the political elite to swallow bitter pills: the liberalization of equity ownership regulations favoring *Bumiputera* is a case in point, and one that may carry a considerable political cost. The outcome of the Anwar-Mahathir power struggle, however, made it clear that far-reaching reforms in the country's political and economic strategies are not on the agenda. Overall, Malaysia's strategy focusing on technological upgrading may be delayed, but is unlikely to be altered in the longer term. The government's policy of selective closure to the forces of international finance is expected to be a temporary solution to the immediate economic problems. Eventually, a return to the basic strategy of riding the waves of globalization by using international capital, technology and markets for its growth—a strategy that has secured it so well far so long—will be the most probable course of action.

Conclusion

Singapore and Malaysia are both outstanding cases of developing countries that have pursued industrial development paths by attracting international capital. This has created an investment climate designed to entice TNCs in search of lower production costs to relocate part of their international production chains to these two countries. Initially, the insertion of the Southeast Asian export processing plants into the changing corporate global division of labor was restricted to labor-intensive activities and low-end component production and assembly operations, without significant linkages to the surrounding domestic economies. Singapore took a lead role in testing the export-oriented industrialization course. The island republic was also among the first to venture beyond the low-tech, labor-intensive activities associated with TNC transplants in Southeast Asia, when from the late 1970s on it used skilled labor and the quality of its infrastructure to upgrade its role in international economic processes. It took a decade for government policies to elicit the desired responses from international capital. Two basic strategies stood at the core of the Singaporean industrial upgrading effort: (1) the increased localization of forward and backward linkages in the production segments of commodity chains, encouraging the emergence of local and regional networks of suppliers; and (2) the move into the nonproduction segments of international commodity chains, adding more remunerative regional management, logistic, and business support services to the spectrum of Singaporean functions. Malaysia's role in the international economy took longer to move toward higher-level functions. The massive internationalization of Japanese corporations from the mid-1980s on, followed later by the similar company strategies of the East Asian Tigers when their economies felt the competitive pressures of higher (wage) costs and appreciating currencies, gave an enormous boost to Malaysia's export-oriented manufacturing. However, it did not succeed in changing the functions of the country within the regional and global division of labor. With the exception of a few very successful industries, namely semi-conductors and selected electrical goods industries, Malaysia's insertion into global commodity chains remained restricted to production operations following the "early" NIC pattern. In a structural sense, during the 1980s Malaysia's position was very much complementary to that of Singapore. Confronted with changing global, regional, and local conditions, Malaysia now aspires to follow a path similar to the one Singapore started to pursue more than a decade ago. New strategies to this effect, such as IMP-2, have been developed. To a large extent, the long-term success of these strategies will hinge on whether the Malaysian state can evoke the corresponding responses from international capital. A wide range of state initiatives in pursuit of this objective were already underway and had left their mark on the landscapes of Malaysia's core economic regions when the Asian financial crisis hit in 1997. At present, the question is whether these policies and projects, partly postponed, are indeed the messengers of the country's future or merely symbols for its high-flying aspirations. The evidence so far would suggest that the restructuring of Malaysia's economy toward a more advanced profile is indeed delayed. Yet this delay in not likely to change the strategy or indeed the direction in which the economy is moving. If anything, the current adversity reinforces the need for Malaysia to move up the technology ladder toward more rewarding activities.

Notes

1. Linda Lim, "Southeast Asia: Success Through International Openness," in *Global Change, Regional Response: The New International Context of Development*, ed. Barbara Stallings (Cambridge: Cambridge University Press, 1995), pp. 238–271.

2. Gary Gereffi, "Global Production Systems and Third World Development," in Stallings, *Global Change, Regional Response*, pp. 100–142.

3. Singapore, Department of Statistics, *Singapore: 25 Years of Development* (Singapore: National Printers, 1995).

4. Department of Statistics, *Singapore: 25 Years of Development*.

5. A good overview of Singapore's second industrial revolution is provided by Garry Rodan in *The Political Economy of Singapore's Industrialization* (London: The Macmillan Press Ltd., 1989).

6. Singapore, Ministry of Trade and Industry, *The Singapore Economy: New Directions* (Singapore: MITI, 1986).

7. Garry Rodan, "Reconstructing Divisions of Labour: Singapore's New Regional Emphasis," in *Pacific Economic Relations in the 1990s: Cooperation or Conflict?* ed. R. Higgot, R. Leaver, and J. Ravenhill (St. Leonards: Allen & Unwin, 1993), pp. 223–249.

8. Singapore, Ministry of Trade and Industry, *The Strategic Economic Plan: Towards a Developed Nation* (Singapore: MITI, 1991).

9. Peter Dicken and Colin Kirkpatrick, "Services-Led Development in ASEAN: Transnational Regional Headquarters in Singapore," *The Pacific Review* 4, no. 2 (1991): 174–183.

10. Phillip Regnier, "Spreading Singapore's Wings Worldwide: A Review of Traditional and New Investment Strategies," *The Pacific Review* 6, no. 4 (1993): 305–312; Tan Chwee Huat, *Venturing Overseas: Singapore's External Wing* (Singapore: McGraw-Hill, 1995).

11. Rodan, "Reconstructing Divisions of Labour"; S. Natarajan and Tan Juay Miang, *The Impact of MNC Investments in Malaysia, Singapore and Thailand* (Singapore: Asean Economic Research Unit, Institute of Southeast Asian Studies, 1992); Leo van Grunsven, "Industrial Change in Southeast Asia: New Spatial Patterns of Division of Labour," in *Processes of Incorporation and Integration in Developing Countries*, ed. Geert Custers and Peter Stunnenberg, Nijmegen Studies in Development and Cultural Change, no. 16 (Saarbrücken: Verlag Breitenbach Publishers, 1993), pp. 65–103.

12. Not only TNCs from the core economies—including Japanese TNCs—but more recently also NIC-TNCs have joined in this process. See, for example, Henri Wai-Chung Yeung, "Hong Kong Firms in the ASEAN Region: Transnational Corporations and Foreign Direct Investment," *Environment and Planning A* 26 (1994): 1931–1956.

13. See, for example, Martin Perry, "New Corporate Structures, Regional Offices, and Singapore's New Economic Directions," *Singapore Journal of Tropical Geography* 16 (1995): 181–196.

14. Some studies into the evolution of supply networks that reveal these trends are: Leo van Grunsven, "Industrial Restructuring in the Asian NIEs, the Behaviour of Firms and the Dynamics of Local Production Systems. The Case of Audio Production in Singapore," in *Regional Change in Industrializing Asia. Local and Regional Responses to Competition*, ed. Leo van Grunsven (Aldershot: Ashgate, 1998), pp. 106–127; Jasper Grotjohann, Tessa Sterkenburg and Leo van Grunsven, *Sourcing Strategies and Local Embeddedness of MNCs in the Asian Pacific Rim: The Case of Philips Electronics in Malaysia*. Geographical Studies of Development and Resource Use, no. 2. (Utrecht University, Faculty of Geographical Sciences, Institute of Development Studies).

15. Gordon Clark and Won Bae Kim, eds., *Asian NIEs and the Global Economy: Industrial Restructuring and Corporate Strategy* (Baltimore: The Johns Hopkins University Press, 1995); Stephen Chiu, Wing-Kai, Ho Kong Chong, and Lui Tai Lok, *City States in the Global Economy: Industrial Restructuring in Hong Kong and Singapore* (Boulder: Westview Press, 1997); Ho Kong Chong, "Industrial Restructuring and the Dynamics of City-State Adjustments," *Environment and Planning A* 25, no. 1 (1993): 47–62; Ho Kong Chong, "Industrial Restructuring, The Singapore City-State and the Regional Division of Labour," *Environment and Planning A,* 26 (1994): 33–51.

16. Regionalization as state response has been discussed by Henry Yeung and Wai-Chung in "The Political Economy of Transnational Corporations: A Study of the Regionalization of Singaporean Firms," *Political Geography* 17, no. 4 (1998): 389–416. Regionalization as firm response has been discussed in Lee Tsao Yuan, *Overseas Investment: Experience of Singapore Manufacturing Companies* (Singapore: Institute of Policy Studies/McGraw-Hill, 1994).

17. The SIJORI growth triangle as a policy device and as a cross-border indus-
     trial complex is well documented in a rather extensive literature on
     Regional Economic Zones in the Asian Pacific Rim. For example, see Chia
     Siow Yue and Lee Tsao Yuan, "Subregional Economic Zones: A New
     Motive Force in Asia Pacific Development," in *Pacific Dynamism and the
     International Economic System,* ed. Fred C. Bergsten and Marcus Noland
     (Washington, D.C.: Institute for International Economics, 1993), pp.
     225–268; Carl Grundy-Warr and Martin Perry, "Growth Triangles, Interna-
     tional Economic Integration and the Singapore-Indonesian Border Zone,"
     in *Global Geopolitical Change and the Asia Pacific,* ed. Dennis Rumley et al.
     (Aldershot: Avebury, 1996), pp. 185–211; Lee Tsao Yuan, ed., *Growth Trian-
     gle: The Johore-Singapore-Riau Experience* (Singapore: Institute of Southeast
     Asian Studies, 1991); Linda Low, "Government Approaches to SIJORI,"
     Asia-Pacific Development Journal 3, no. 1 (1996): 1–20; Myo Thant, Min Tang,
     and Hiroshi Kakazu, eds., *Growth Triangles in Asia. A New Approach to
     Regional Economic Cooperation* (Hong Kong: Oxford University Press / Asian
     Development Bank, 1994); Kenichi Ohmae, *The End of the Nation State: The
     Rise of Regional Economies* (New York: The Free Press, 1995); Toh Mun Heng
     and Linda Low, eds., *Regional Cooperation and Growth Triangles in ASEAN*
     (Singapore: Times Academic Press, 1993); Leo van Grunsven, Shuang-Yann
     Wong, and Won Bae Kim, "State, Investment and Territory: Regional Eco-
     nomic Zones and Emerging Industrial Landscapes," in *The Pacific Rim and
     Globalization: Enterprise, Governance and Territoriality,* ed. R. le Heron and
     Sam Ock Park (Aldershot: Avebury, 1995), pp. 151–178.
18. For more critical treatments of the growth triangle see Scott MacLeod and
     Terry G. McGee, "The Singapore-Johore-Riau Growth Triangle: An Emerg-
     ing Extended Metropolitan Region," in *Emerging World Cities in Pacific Asia,*
     ed. Fu-Chen Lo and Yeung Yue-Man (Tokyo: United Nations University
     Press, 1996), pp. 417–464; Martin Perry, "The Singapore Growth Triangle:
     State, Capital and Labour at a New Frontier in the World Economy," *Sin-
     gapore Journal of Tropical Geography 12* (1991): 138–151.
19. Singapore, Department of Statistics, *Singapore's Investment Abroad
     1990–1993* (Singapore: Department of Statistics, 1996); Pang Eng Fong,
     "Staying Global and Going Regional: Singapore's Inward and Outward
     Direct Investments," in *The New Wave of Foreign Direct Investment in Asia* ed.
     Nomura Research Institute & Institute of Southeast Asian Studies (Singa-
     pore: ISEAS, 1995), pp. 111–129.
20. *Times,* "Singapore's External Wing in Full Flight," Sunday, April 13, 1997
21. "Leaving Home: Singapore Inc. Goes Global," *Far Eastern Economic Review,*
     April 25, 1996, p. 5.
22. Kwome Sundaram Jomo, "Malaysian Industrialisation in Historical Per-
     spective," in *Industrialising Malaysia. Policy, Performance, Prospects,* ed.
     Kwome Sundaram Jomo (London: Routledge, 1993), pp. 14–39.
23. Ibid.
24. David O'Connor, "Electronics and Industrialisation: Approaching the 21st
     Century," in Jomo, *Industrialising Malaysia,* pp. 210–233.

25. S. Jayasankaran, "Made in Malaysia: The Proton Project," in Jomo, *Industrialising Malaysia*, pp. 272–285.
26. See discussion of Singapore above.
27. Malaysia, Ministry of International Trade and Industry, *Second Industrial Master Plan (IMP-2)* (Kuala Lumpur: MITI, 1996), p. 8.
28. Ibid., pp. 4–6.
29. David O'Connor, "Electronics and Industrialisation: Approaching the 21st Century," in Jomo, *Industrialising Malaysia*, pp. 210–233.
30. Jomo, *Industrialising Malaysia*, p. 7.
31. Malaysia, Economic Planning Unit, *Second Outline Perspective Plan, 1990–2020* (Kuala Lumpur: EPU, 1996), pp. 34, 103.
32. Malaysia, Ministry of International Trade and Industry, *Second Industrial Master Plan (IMP-2)*, p. 9.
33. Paul Krugman, "The Myth of Asia's Miracle," *Foreign Affairs*, November/December, 1994, pp. 62–78.
34. Malaysia, Ministry of International Trade and Industry, *Second Industrial Master Plan (IMP-2)*, p. 13.
35. Linda Lim, "Southeast Asia: Success Through International Openness," in Stallings, *Global Change, Regional Response*, pp. 246–247.
36. Jayant Menon, *Restructuring Towards AFTA* (Singapore: ISEAS, 1996).
37. Malaysia, Ministry of International Trade and Industry, *Second Industrial Master Plan (IMP-2)*, p. 23.
38. Michel Porter, *The Competitive Advantage of Nations* (London: Macmillan, 1990), p. 23.
39. See, for example, *Far Eastern Economic Review*.
40. Lim, "Southeast Asia," p. 266.
41. Menon, *Restructuring Towards AFTA*, p. 78.
42. Malaysia, Ministry of International Trade and Industry, *Second Industrial Master Plan (IMP-2)*, p. 22.
43. Proposals for immediate action and longer term strategies are extensively dealt with in the *Report of the Committee on Singapore's Competitiveness*, Ministry of Trade and Industry, Republic of Singapore, November 1998.

PART THREE

Latin America and the Caribbean

8

Globalization, Neoliberalism, and Regional Response in the Americas

Latin America

Robert Gwynne

At the close of the twentieth century, the international integration of the world market economy is progressing at a rapid pace. Perhaps it is because of the speed of this integration that the process has become termed "globalization." This process encompasses economic transformations in production, consumption, technology, and ideas. It is also intimately linked with transformations in political systems as well as with sociocultural and environmental change.[1]

What is globalization? According to H. A. Watson, "globalization is not reducible to terms like international, multinational, cross-border, or off-shore."[2] Richard O'Brien argues that it is a tendency that refers to "operations within an integral whole," since "a truly global service knows no internal boundaries, can be offered throughout the globe, and pays scant attention to national aspects."[3] This radical position gives globalization a clear definition but it also limits globalization to those global corporations that have a presence in most countries of the world—as in international banking. This approach essentially sees geographical variations in the world as becoming less and less significant. Indeed, O'Brien argues that "the closer we get to a global, integral whole, the closer we get to the end of geography."[4] According to this view, globalization will become synonymous with a homogenized world of global corporations.

Opposing views of globalization stress the notion of the "shrinking world," focusing on a growing integration and compression of the world's peoples, places, and nation-states and a blurring of their territorial boundaries.[5] Territory and geography are still important in this view, but there is an increasing connection between local events and global phenomena. Thus Anthony Giddens defines globalization as an "intensification of world-wide social relations which link distant localities in such a way that local happenings are shaped by events occurring many miles away and vice versa."[6] Complex networks now link the locality with global spaces. In the economic sphere, this can lead to increasing competition between localities and a greater unevenness in development. In this view, globalization is transforming geographical space at a variety of levels—regional blocs, nations, regions, and localities.

Globalization and the Americas

This chapter attempts to examine the globalizing tendencies of capitalism—the dominant socioeconomic system in the global economy—in Latin America at the end of the twentieth century. It could be argued that nation-states in Latin America must increasingly pursue national goals and objectives within globally defined parameters and structures.[7] For developing countries in particular, the impact of a more comprehensive integration into the global economy increasingly reduces the room for policy maneuver. In part this is because the governments of developing countries are more dependent on the policy approval of the global institutions that "supervise" the world economy—such as the IMF, the WTO, and the World Bank—and on the investment decisions of multinational companies that can be persuaded by the verdicts of these international institutions.

Of course, the idea that global constraints are placed on the policy options of developing countries is nothing new in Latin America. The tradition of development theory that has emanated from Latin American writers, through structuralism and dependency, has emphasized the asymmetric and unequal economic relations suffered by members of the periphery within a global core-periphery model.[8] But it is increasingly popular to claim that the traditional division between core and peripheral regions of the world is no more and to justify this claim through reference to the process of globalization.[9] According to Michael Kearney, "globalization implies a decay in the distinction" between core and periphery.[10] The East Asian model of rapid economic growth through increased trade, manufacturing production, and technological capability has been significant in this respect. In Latin America, the rise of substantial manufacturing sectors and technological capability in Brazil and, to a lesser extent, Mexico and Argentina has also served to obscure the core-periphery model, at least in terms of its original formulation, based on the location of manufacturing capacity.[11]

The core-periphery model in Latin America was intimately linked to structuralism and dependency theory. During the latter half of the 1980s and the 1990s, these theories have been replaced by neoliberalism as the dominant theoretical paradigm and method of analysis. Emblematic of this change has been Fernando Cardoso's shift in policy perspective, from key dependency writer[14] to head of a Brazilian government committed to neoliberal reform. Latin American countries, including Brazil, have thus been less likely to move away from the policy orthodoxies recommended by the global institutions, both public and private. Economic and political transformations in Latin America have been intimately linked to the policy recommendations of these institutions. This has been called the period of neoliberal reform, which started in the late 1980s and has become particularly pervasive during the 1990s.

However, among the ways in which dependency theory has evolved is a conceptualization of a world system integrated by commodity chains.[12] The analysis of commodity chains in relation to Latin America as a whole demonstrates the following:

1. The export profile of virtually all of the smaller countries of Latin America is dominated by primary products, much as it was in the 1950s.
2. The export profile of the larger, more industrialized countries of Latin America is characterized by labor-intensive consumer products or components. Certainly the case of Mexico and particularly the type of industrialization experienced in its northern cities has been well documented in this respect.[13]

Given this continuation of the core-periphery pattern, why has neoliberalism become the dominant paradigm of the 1990s in Latin America? There seem to be a number of historical and comparative factors. First of all, in the 1980s, neoliberal policies provided a framework to extricate Latin American economies from the severe debt crisis of that decade, in which access to external finance was suddenly curtailed. Neoliberal economic policies that favored rapid export growth, high interest rates, privatization, and reductions in government spending were designed to ameliorate the severe effects of the sudden drop in external finance and increased government indebtedness.

The adoption of neoliberal policies could thus be seen as a specific response to the impact of the 1980s debt crisis. In many countries, the adoption of a new paradigm also constituted a wider response to the perceived economic failure of the previous political economy paradigm of inward orientation.[15] The intellectual justification of inward orientation came from structuralism and dependency theories, and it called for governments to give protection to industrial enterprises in the home markets and hence to mediate between the national and global economies. However, in the wake of the debt crisis, this policy package, which had been highly successful in East Asia with certain modifications, demonstrated two key economic problems. The first was that of stagnant export trade, partly linked to the historical pattern of overvalued exchange rates and partly linked to government neglect of export growth during inward orientation. Secondly, the inward-oriented model had left a legacy of very high inflation in many countries, particularly in the 1980s, and increased the problems of economic instability in Latin America.

The decade of the 1990s has witnessed big advances in the globalization of the Latin American economy, with capital flows, trade, and investment increasing significantly.[16] The inward-oriented model had been effectively cutting off Latin American economies from the advantages (and problems) of being more fully inserted into a globalizing world economy. Neoliberal policies provided the framework for Latin American economies to increase trade with other world regions and increase inward investment and capital inflows from firms and banks in those regions. It was often argued, incorrectly, that such openness had led to the economic success of the newly industrializing countries of East Asia and their rapid recovery from the debt crisis of the 1980s.[17] Nevertheless the East Asian model was "consumed" in Latin American policy circles because East Asian countries were thought to have been more successful in developing dynamic and technologically innovative economies, at least in part due to their insertion into the world economy through trade, investment, and technology flows.

Brief Perspectives on the
Political Economy of Neoliberalism

The political economy of Latin American countries seems increasingly characterized by neoliberal approaches. But the use of the term *neoliberal* has numerous problematic ideological connotations. For example in international policy circles, the term *Washington consensus* tends to be used to indicate a neoliberal package of reforms.[18] These reforms emphasize economic reforms as opposed to social policies or political reform.[19] Hence some writers have talked about the "new economic model."[20]

The neoliberal package of economic reforms is strongly supported by international institutions such as the World Bank and the IMF—hence the suggestion that the consensus was forged in Washington.[21] The package tends to emphasize reforms in areas of fiscal management, trade, financial markets, and the privatization of state firms. In fiscal reform it emphasizes the reduction of budget deficits, the creation of strong budget and tax offices and an independent central bank, as well as the need to slash public expenditure in economic sectors and concentrate funding on social areas—the main targets for social expenditure being education and health. Neoliberal trade reform is concerned with making Latin American economies more outward looking by promoting exports through more effective exchange rates and by reducing tariffs on imports. Governments are supposed to avoid interventionist industrial policy, reduce their intervention in trade, and abolish barriers to FDI, both inward and outward. Neoliberal financial market reform also had the objective of reducing government intervention and aiming for the operation of free markets—working toward market-determined interest rates. However, after the Mexican crisis of 1994, the policy emphasis changed. It is now understood that financial deregulation needs to be combined with stronger oversight of banks through an effective and efficient Superintendency of Banks.

The reduction of direct government influence in the economy was also furthered through privatization. This reform has had two objectives: eliminating inefficient and insolvent state enterprises and boosting government income in the short term through the sale of these firms to the private sector. However, strong regulatory bodies are needed to ensure that in areas of potential monopoly, such as electricity production and distribution, the private sector companies will actually work more efficiently than those of the former public sector. Reforms to the labor market and the national institutional framework (such as laws protecting property rights) are also seen as vital.[22]

These represent the core of the neoliberal reforms that are recommended by international institutions. However, over the last fifty years the IMF and the World Bank have often made such recommendations for the management of Latin American economies—recommendations which have often been ignored. Why are they more acceptable now? The following five contextual points about neoliberal reform and globalization in Latin America today may help answer this question.

First, the commitment to and the extent of neoliberal reform in Latin America varies substantially; for example, Chile has experienced over two decades of reform and a shift from authoritarian to democratic governance, whereas in Venezuela, conversion to neoliberal reform between 1989 and 1992 was short-lived and became closely involved with corruption. Most Latin American countries are somewhere between these two extremes. Sebastian Edwards has tabulated the main parameters of neoliberal reform for each country.[23] He concludes that as a continent Latin America is shifting toward a closer integration with world markets, but its constituent parts are doing so at very different rates. Mexico and Chile have the fastest rates of integration, Venezuela the slowest. Many governments justify their shift to neoliberal policies by complaining of the lack of an alternative.

Second, there is a link between neoliberal reform and governance. During the late 1980s and 1990s, the link between neoliberal policies and democratic governance has become particularly strong in Latin America—particularly through transitions to democracy in former authoritarian governments.[24] Geopolitical factors are important here.[25] There have been significant shifts from authoritarian to democratic governance in all Southern Cone countries and Brazil during the 1980s and 1990s. In each case there has been either a shift toward or a maintenance of neoliberal economic policies in the aftermath of the democratic transition. Political parties that have come to power after authoritarian governments but have maintained neoliberal policies—as in the case of the *Concertación* in Chile—have argued that democratic governance allows for and encourages greater public participation and representation in the policy process. Democratic transitions have been important because they have allowed responses from the citizenry to policies that have often created widespread hardship in terms of increased unemployment and poverty and a more unequal distribution of economic benefits.

This introduces a third theme: the negative effects of neoliberal reforms on income distribution and poverty. Victor Bulmer-Thomas has shown that the social impacts of neoliberal reform have overall been negative—pressures on the minimum wage, declining real wages, higher unemployment, and an expanded informal sector alongside a significant wealth effect among the economic and financial elites.[26] Within states that have shifted from authoritarian to democratic governance, there is greater evidence that social policies have been integrated into neoliberal reform packages with the objective of achieving greater social equity—or "neoliberalism with a human face," as it has been called. The democratic transition in Chile after 1990, for example, saw a significant shift in social priorities, as taxes were increased to pay for greater spending on social welfare, education, and health care. However, there seems to be less commitment to social policies in the other countries experiencing neoliberal reform.

Fourthly, it could be argued that in order to make Latin American countries more competitive in a globalizing world, neoliberal reform cannot simply be about making economies more market-oriented. The Chilean case shows that substantial and critical institutional reforms have to take place over a long period of time in order for a Latin American country to become more competitive and less prone to international crises. Institutional reform in Chile has stretched over a period dating from 1964 and has emerged from a wide variety of political ideologies. Reforms of the law regarding landholding and the ownership of national mineral wealth (notably copper), reform of health and personal pensions, financial institutions, and taxation have all occurred under governments of widely different ideologies. J. Martinez and A. Diaz have argued that the combination of these profound institutional reforms with market-oriented neoliberal policies lies behind Chile's economic success during the 1990s.[27] This has great significance for the challenge of sustaining economic growth within an increasingly competitive world. In this context, there is some connection between Chile and certain East Asian countries, where institutional change has been fundamental in creating a competitive economy and society within a globalizing world.

The fifth element of neoliberal reform and globalization in Latin America is the formation of regional trade blocs. The original conception of trade liberalization as a policy called for each country to abolish trade barriers, reduce tariffs to low levels, and promote a multilateral system of trade with all major world regions and countries.[28] This was very much the model followed by Chile under the Pinochet dictatorship during the 1980s. However, regionalism has emerged as a potent new force in Latin America during the 1990s, allied in general with neoliberal policies at the national level. Trade liberalization is emphasized, but particularly at the regional level.

Geopolitical considerations have been as important as the demands of neoliberal reform. This is indicated by the early years of Mercosur, the Southern Cone Common Market—comprising Argentina, Brazil, Paraguay, and Uruguay, with Chile as associate member. The shift to regional integration was initiated by the two key members, Argentina and Brazil, in the early 1990s, when both governments were more ideologically committed to neoliberal strategies. However, as Jeffrey Cason points out, state officials in Argentina and Brazil pursued regional economic integration policies for very different reasons.[29]

In Argentina, the radical free-market views of Economy Minister Domingo Cavallo dominated policy making. He hoped to use economic opening to discipline private firms and make them more efficient, to subject them to the competition that they had avoided in the traditionally protected Argentine economy.[30] Thus the strategy of the Argentine government, organized through the Ministry of Economy, was to use the Mercosur process to discipline both business and labor in order to transform and "modernize" the Argentine economy and make it more competitive.

In contrast, the Brazilian government through the 1990s has seen Mercosur as playing much more of a geopolitical role—as is evidenced by the fact that it was the Foreign Ministry, Itamaraty, that coordinated the process of regional economic integration. "Itamaraty has tended to view South American integration in a much more global and strategic context than the Argentine Economy Ministry. This is largely a function of the fact that Brazil is a much larger country than Argentina; it has a much larger industrial base, and it views itself as a global player to be reckoned with."[31] Thus the Brazilian government has seen Mercosur as a way to expand its economic influence in South America. Regional economic integration is seen in geopolitical terms, and indeed, Brazil sees itself as the country to integrate South America leading up to the discussions for western hemispheric integration in the year 2005. In contrast, policy makers in Argentina see economic integration as a way to justify the incorporation of neoliberal reforms, arguing that regional competition will make the Argentine economy more efficient.

Globalization, Neoliberal Reform, and Regional Development

An analysis of the development of export positions in global markets can allow us to examine global-local relations in the context of the neoliberal policies that are integrating Latin American economies more closely with the global economy.

The Growth of Nontraditional Exports in Global Markets

The shift to outward orientation is normally associated with the growth of what have been termed *nontraditional exports*. These are distinguished from *traditional exports*, which were traded internationally under the inward-oriented model. These traditional exports are usually raw materials that are traded on world markets despite overvalued exchange rates in their country of origin. They tend to be nonrenewable resources—oil and minerals in particular—whose international price reflects the global balance of supply and demand in the commodity rather than the costs of production. By contrast, the growth of nontraditional exports is very much influenced by their costs of production. As a result, nontraditional exports have benefitted from the shift to outward orientation and effectively valued exchange rates. The quality and reliability of the export product are important considerations as well, but the relative cost of production is the crucial factor behind the early growth of a nontraditional export sector.

Nontraditional exports can best be divided into two groups—those based on renewable resources and those based on manufacturing products. Renewable resources include such sectors as agriculture,[32] fishing (if extraction rates are controlled), aquaculture, and plantation forestry.[33] Exports within these sectors tended to be discriminated against during the inward-oriented phase because overvalued exchange rates made them more expensive on world markets. However, with the shift to neoliberal policies, these exports have become particularly important for the smaller countries of Latin America.[34] Michael Carter and his colleagues have pointed out that from the middle to late 1980s, nontraditional agricultural exports grew at rates of 222 percent in Chile, 78 percent in Guatemala, and 348 percent in Costa Rica.[35] Due to the renewable nature of these primary exports, the question of environmental sustainability has become an important issue.

Primary resource exports remain important for smaller countries that have generally been unsuccessful in promoting manufacturing exports.[36] For these countries, the previous inward-oriented phase based on manufacturing had been characterized by high-cost and small-scale industrial plants that were weak in terms of industrial competitiveness on a world scale and found it difficult to lift their horizons from domestic to international markets.

However, the shift to neoliberal policies has boosted nontraditional manufacturing exports from the larger countries of Latin America, particularly Mexico and Brazil. In these two countries, the inward-oriented phase of manufacturing development was much more successful in creating effective manufacturing sectors. In the shift to outward orientation, many firms have been unable to compete in international markets and have closed down plants. Other firms, however, have been able to restructure successfully and achieve levels of international competitiveness. Such firms have required access to capital, new technology, best-practice in management, and a range of labor skills.

However, the key factor in the international competitiveness of these firms has been low labor costs. For example, wage levels in Mexican industrial plants have been approximately one-tenth of those in equivalent plants north of the border in the United States.[37] Such labor-cost differentials have attracted much investment from foreign firms, particularly since the signing of NAFTA in 1993 and Mexico's privileged access to the United States market; as a result, labor markets, the gender division of labor, and social relations have changed dramatically in Mexico's northern border towns.[38]

Global-Local Relations and the Growth of Nontraditional Exports

The study of global-local relations in contemporary Latin America presents a number of interesting questions. How much change has there been in patterns of uneven development, most notably the core-periphery model so characteristic of Latin America's previous phase of inward-oriented

industrialization?[39] Has the shift to market-led and outward-looking development expanded the manufacturing or primary resource sectors in Latin
America? What kind of nontraditional exports have emerged in Latin
America, and what have been their locational characteristics? Have peripheral regions gained from the increased role of the private sector in export-
oriented activity? Furthermore, at what levels and on what geographical
scale do we need to discuss globalization? It is often at the local scale that
the impacts of globalization can best be seen in terms of changing social
relations—for example, through changing labor markets (both paid and
unpaid labor) and land markets. However, one then has the methodologi-
cal problem of generalizing from the particular impact of globalization at
one locality to its impact at other localities.

In broad terms, the outward-oriented nature of this phase of economic
growth has had an impact on peripheral regions according to the ability of
producers in those regions to export successfully to international markets.
In those regions where producers have made the shift from domestic to
international markets, usually with the assistance of international intermediaries, significant increases in regional investment and labor productivity have often followed. However, in regions where producers remain
geared to the domestic market, often no such transformation has occurred.
Thus, outward-oriented growth has resulted in uneven development
without unduly affecting the inherited core-periphery relationship.[40]

Neoliberal reform has tended to accentuate the economic importance
of the core region or main city of each country. According to Carlos De
Mattos, foreign investment in Chile (aside from mining) has been heavily concentrated in the metropolitan region of Santiago during the
period of neoliberal reform, and particularly during the late 1980s and
1990s.[41] Between 1974 and 1993, nearly two-thirds (62.7 percent) of foreign investment in manufacturing and services was concentrated in the
Santiago region, causing that region to receive the largest benefits in
terms of regional economic growth, employment, construction, and
labor productivity.

Away from the core region, a complex patchwork of regions and subregions has evolved as a result of their comparative advantage and factor endowments in world markets. Prosperity has become linked to an
area's ability to attract investment and produce for export markets. In
regions that did well under the inward-oriented model but found it difficult to attract export-led capital and to restructure production for
global markets, economic stagnation and decline relative to other
regions has occurred, particularly in terms of labor productivity. Furthermore, the old reliance on supplying domestic markets has became
more problematic as regional producers have to face competitive import
goods and products.[42]

Globalization in Latin America:
Some Concluding Remarks

During the 1990s in Latin America, globalization has been intimately linked with the shift to neoliberal policies. The governments of most of the larger countries of Latin America have integrated their national economies more closely with the global economy. In particular this has been achieved through trade liberalization and the deregulation of financial markets, and increased trade, capital flows, investment, and technology transfer have generally been the result.

The globalization of Latin American economies has coincided with a shift from authoritarian governments (which were still numerous in the 1980s) to democratic governance; at present all sixteen countries in Central and South America have governments elected through the ballot box. Thus in general terms, the Latin American state in the 1990s has transformed itself into a democratic system and at the same time has reduced its direct influence over the economy through privatization and deregulation and has cut the size of the public sector through fiscal reform. Globalization, or Latin America's closer integration with global markets, has thus been associated with a shift to a more representative and participatory political system.[43] To a certain extent this may have obscured the negative social impacts of neoliberal reform, which include increased unemployment and poverty, an even more unequal distribution of income, and a further rise in the informal sector. However, democratic governments have attempted to explain or justify this in two ways.

First of all, there is the argument that the negative social impacts reflect a short-term adjustment to new conditions and will be soon turned around. Unemployment and poverty will increase only while the economy adjusts to new external realities and as the country forges a more competitive economy. The case of Chile can be brought in to justify this argument, given that the shift to democratic governance in the 1990s made reducing social inequity a priority, resulting in increased investment in social programs; consequently poverty levels have been significantly reduced and the distribution of income has become more equitable.[44]

The second argument is that there is a lack of alternatives. Latin American governments point out that the political economy of neoliberalism has become the basis for policy in other areas of the world that are identified as "competitor" regions in the world economy: Eastern Europe and East Asia, in particular. Thus Latin American governments following neoliberal policies argue that they must "modernize" their economies in order to make them more competitive in world markets and better able take advantage of globalization. Such modernization is necessary in order to successfully attract foreign investment from global corporations, which have a wide range of investment options.

There is at least one conceptual problem with the logic of these two arguments. It concerns the relationship of the state with the process of economic change. The neoliberal paradigm stresses that the state should avoid, as much as possible, intervening in and guiding the economy. However, the East Asian model and the Chilean experience show that in order to transform an economy and make it more competitive in the global market, governments must intervene by reforming institutions, such as land ownership, pensions, and education. With this in mind, Robert Wade emphasizes the role of the state in "governing the market."[45] Hence the ideological shift to limited government involvement in the economy may not produce the modernized, competitive economy that is anticipated in neoliberal reform. Without a modernized, competitive economy, sustained economic growth will not occur—and sustained economic growth is seen as the prerequisite for addressing the social debt and beginning to rectify the highly unequal patterns of income distribution.

The question of the relationship between economic integration, neoliberalism, and globalization also remains before us. It is expected that by the year 2005, the Americas will be one large free-trade zone. This would involve integrating the dominant economies of the twentieth century with sixteen much smaller but highly diverse countries in Latin America. As has been pointed out, geopolitical reasons have become important factors in this process. It is true that neoliberal reform and the opening up of formerly inward-oriented economies have produced a more successful record of economic integration in the 1990s than in the 1960s, when economic integration was also seen as a key international policy in Latin America.[46] In geopolitical terms, however, it will still be necessary to resolve the problems inherent in a strong core-periphery pattern that, without massive corrective action, will continue to characterize economic integration of the Americas.

Notes

1. Ronald J. Johnston, Peter J. Taylor, and Michael J. Watts eds., *Geographies of Global Change* (Blackwell, 1995).
2. H. A. Watson, "Globalization, New Regionalism, Restructuring and NAFTA," *Caribbean Studies* 29 (Spring 1996): 5–48.
3. Richard O'Brien, *Global Financial Integration: The End of Geography* (New York: Council on Foreign Relations, 1992).
4. Ibid.
5. Thomas Klak, ed., *Globalization and Neoliberalism: The Caribbean Context* (Boulder: Rowman & Littlefield, 1997).

6. Anthony Giddens, *The Consequences of Modernity* (Stanford: Stanford University Press, 1990).
7. Watson, "Globalization, New Regionalism, Restructuring and NAFTA."
8. Cristobal Kay, *Latin American Theories of Development* (London: Routledge, 1988).
9. Klak, *Globalization and Neoliberalism.*
10. Michael Kearney, "The Local and the Global: The Anthropology of Globalization and Transnationalism," *Annual Review of Anthropology* 24 (1995): 547–565.
11. Raul Prebisch, "The Economic Development of Latin America and Its Principle Problems," *Economic Review of Latin America* 7 (1962): 1.
12. Gary Gereffi and Michael Korzeniewicz, *Commodity Chains and Global Capitalism* (Westport, Conn.: Praeger, 1994).
13. Lesley Sklair, *Assembling for Development* (London: Unwin, 1988); and Otto Verkoren, "Trends in Manufacturing Employment on the US-Mexico Border," (paper presented at the annual meeting of the Latin American Studies Association, Guadalajara, Mexico, 1997).
14. Fernando H. Cardoso and Enzo Faletto, *Dependency and Development in Latin America* (Berkeley: University of California Press, 1979).
15. Kay, *Latin American Theories of Development;* James Dietz, ed., *Latin America's Economic Development: Confronting Crisis* (Boulder: Lynne Rienner, 1995).
16. Sebastian Edwards, *Crisis and Reform in Latin America: From Despair to Hope* (Oxford University Press, 1994).
17. Gary Gereffi and Donald Wyman, eds., *Manufacturing Miracles: Paths of Industrialization in Latin America and East Asia* (Princeton: Princeton University Press, 1994).
18. John Williamson, *Latin American Adjustment: How Much has Happened?* (Washington, D.C.: Institute for International Economics, 1990).
19. Cristobal Kay, "For a Renewal of Development Studies: Latin American Theories and Neoliberalism in the Era of Structural Adjustment," *Third World* 14 (Winter 1993): 691–702.
20. Victor Bulmer Thomas, ed., *The New Economic Model in Latin America and Its Impact on Income Distribution and Poverty* (London: Macmillan, 1996).
21. Edwards, *Crisis and Reform in Latin America.*
22. Ibid.
23. Ibid.
24. Stephan Haggard and Robert Kaufman, *The Political Economy of Democratic Transitions* (Princeton: Princeton University Press, 1995).
25. John Barton, *The Geopolitics of South America* (London: Routledge, 1997).
26. Bulmer Thomas, *The New Economic Model in Latin America.*
27. J. Martinez and A. Diaz, *Chile: The Great Transformation* (Washington, D.C.: The Brookings Institution, 1996).
28. E. V. K. Fitzgerald, "The New Trade Regime, Macroeconomic Behaviour and Income Distribution in Latin America," in Bulmer Thomas, *The New Economic Model in Latin America.*
29. Jeffrey Cason, "Mercosur and the Redefinition of Economic and Political Interests in South America," (paper presented at the annual meeting of the Latin American Studies Association, Guadalajara, Mexico, 1997), p. 8.

30. Ibid.
31. Ibid.
32. Robert N. Gwynne, "Outward Orientation and Marginal Environments: The Question of Sustainable Development in the Norte Chico, Chile," *Mountain Research and Development* 13 (Autumn 1993): 281–293.
33. Robert Clapp, "Creating Competitive Advantage: Forest Policy as Industrial Policy in Chile," *Economic Geography* 71 (Autumn 1995): 273–296; Robert Gwynne, "Direct Foreign Investment and Non-Traditional Export Growth in Chile: The Case of the Forestry Sector," *Bulletin of Latin American Research* 15 (Autumn 1996): 341–357.
34. Bradford Barham, Mary Clark, E. Katz, and Rachel Schurman, "Non-Traditional Agricultural Exports in Latin America," *Latin American Research Review* 27 (Summer 1992): 43–82; Robert Gwynne, "Non-Traditional Export Growth and Economic Development: The Chilean Forestry Sector since 1974," *Bulletin of Latin American Research* 12 (Summer 1993): 147–169.
35. Michael Carter, Bradford Barham, and Dina Mesbah, "Agricultural Export Booms and the Rural Poor in Chile, Guatemala and Paraguay," *Latin American Research Review* 31 (Spring 1996): 33–65.
36. Robert N. Gwynne, *Industrialisation and Urbanisation in Latin America* (London: Routledge, 1985).
37. Harry Shaiken, "Advanced Manufacturing in Mexico: A New International Division of Labour," *Latin American Research Review* 29 (Summer 1994): 39–72.
38. Sklair, *Assembling for Development*; Verkoren, "Trends in Manufacturing Employment on the US-Mexico Border."
39. Gwynne, *Industrialisation and Urbanisation in Latin America*; Arthur Morris, *Latin America: Economic Development and Regional Differentiation* (London: Routledge, 1981).
40. C. Scott, "The Distributive Impact of the New Economic Model In Chile," in Bulmer-Thomas, *The New Economic Model in Latin America*; Uribe Echevarria, "Reestructuración Económica y Desigualdades Interregionales: El Caso de Chile," *EURE, Revista Latinoamericana de Estudios Urbano Regionales* 22, no. 65: 11–38.
41. Carlos De Mattos, "Avances de la Globalización y Nueva Dinámica Metropolitana: Santiago de Chile, *EURE, Revista Latinoamericana de Estudios Urbano Regionales* 22, no. 65: 39–64.
42. A. Apey, *Agricultural Restructuring and Coordinated Policies for Rural Development in Chile* (Ph.D. diss., University of Birmingham, 1995).
43. Haggard and Kaufman, *The Political Economy of Democratic Transitions*.
44. Scott, "The Distributive Impact of the New Economic Model in Chile."
45. Robert Wade, *Governing the Market: Economic Theory and the Role of Government in East Asian Industrialization* (Princeton: Princeton University Press, 1996).
46. R. Gibb and W. Michalak, eds., *Continental Trading Blocks: The Growth of Regionalism in the World Economy* (New York: Wiley, 1994).

9

Globalization and Regionalization in Central America

Helmut Nuhn

Central America consists of a number of small states with internal economic, social, and political structures that have been heavily influenced by their extreme dependence of a limited range of agrarian export products—mostly bananas and coffee. Their integration into the world economy was brought about by coffee exports to Europe from the mid-nineteenth century onwards. Coffee exports still account for one-quarter of the foreign trade income of the region. The establishment of extensive banana plantations before the end of the last century caused a new export boom. After the major restructuring of banana production, banana exports still account for one-fifth of the total trade income. In some Central American countries these exports are the major source of foreign currency income. After the Second World War, new agrarian products opened additional opportunities for economic growth. These new exports included cotton, important after the Suez crisis in 1956 eliminated Egypt as an exporter, cane sugar after Cuban sugar quotas on the U.S. market were cancelled, and beef products in response to the needs of the rapidly growing fast-food industry in the United States.

Although the Central American nations have similar foreign trade patterns, their socioeconomic and sociopolitical structures show considerable variation. In Costa Rica the coffee industry has been based on family businesses, a major factor behind the development of a political democracy in that country. In Guatemala, on the other hand, the domination by large-scale companies employing indigenous labor has contributed to the prevalence of authoritarian structures. In Honduras, with an economy heavily relying on banana exports, decisionmaking was strongly influenced by big companies operating in externally controlled enclaves. In El Salvador, coffee, sugarcane, and cotton production was controlled by national oligarchies.

The governments of these small countries took an active part in opening their economies to foreign capital and acquiring the know-how needed for the exploitation of their agrarian potential and the reservoir of cheap manual labor. In times of high market demand and rising prices, this strategy did contribute to great affluence among those in control of the agrarian sector. The lower social classes, however, were left out. Actually, many smallholders and agricultural workers lost their income as a result of the expansion of agrarian exports in combination with the increasing mechanization and rationalization of these sectors. The export economy had boom-bust characteristics with an absence of sustained development.

In the late 1950s, the Central American countries decided upon an alternative model of development. Its central element involved the establishment of import substituting industries in combination with a project of regional integration and the creation of a common market.[1] However,

Figure 9.1   Offshore Assembling Operations in Central America. 1994

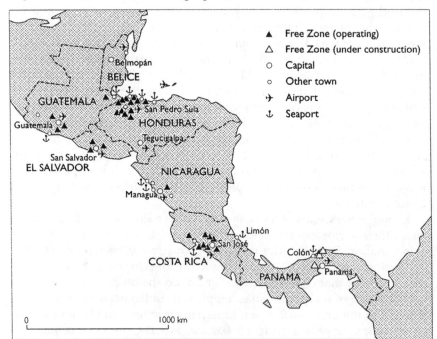

the success of this strategy was only temporary; the limits of growth under this model were already reached by the 1970s. At the same time, the uneven distribution of the positive results gained by the regional integration project led to far-reaching conflicts between and within the countries concerned.

The economic situation further deteriorated as a result of increasing energy costs and falling world market prices for traditional exports, in addition to a growing foreign debt. In the early 1980s, a radical change in development strategy was indicated. In the course of this process several major factors had to be confronted:

1. the developmental problems resulting from the small size of the countries concerned and the efforts to overcome them through regional cooperation;
2. the organization of programs of structural adjustment and integration into the international economy;
3. the role of regional integration in a strategy of sustainable development for the countries of Central America.

In this chapter we will analyze these issues and describe how they have been addressed within the region.

Small Countries and
Regional Economic Integration

In addition to typical developmental problems, the Central American countries have to cope with the disadvantage of the small size of their internal markets. Although the correlation between country size and the general state of development is not strong, the small, less developed countries have a number of specific problems to overcome that affect their macroeconomic performance.[2]

Small West European states with democratic structures, political stability, a strong social commitment, and an open competitive economy have proven able to adjust flexibly to world market fluctuations.[3] However, cross-country comparative data show that small developing countries are more vulnerable to international economic influences. In addition, small population size and reduced purchasing power will limit the development of the domestic market, impede the growth of some companies and production lines, and restrict the possibilities of the developing economies of scale.[5] Because only a few businesses of the same industrial branch can survive in a small economy, intra-industrial specialization and integration are limited and small states are at risk of developing monopolies (see Table 9.1).

Table 9.1   Factors Inhibiting Growth and Industrialization in Small, Less Developed Countries

Small domestic market
- Impedes growth in some production lines;
  No large-scale production feasible
- Small number of companies;
  Weak intraindustrial linkages;
  Danger of monopoly formation
- Dominance of small-size enterprises;
  Competitive disadvantages in comparison with large companies

High levels of external dependence
- High demand for imports that cannot be produced cheaply within the country
- High export volume necessary to achieve a balance of payments
- Selective export specialization in few products
- Reliance on a small number of trading partners

Low market power
- No impact on commodity pricing due to modest export shares in the world market
- Lack of counterbalancing effects from the domestic market
- No headquarters of multinational companies

Limited financial resources
- Deficient public services and infrastructures
- Poor scientific and technological research development
- Antiquated machinery and labor organization
- Reliance on license contracts

Archaic social structures
- Key positions controlled by a small number of families
- Minimal social and political mobility
- Emigration of qualified workers and specialists

The creation of a free trade area and improvement of technological competence could possibly counterbalance the negative effects of small size.

The lack of opportunities to produce cheaply in a small country will generate an increasing demand for foreign imports, maintaining the need for large export volumes in order to avoid trade and balance-of-payments deficits. This emphasis on exports is an absolute necessity for those small countries confronted with the drawbacks of a narrow domestic market. In many cases, however, exports will be directed toward a small number of trading partners, creating dependence relationships. Since export shares are generally modest in relation to the volumes on the overall world market, commodity prices can barely be influenced. Consequently, small countries are "price takers" without market power, compelled to adapt to conditions as they are presented to them.

Those companies with a strong presence on the world market usually operate from headquarters in larger countries. In the smaller countries, most companies tend to be small to medium-sized and often have difficulties keeping abreast of market developments.[6] Furthermore, the lack of diversified economic structures generally coincides with a deficiency or even absence of specialized service companies in the areas of design, marketing, consulting, and R&D, which are crucial for international competitiveness.

Additional economic problems often encountered by small countries result from the lack of financial resources available for public expenditure, especially affecting the quality and differentiation of public services and infrastructure. Basic services, such as water, energy, health care, and education, are often under-supplied. Research and technological development are limited by the small operational basis and the out-migration of qualified staff, creating a brain drain that has a negative impact on society as a whole.

In many Central American countries, key economic and political positions have been controlled by traditional family-clans for a greater part of their history since Independence. We find an extreme example with the Somoza family, who dominated Nicaraguan economy and society from the mid-1930s until the Sandinista Revolution in 1979. In El Salvador and Guatemala as well, archaic social and political structures and the lack of an open, diversified society have obstructed developments that would be necessary to counterbalance the disadvantages generated by the countries' small size.

Many structural barriers to development in small states can be overcome through economic and political cooperation—at least that was the general idea in the 1950s. In those years, after repeated efforts at political integration had failed, the small Central American countries now began preparations for economic integration. It was hoped that the ensuing extension of the internal market would lead to the increased use of local resources and a diversification of production and would stimulate the industrialization process in general. At the time, conditions for such an economic integration were perceived to be favorable, given the countries' size, stage of development, shared cultural and historical heritage, and matching interests in the international economy.

In 1960, a general treaty was concluded that aimed at a gradual reduction of tariffs within the member states, the creation of a free trade zone, as well as the organization of a customs union through the alignment of external tariffs. Industrialization was promoted as part of the import substitution model, including protectionist state intervention. Investment increased, considerable economic growth was registered, and intraregional trade relations intensified. The metropolitan areas in particular, as locations of industry and service trade, profited from this development. The rural areas were left behind.[7]

However, as elsewhere in Latin America, the import substitution industrialization strategy did not meet expectations. Imports of consumer goods continued to be voluminous. High duties on these goods combined with subsidies on the imports of investment goods to stimulate local production failed to turn this situation around. Usually, foreign investors and national governments, instead of local entrepreneurs, were involved in the process. The positive effects on employment were rather meager. The exchange and price policies that were used failed to stimulate production and put the agrarian sector at a disadvantage. Policies were one-sidedly concentrated on the necessity of integration, bypassing the need for economic and social reform.

A negative trade balance and increased public spending was compensated for at the time through external lending. The foreign debt grew dramatically and by the end of the 1970s it had become clear that the strategy of import substitution industrialization in combination with strongly protectionist government intervention had failed.[8] The economies had entered into a severe economic crisis that conventional methods were unable to resolve. The resulting decreases in real income, rampant inflation, and shortages in supplies of basic staples triggered grave social unrest.

Structural Adjustment and the Opening to World Competition

In Central America, as in most developing countries, the implementation of fundamental reform as part of an outward-oriented structural adjustment was initiated in the 1980s. The strategy was, to a great extent, determined by international financial institutions. Short- and medium-term loans meant to stabilize the economies were advanced by the IMF and the World Bank under rigid conditions that included application of the adjustment programs and neoliberal economic reforms. The old structuralist policies that had been oriented to the domestic market were abolished. Instead, reforms aimed at opening the economy were introduced with the objective of increasing competitiveness and sustained growth. Tariffs were gradually reduced, exchange rates liberalized, financial markets deregulated, and banks and public service sectors privatized. At the same time, direct and indirect state subsidies were largely eliminated. Incentives were given for productivity increases. Nontraditional exports were supported (see Table 9.2).

Government intervention was reduced through the privatization of state-owned companies and by the reduction of the state apparatus through financial cuts and layoffs. Comprehensive sectoral and regional planning strategies were replaced by limited macroeconomic frameworks and isolated strategic projects that were thought to provide sufficient direction to economic development. Further economic guidance was left to market forces. Only those programs directed toward the alleviation of extreme poverty were left to the state.[9]

The structural adjustment strategy generated intensive debates on the correctness of the approach and the instruments used. Eventually, international financial institutions and the community of critics found more common ground. In 1987, the IMF development committee identified a number of fundamental deficiencies in the strategy, namely those resulting from the exclusion of social matters. This lead to compensational measures for the "vulnerable groups."[10]

Structural adjustment measures were implemented at different times and with varying intensity in different countries in the region.[11] In Costa Rica, these measures were gradually introduced from 1982 on, while in Honduras, the introduction of structural adjustment policies in 1990 had "shock" characteristics with a sudden currency devaluation and the removal of tariffs and subsidies. In hindsight, the Costa Rican strategy of a slow, stepwise, and coordinated introduction of measures, employing temporary regulations and subsidies for the transitional phases, appears to have worked better and to have had fewer negative effects than the Honduran shock-therapy approach, which had been advocated by the country's creditors. In Honduras, privatization—leading to the dissolution of cooperatives and the sale of large estates to the plantation companies—annulled the results of earlier agrarian reforms. Also, restructuring the agrarian sector did not produce the expected results. Growth rates of nontraditional exports were rather modest compared to those of Costa Rica.

Conditions for the success of this model seem to have been more favorable in Costa Rica, where the existence of already competitive small enterprises and cooperatives has contributed significantly to integration into the global economy. It remains to be seen whether this trend will continue or will end again with a concentration of ownership and foreign control—as was the case with the former traditional exports.[12] In the meantime, both Honduras and Costa Rica have experienced a rapid growth of the offshore assembling, or *maquila*, industry. This development has provided new employment opportunities in the vicinity of the urban agglomerations that have a functioning infrastructure and a differentiated labor market. The analysis of the *maquila* boom in Costa Rica and Honduras indicates that the new employment has benefitted mainly the

Table 9.2   Political-Economic Objectives Based on the Neoliberal Economic Model

Concepts: Opening the economy to the world market; deregulation
Promoters: IMF and the World Bank (1980s)

Trade policy	Orientation to the world market
	International free trade
Tariff policy	Trust in self-regulation through market forces
	General reduction of tariffs to a low level
Currency policy	Devaluation of the national currency
	Free sale and purchase of currencies
Pricing policy	Liberalization of pricing
	Liberalization of the money market
Banking and lending policy	Privatization of banks
	Support for improved exports and productivity
Industrial policy	Privatization of state-owned companies
	Reduction of direct and indirect subsidies
	Competition between companies
Agrarian policy	Removal of export barriers
	Support for nontraditional exports
Role of the state	Limited to macroeconomic frameworks
	Reduction of state institutions
Infrastructure policy	Further development through private companies
	Levying of fees
Education, training, and technology	Partly taken over by private services

former underemployed marginal groups. Next to these employment effects, no other linkages have developed in the local economy.[13]

Interestingly enough, the traditional industrial sector did not collapse completely after the abolition of protectionism, as many feared it would. Very few of the larger firms went bankrupt and most of them seemed capable of adapting to the new conditions. Some firms have already succeeded in achieving international competitiveness. Many small companies also managed to adjust to the new economic situation. Major problems appear to have arisen for trade firms when cheap imports undermined the competitiveness of the native companies, long in need of technical modernization.[14]

The concentration on industrialization and the neglect of the agrarian sector came to an end when exchange rates and prices were liberalized and measures for the stimulation of exports were implemented. This liberalization did open up new possibilities for the marketing of traditional and nontraditional export products. On the other hand, it also permitted the imports of fodder and grains, jeopardizing the interests of small local producers. It appears that in some cases these losses are being compensated for by new nontraditional exports, such as fruit and ornamental plants.

An overall evaluation of the effects of the adjustment policies would show crises severely affecting the lower and middle classes, followed by a general improvement in economic performance (see Table 9.3). However, substantial differences can be observed among the Central American countries. While the Nicaraguan economy has not yet been able to register consistent growth, results have been quite positive in El Salvador, where reconstruction after the civil war has stimulated economic growth. Costa Rica also has experienced economic success, which is not surprising given the initial conditions in the country and the early introduction of measures to stimulate the local market and exports.

This again illustrates that the success of a national reform process is strongly dependent on the country's internal conditions.

It explains why development strategies like the neoliberal adjustment strategies, thought to be universally applicable, do not work in all cases.[15] Although fundamental reforms of the public sector can be initiated externally, they are always tied to internal sociopolitical processes, and these are rather inflexible.

The neoliberal model, with its strong reliance on market forces and static comparative cost advantages, will not be able to bring about sustainable development, at least not in the medium term.[16] Inexpensive exports and cheap labor are poor guarantees of long-lasting competitiveness in international markets.

Economic Integration and Open Regionalism

In the wake of the neoliberal offensive, there was certainly no lack of recommendations for revitalizing and restructuring Central American economic integration. The UN Economic Commission for Latin America (CEPAL), the Secretary of the Common Market (SIECA), as well as regional interest groups and economists all made their suggestions.[17] Public opinion surveys in Central America also confirmed that economic cooperation is generally considered to be necessary and desirable. Political integration, on the other hand, was not that easily embraced.[18]

From 1984 onward, not only the United States but also the EU showed increased interest in the Central American region. In the course of political dialogues between the EU and the Central American states, it was repeatedly emphasized that economic cooperation was crucial as a basis for the consolidation of the peace process and a successful democratization.[19] After the United States reduced its aid programs, the EU economic

Table 9.3   Effects of Structural Adjustment Policies in Central America

Short term stabilization of the fiscal crsis
- Reduction of inflation rates to acceptable levels
- Cuts in public spending through labor layoffs and the reduction of subsidies
- Problems with regard to state income, due to tax cuts and changes in tax legistlation

Industrial collapse did not happen
- Traditional industries have been able to adapt, however a new dynamism has not yet developed
- Strong increase of maquila industry should be evaluated with caution (limited preferences to the US-market)
- Small-scale trade industry temporary threatened by cheap imports

Discrimination of agriculture has been eliminated
- Impressive success of nontraditional agrarian exports, which, however, still have to be stabilzed
- Unfavorable perspectives for traditional agrarian exports (EU banana regulations)
- Danger for staple food production owing to cheap imports

High social costs of structural adjustment policies
- Decreasing real income and increasing job loss, which economic development has so far not compensated for
- The privatization of public services endangers the supply of basic goods to lower social classes
- Social and spatial disparities are on the increase

Long-term consequences of structural adjustment have proven problematic. The main threat has come from global competition.

cooperation came to play an important role in supporting the integration of the Central American economies into the international economy, as well as supporting their regional integration.[20]

Regular summit meetings of Central American presidents have repeatedly called for economic integration. At the Antigua summit in June 1990, the presidents adopted the Central American Economic Action Plan (PAECA), which had as objectives the renewal of the Regional Payment System, participation in the GATT, and the coordination of economic policies. The summit in El Salvador, one year later, prompted the adoption of a new action plan for agriculture (PAC) and the introduction of common external tariffs of between 5 percent and 20 percent for raw materials and finished products, starting in 1993. In October 1993, the presidents agreed to adopt a flexible modernization of the System of

Regional Integration (SICA). In addition, the wish to become members of NAFTA was expressed.[21]

These dialogues do not cancel previous integration agreements, but modify or replace them with bilateral and multilateral arrangements. By 1991, all countries in the region had signed general agreements with the United States to strive for long-term free trade based on President Bush's Enterprise for the Americas initiative. In subsequent years, extraregional trade has experienced a stronger growth than intraregional trade. However, in the early 1990s all Central American countries, with the exception of Costa Rica, registered significantly lower overall trade volumes than before the crisis of the 1980s. Attempts to strengthen regional institutions, including the SIECA, the ODECA, and the Central American Parliament (PARLECEN), have been half-hearted. The rhetoric for integration at all levels unfortunately contradicts the actions that are actually being taken. With such ambivalence underlying it, the task of fundamental economic integration may prove to be almost a mission impossible.

Yet cooperation that will remain limited to certain areas appears to be promising. Examples include an extended distribution of the energy supply, the improvement of communication and transport networks, the agreements on common interests regarding foreign trade, and in the case of joint ventures and multilateral projects, the support of production and services. Cooperation between state departments, chambers, and unions that remains restricted to factual questions on a regional scale have a positive tradition and will continue to be effective. There is hope for the gradual implementation of limited short to medium-length projects that are of common interest and are partly founded on the former, more comprehensive integration agreements.[22]

This mode of cooperation is usually referred to as *Acción Conjunta Regional*. Meanwhile, since 1994 there has also been a shift toward more substantial political-economic targets, which are propagated under the slogan *Regionalismo Abierto*.[23] Unlike the MCCA (Mercado Común Centroamericano), which was in favor of cutting extraregional relations and protecting intraregional development, the *Regionalismo Abierto* seeks to establish an open regional cooperation in the economic-political arena. Starting points for such a development are derived from the combined strength of the participants in asserting their interests against foreign trade partners and international organizations.

This concept, which was favored particularly by CEPAL, combines structuralist positions with neoliberal elements.[24] It is supported by analyses of the development process in traditional and newly industrialized countries[25] and emphasizes the need to redefine the way the economies of small countries are integrated into the world economy—as a result of decisionmaking in democratic institutions and accompanied by social compensation. In this context, development is interpreted as a multidimensional process that needs long-term planning and is being influenced equally by sociocultural and political variables as well as economic factors. The importance of these last mentioned factors is especially pronounced in the Central American region, where the lack of social coherence and political stability forcefully intervenes into the workings of economic variables. Here lies an important task for the governments of the respective countries. They should focus on securing stable political and social conditions and providing the material and institutional infrastructures that private companies rely upon for their operations and their economic linkages. Apart from that, the state should serve as an engine, coordinator, stimulator, and guarantor of a free market. This should be an essential part of the regional project also.

Notes

1. Bela Balassa, *The Theory of Economic Integration* (London: Macmillan, 1962); *El Desarrollo Integrado de Centroamérica en la Presente Decada*, vol. 1–11, (Buenos Aires: SIECA/BID/INTAL, 1973; Eduardo Lizano, *Escritos sobre Integración Económica* (San José: Planeta, 1982).
2. Eduardo A. G. Robinson, ed., *Economic Consequences of the Size of Nations* (London: Routledge, 1960); G. Ashoff, *Entwicklungs- und Industriestrategische Optionen Kleiner Länder der Dritten Welt.* (Berlin: DIE, 1988); René Escoto and Pedro Vuscovic, *PPP Pequeños Países Periféricos en América Latina*, (Caracas: Nueva Sociedad, 1990).
3. Pedro J. Katzenstein, *Small States in World Market: Industrial Policy in Europe* (London: Sage, 1985).
4. Robert E. Looney, "Macro-Economic Consequences of the Size of Third World Nations, with special reference to the Caribbean," *World Development* 17 (1989): 69–83; Dwight W. Perkins and Moshe Syrquin, "Large Countries. The Influence of Size," in *Handbook of Development Economics*, vol. 2, ed. Hollis Chenery and Thomas N. Srinivasan (Amsterdam: North Holland Publishing Company, 1989).
5. Simon Kuznets, "Economic Growth of Small Nations," in Robinson, *Economic Consequences of the Size of Nations*, pp. 14–32; Christopher D. Edwards, "Size of Markets, Scale of Firms, and the Character of Competition," in Robinson, *Economic Consequences of the Size of Nations*, pp. 117–130.
6. Christopher Freeman and Bernt-Ake Lundvall, eds., *Small Countries Facing the Technological Revolution*, (London: Pinter, 1988).
7. Helmut Nuhn and Jürgen Obenbrügge, eds., *Polarisierte Siedlungsentwicklung und Dezentralisierungspolitik in Zentralamerika*, vols. 1 and 2 (Hamburg: Geo-Center, 1987–1988).

8. Peter Greiner, *Handelsliberalisierung, Oekonomische Integration und Zwischenstaatliche Konflikte*, (Münster: LIT Verlag, 1992).

9. Peter Waller, "Zum Gegenwärtigen Stand der Diskussion über die Strukturanpassungspolitik," *Zeitschrift für Wirtschaftgeographie* 34 (1990): 1–5; John Williamson, ed., *Latin American Adjustment: How Much has Happened* (Washington, D.C.: Institute for International Economics, 1990); Hermann Sautter and Rolf Schinke, "Die Sozialen Kosten Wirtschaftlicher Reformen - ihre Ursachen und die Möglichkeiten einer Abfederung," *IAI-Diskussionbeiträge*, no. 63, 1994.

10. Eliane Zuckerman, *Adjustment Programs and Social Welfare*, (Washington, D.C.: World Bank, 1989).

11. Roberto López, *El Ajuste Estructural de Centroamérica. Un Enfoque Comparativo*, (San José: Planeta, 1989); Simon Saborio, "Central America," in Williamson, *Latin American Adjustment*, pp. 279–302; Eliana Franco and Carlos Sojo, *Gobierno, Empresarios, y Políticas de Ajuste* (San José, Costa Rica: FLACSO, 1992); Simon Buttari, "Economic Policy Reform in Four Central American Countries. Patterns and Lessons Learned," *Journal of Interamerican Studies and World Affairs* 34, no. 1: 179–214.

12. Andreas Stamm, "Weltmarktinduzierte Innovationen im Costaricanischen Agrarsektor: eine Neue Dynamik für den Ländlichen Raum?" *Zeitschrift für Wirtschaftgeographie* 39 (1995): 82–91; Helmut Nuhn and Andreas Stamm, eds., *Apertura Comercial en Centro América: Nuevos Retos para la Agricultura* (San José: FLACSO, 1996).

13. Tilman Altenburg and Ian Walker, "Nationale und regionale Entwicklungsimpulse durch Weltmarktfabriken. Beispiele aus Zentralamerika," *Zeitschrift für Wirtschaftsgeographie* 39 (1995): 102–112; Tilman Altenburg and Helmut Nuhn, eds., *Apertura Comercial en Centroamérica. Nuevos Retos para la Industria* (San José: FLACSO, 1995).

14. Tilman Altenburg, "Vom Protektionismus zum Freihandel: Industrie und Kleingewerbe in Honduras und Costa Rica," *Zeitschrift für Wirtschaftsgeographie* 39 (1995): 113–123; Geske Dijkstra, "La Industria Tradicional ante los Condiciones de Competencia: El Caso de Nicaragua," in Altenburg and Nuhn, *Apertura Comercial en Centroamérica*, pp. 111–126.

15. Peter Wolf, *Strukturanpassungsprogramme. Versuch einer Bilanz nach Zehn Jahren* (Berlin: DIE, 1991).

16. Christopher Colclough, "Structuralism Versus Neo-Liberalism: An Introduction," in *States or Markets? Neo-Liberalism and the Development Policy Debate*, ed. Christopher Colclough and John Manor (Oxford: Oxford University Press, 1993) pp. 1–25.

17. José Manuel Salazar, "Present and Future Integration in Central America," *CEPAL Review* 42 (1990): 157–180; CEPAL, *Bases y Propuestas para la Reestructuración del Sistema Centroamericano de Integración* (Mexico City: CEPAL, 1991); CEPAL, *Centroamérica. El Camino de los Noventa* (Mexico City: CEPAL, 1993); CEPAL, *El Regionalismo Abierto en América Central. El Desafio de Profundizar y Ampliar la Integración* (Mexico City: CEPAL, 1995); Rómulo Caballeros, "Reflexiones sobre la Integración Centroamericana en

la Década de 1990," *Integración Latinoamericana* 17 (1992), no. 185: 17–22; Alfred Guerra Borges, "Integración Centroamericana en los Noventa: De la Crisis a las Perspectivas," *Revista Mexicana de Sociologia* 54, no. 3 (1992): 115–127; FLACSO, ed., *Una Contribución al Debate: Integración Regional* (San José: FLACSO, 1993).

18. Victor Bulmer-Thomas, Rodolfo Cerdas, Eugenia Gallardo, and Mitchell Seligson, *Central American Integration. Report for the Commission of the European Community* (Miami: North-South Center, 1992); Helmut Nuhn, ed., *Zentralamerika Oekonomische Integration und Regionale Konflikte* (Hamburg: Geo-Center, 1991).

19. Hans Kreft, "Europa und Zentralamerika: 12 Jahre San José-Dialog," *Aus Politik und Zeitgeschichte* B 48–49/96(November 22, 1996): S.3–11.

20. IRELA, *The San-José Process. Current Situation and Prospects* (Madrid: IRELA, 1996).

21. *Revista de la Integración y el Desarrollo de Centroamérica*, no. 50, 1996.

22. Victor Bulmer-Thomas, "Un Modelo de Desarrollo de Largo Plazo para Centroamérica," *Política Económica* 1, no. 7 (1991): 2–40; Luis-René Caceres, "Central American Integration: Its Costs and Benefits," *CEPAL Review* 54 (1994): 111–128.

23. CEPAL, *El Regionalismo Abierto en América Latina y el Caribe. La Integración Económica al Servicio de la Transformación Productiva con Equidad* (Santiago de Chile: CEPAL, 1994); Juan Alberto Fuentes, "Reconciling Subregional and Hemispheric Integration," *CEPAL Review* 45 (1991): 99–120; Juan Alberto Fuentes, "Open Regionalism and Economic Integration," *CEPAL Review* 53 (1991): 81–89.

24. Maurice Rosenthal, "Central America," in *Latin American Adjustment*, ed. John Williamson (Washington, D.C.: Institute for International Economics, 1990), pp. 279–302.

25. Fernando Fajnzylber, *La Industrialización Trunca de América Latina.* (Mexico City: ERA, 1989).

10

Globalization and Regional Integration: The Brazilian Industry and Mercosur

Kees Koonings

For half a century Brazil has been one of the classic cases of import substituting industrialization (ISI). This process was based on a "triple alliance" between state, foreign, and domestic private capital[1] and resulted in a closed economy heavily biased toward the urban sector and toward those industries producing durables and capital goods for the domestic market. Between the 1950s and the early 1980s, this model managed to realize an impressive industrial growth and overall economic transformation, driven by state intervention and, especially since the early 1970s, financed through extensive external borrowing.[2] In those years, the "politics of industrialization" united state technocrats, industrialists, the military, and national and regional politicians under the protection of the huge regulatory apparatus of the state.[3]

Brazilian ISI was marked by a substantial spatial concentration of economic activities in the São Paulo–Belo Horizonte–Rio de Janeiro triangle, where the largest and most dynamic industries were located. However, some regional economies experienced noteworthy industrial growth as well. States like Pernambuco and Bahia and especially the three southern states of Paraná, Santa Catarina, and Rio Grande do Sul managed to play a significant role in national industrialization. Their industrial economies were based on a combination of historically established local manufacturing and more recent activities linked to specific regional conditions (such as a strong agriculture in Rio Grande do Sul) or to large-scale investments by the state or large firms from the center (as happened in Bahia, Pernambuco, and Amazonas).

This intricate and complex structure supporting ISI wore thin to the verge of breaking down with the "debt crisis" of the early 1980s. However, it took more than an additional decade for Brazilian policy makers and businessmen to abandon the ISI logic in favor of the new dogmas of liberalization, deregulation, and globalization. The sheer weight of the Brazilian economy complicated restructuring while the relatively rapid growth of the export sector in the 1980s had made the debt burden "manageable." Initially, strong neoliberal convictions were rare among Brazil politicians and technocrats and the adjustment to changing international economic conditions was slow. In fact, much of their attention was absorbed by the paramount problem of hyperinflation. Only after the successful attack on inflation through the *real* stabilization plan in 1993–1994 and the subsequent election of finance minister Fernando Henrique Cardoso to the presidency was a more long-term substantial adjustment and reform policy defined. Within this context, the decision in 1991 to join Argentina, Paraguay, and Uruguay in the formation of a common market was a most interesting initiative. Argentina and Brazil had made prior attempts to establish bilateral economic cooperation and integration but they had never gone that far. Both countries were being pushed toward closer eco-

Figure 10.1   Bilateral Trade between the Mercosur Countries, 1990–1993

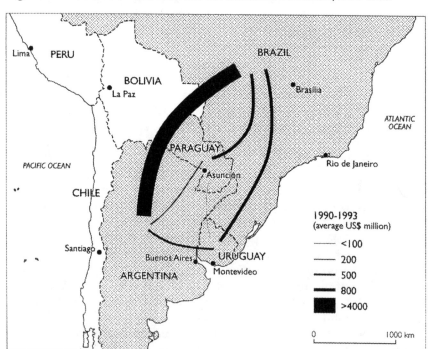

nomic and political cooperation by a complex of coinciding factors. Both had passed through a transition toward democracy after a long period of military rule and had put an end to traditional geopolitical rivalries. Both had experienced the exhaustion of the ISI model and were confronted with the pressures for economic adjustment. Finally, globalization generated a tendency toward regionalization in this part of the world.

Within the context of these dynamics, Brazil's south, and especially the state of Rio Grande do Sul, has been playing an interesting role. During the ISI period, the region was subordinated to the powerful economic and industrial center in the São Paulo–Belo Horizonte–Rio de Janeiro triangle. Yet, Rio Grande do Sul's industrial economy showed considerable dynamism, supported by a booming agricultural sector and led by a strong group of regional entrepreneurs. However, the region did not remain unaffected by the crisis, stagnation, and instability that characterized the 1980s and early 1990s. The need to meet these challenges led to new forms of regional awareness among the political and business elites of the state, especially after 1985 with the end of military rule. Mercosur offered a new platform for this regionalism, which presented Rio Grande do Sul as the natural core region of this trade block—strategically located halfway between the poles São Paulo and Buenos Aires and with the presence of a strong agricultural and industrial tradition, a relatively well-qualified workforce, and with a quality physical infrastructure. In recent years, this potential appears to be paying off. The Cardoso reform agenda did enable the regional government to actively support participation in Mercosur and to successfully promote a process of industrial renewal. However, the present international economic-financial conjuncture, in addition to the opposition against the restructuring process within Rio Grande do Sul's political arena, has been generating uncertainties and may yet complicate this region's insertion, by way of Mercosur, into the global economy.

This chapter focuses on the complexities of adjustment of the Brazilian (industrial) economy in the face of globalization and the pressures toward regionalization. The industrial dynamics of Rio Grande do Sul will be examined as an example of sub-regional responses to world economic processes.

Brazilian ISI, Crisis, and Adjustment

"Deepening" the ISI strategy rather than entering into an export-led industrialization strategy made sense economically as well as politically in the mid-1950s. In taking this course, Brazil joined other Latin American countries like Argentina, Colombia, and Mexico that had already experienced decades of sustained import-substituting industrialization in the early 1950s and at the time had good reason to expect a continuation of this industrial growth.[4] Industrialists and governments were committed to ISI, multinationals were willing to invest in the protected markets, and the agro-export sector continued to provide part of the necessary foreign exchange. In Brazil, ISI's second phase started in the second half of the 1950s and lasted until the early 1980s. Throughout this period, the basic industrialization pattern remained the same, despite some changes in macro-economic orientation and in the relation between private domestic, state, and foreign capital. The dramatic regime change through the military coup of March 1964 left the course of industrialization untouched. While responding to the changes affecting the external sector during the oil-crisis of 1973–1974, the regime even promoted an expansion of the ISI process through state-owned firms in strategic sectors, such as steel, petrochemicals, energy, communications, and in some high-tech activities such as aviation and computers. The worsening external conditions did not impede the continuation of industrial growth.[5]

Toward the end of the 1970s, however, ISI was meeting its limits as a result of internal structural problems and externally induced difficulties. Severe balance of payments problems in 1979 emphasized the urgency of radical adjustments. However, political considerations again intervened with economic rationality. Economic adjustment, defended by the regime's technocrats, had to be reconciled with the requirements of the transition toward democracy. The government formally accepted the IMF dictamen in 1983, but in practice it backed away from too rigorous a compliance. Two years later, civilian rule was reinstalled. However, economic recovery along alternative, less debt-prone and more equitable lines was slow in coming. Government attention was almost exclusively focused on the need to control inflation and in fact postponed adjustment to a post-ISI era by another ten years.

Inflation became the principal symptom of Brazil's economic problems. The inability to deal with it contributed to the erosion of the credibility and the popularity of the government. Inflation eroded the fiscal capacity of the state, led to a decline of real investment, and undermined the living standards of wage earners. It was clear that the effectiveness of any government would be measured against its ability to bring inflation under control. It took scores of finance ministers and as many reform packages before finally in 1994 inflation was forced down to historically low levels. The broad political support for the Cardoso presidency that resulted could now be used to implement a more substantial adjustment of economic policies which, in fact, are changing the basic rationale of the Brazilian model of development.

A first round of structural economic reforms directed toward trade liberalization and privatization of state-owned firms had already been carried out by the Collor government, beginning in 1990. In addition, measures were taken to enhance industrial technological development and competitiveness, to end domestic monopolies, and to regulate industrial property.[6] This process continued with more vigor under the Cardoso administration in 1994. External trade boomed as a result of the successful currency stabilization which included an overvalued semi-fixed exchange rate with the U.S. dollar. Privatization was planned to affect, eventually, all major public companies. This included the icons of state-led ISI in branches such as steel, petrochemicals, transportation, aircraft manufacturing, energy, telecommunications, and mining. The presence of state-owned firms among the largest companies in the country, the result of half a century of ambitious ISI, would end.[7] As the 1988 constitution had established state ownership for these strategic companies, and—in the case of oil and electricity even had stipulated a virtual monopoly position—a constitutional reform program was called for. Foreign capital was allowed to take part in the privatization schemes, although generally through a minority participation. Through painstaking political negotiations, involving complex political trade offs and "traditional" forms of patronage, the Cardoso government managed to advance considerably on the road toward trade liberalization and privatization. Import duties were lowered and a large number of import restrictions were abolished. However, with some exceptions including Rio Grande do Sul, privatization has barely started on the state and municipal levels. On these lower levels of government, anti-privatization interests are strongly articulated and the required consensus on privatization issues is as yet at a very primary stage.

Despite the success of Cardoso's presidency in combating inflation and propelling reform (reflected in his easy re-election in October 1998), three main problems affecting the adjustment program have remained. First, the fixed and high exchange rate of the *real* to the dollar means monetary stability but it has been affecting the balance of payments negatively. Second, the huge fiscal deficit and lack of a balanced budget will prevent interest rates from dropping. Third, too little systematic attention has been paid to the need for industrial restructuring, given the pressures toward liberalization and participation in globalized competition.

The effects of these problems on the balance of trade have been substantial. Exports continued to expand and increased from US$31 billion in 1990 to US$46 billion in 1995. The composition of these exports remained stable and continued to depend on manufacturing products. However, the deregulation of imports, the gradual lowering of tariffs, and above all, the overvaluation of the currency and the enhanced domestic purchasing power—both the result of the Cardoso economic recovery plan—had a stimulating effect on the level of imports. Brazilian imports increased sharply from US$16 billion in 1987 to US$22 billion in 1990 and to almost US$54 billion in 1995. The large trade balance surpluses that had been built up between 1983 and 1994 have evaporated. Beginning in 1994, the current account has started to show sizable deficits that are being compensated only partly by the large foreign currency reserves and the sizeable inflow of foreign capital and lending (see Table 10.1).

The Cardoso government has responded by curbing internal demand through high domestic interest rates and by reintroducing strategic import controls. It has become clear that the policy of controlling inflation by maintaining a tight exchange rate of the domestic currency to the dollar was sacrosanct: the trauma of hyperinflation had a larger political impact on government decisions than the long-term strategy of global commercial integration. Another danger of founding domestic price stability on a fixed and overvalued exchange rate came to the fore in 1997 and 1998 when successive shock waves sent out by the Asian crisis hit the Brazilian stock markets. The government had to further raise interest rates and increase taxes to maintain the position of the *real* and had to use its foreign currency reserves to support the domestic currency.

The impact of the macroeconomic reforms on the structure and shape of the industrial sector has not been strong, despite the fact that many firms have started adjusting to the new pressures of global competition.[8] In this light, and also in view of the recent uncertainties brought to Brazil's economy by global exposure, Mercosur is an attractive intermediary mechanism through which the domestic industrial economy can be exposed gradually, and in a more controlled way, to the exigencies of liberalization and international competition. At the same time, Mercosur may, at least from the Brazilian perspective, allow the continuation of some of the instinctive strategies of protection and regulation inherited from the ISI period.

Brazil and Mercosur: Responding to Globalizing Pressures

Brazil's participation in supranational economic integration schemes has been part of the overall agenda of crisis management and adjustment followed since the mid-1980s. Supranational economic cooperation (which until 1990 mainly meant stepping up bilateral cooperation with Argentina) initially was conceived of as one of the solutions for the problems with ISI that did not require revamping the entire model. After 1990, however, supranational economic integration was embraced as a useful ingredient of liberalization in general. Mercosur was meant to create an environment where trade liberalization, deregulation, and transnationalization of economic activity could be pursued in a more or less controlled

Table 10.1 Trade Between Brazil and the Other Mercosur Countries (all values in millions of U.S. dollars f.o.b.)

Year	Exports to Mercosur Countries	Percentage of Total Exports	Imports from Mercosur Countries	Percentage of Total Imports	Trade Balance with Mercosur Countries	Percentage of Total Trade Surplus (or Deficit)	Manufacturing Exports to Mercosur Countries (as Percentage of Total Exports to Mercosur)
1980	1,811	9	1,044	5	767	(–27)	70
1985	990	4	684	5	307	2	80
1990	1,320	4	2,320	11	–999	–9	82
1991	2,309	7	2,268	11	41	less than 0.5%	84
1992	4,097	11	2,229	11	1,869	12	90
1993	5,386	14	3,378	13	2,009	15	90
1994	5,921	14	4,583	14	1,338	13	90
1995	6,154	13	6,844	14	–690	(20)	89
1996	7,305	15	8,267	16	–962	(17)	90
1997	9,044	17	9,624	16	–580	(7)	90

Source: Elaboration of data from Secretaria de Comércio Exterior, Ministério da Indústria, do Comércio e do Turismo, online posting, available from www.mict.gov.br/secex, September 1998.

way. In addition, the consolidation of Mercosur would provide the member countries with instruments that would allow them a greater scope for (defensive) regulation within the globalizing economy than would have been possible in the case of unilateral liberalization and global insertion. The example of the European Community had made it quite clear that the neoliberal world order would not be one level playing field, but would be carved up in large protected areas formed by the main trade blocs. Brazil and Argentina decided that the formation of Mercosur should be an indispensable corollary to the new agenda of economic liberalization.

The signing on March 26, 1991, of the Asunción Treaty establishing Mercosur inaugurated a new era in Brazil's foreign economic policy and its international relations in general. The entry into Mercosur meant a clear break with Brazil's international economic, diplomatic, and political orientation that had prevailed during much of the twentieth century and that in the first place had been guided by the logic of national development, especially industrialization, under the ideological banner of "pragmatic nationalism."[9] Engagement in supranational economic integration prior to Mercosur had remained limited to formal participation in largely inoperative continental commercial agreements such as the Latin American Free Trade Association (LAFTA—Montevideo, 1960) and its successor, the Latin American Integration Association (LAIA-Montevideo, 1980). During the second half of the 1980s, however, Brazil and Argentina engaged in a program of economic and political rapprochement. Both countries shared similar economic problems flowing from the exhaustion of ISI. Also, in both countries the civilian governments that had succeeded the military dictatorships were facing strong social demands and were reluctant to adopt the neoliberal adjustment recipe. In 1986, the countries agreed on an integration and the Economic Cooperation Program Argentina-Brasil (PICAB). The main objective of this program was to combine the domestic markets of both countries and to develop industrial sector programs jointly, especially in the area of capital goods, cars, and foodstuffs, without abandoning the basic logic of the ISI strategy. The results were modest, due to the continuing economic problems of both countries and the difficulties of negotiating the details of sectoral agreements that had to include the participation of the private sector on both sides.[10]

In November 1988, both countries, with Uruguay as observer, signed a bilateral treaty on integration, cooperation, and development. This agreement aimed at forming a common market within ten years. However, with the election to the presidency of Carlos Menem in Argentina and Fernando Collor in Brazil, the process of regional economic integration in the Southern Cone gained an unexpected momentum. From the Brazilian perspective, this momentum was based upon policies in favor of economic liberalization and international integration supported by the Collor government. The formation of trade blocks was seen as a useful mechanism to strengthen Brazil's position in the global economic order.[11] The Menem government in Argentina, espousing a kind of "neoliberal populism" after having freed itself of traditional peronist tenets, more or less adhered to the same notion. As a result, the formation of Mercosur was decided upon within a relatively short period of time by the countries concerned: Argentina, Brazil, Paraguay, and Uruguay. The basic design of Mercosur included, first, the establishment of a free trade zone by gradually lowering the import duties for trade among the four countries. This free trade zone would come into being on January 1, 1995. Second, a custom union was to be established by agreeing upon a common external tariff. This posed considerable difficulties, given the differences in economic structure and trade protection regimes between Brazil and Argentina and between these two large economies and the smaller and more open economies of Paraguay and Uruguay. Finally, in the long run, Mercosur was intended to evolve into a genuine common market through the coordination of macroeconomic and sectoral policies of the participating countries and the harmonization of the relevant legislation.[12] After the signing of the Treaty of Asunción, additional agreements and protocols were adopted to further specify and regulate the implementation of Mercosur.

Since 1991, the Mercosur project has encountered a number of obstacles. First, the move from the high-level political and diplomatic origins of Mercosur to the more technical (but no less political) resolution of specific problems, such as the external tariff, verification of commodity origins, lists of exceptions to the liberalization scheme and the external tariff, and arbitration of trade conflicts, has been at times a complicated affair.[13] Second, a workable institutional structure had to be created in a short period of time. Mercosur's institutions bear some resemblance to those of the early European Community, although the governance principle of Mercosur is firmly intergovernmental, with no real supranational dimension.[14] Third, the Mercosur project was defined without participation by relevant actors from civil society in the member countries.[15] Only afterwards have representatives from business sectors, trade unions, social movements, and regional and local governments become increasingly active with regard to Mercosur-related issues, such as social and environmental policies, labor mobility and labor rights, and border regions.

Yet Mercosur has become an immediate success in terms of fostering increasingly liberalized economic relationships—especially trade relationships—among the four member countries, although full implementation (that is, without exceptions) of the custom union and the common external tariff has been postponed to the year 2005. Mercosur also has strengthened the individual international trade and investment-related position of its member states, especially Brazil and Argentina. In 1994, Mercosur acquired international legal status. Trade agreements were signed with Chile and Bolivia, followed by a long-term trade liberalization agreement with the EU in 1995. Mercosur has become a countervailing power against the U.S.-dominated agenda for hemispheric trade liberalization through the establishment of a Free Trade Association of the Americas by 2005. The Mercosur countries, led by Brazil, pressured for a more gradual implementation of the Association based upon the cooperation between the existing trade blocks rather than through the adherence of individual countries. Finally, Mercosur expressed its adherence to the principles of democratic government within its boundaries, following the diplomatic pressure to avoid a military coup in Paraguay against the government of President Waismody in April 1996.

The economic significance of Mercosur for Brazil has been notable (see Table 10.1). The drop in exports to the three other member countries during the 1980s was followed by a steady increase in the value of trade from 1990 on. However, we have to insert a caveat here. Certainly, Brazil can be seen as the industrial "powerhouse" of the Mercosur area; Brazil's exports to Mercosur consist almost exclusively of manufactured products. In fact, observers have cautioned against Mercosur becoming something of a Brazilian backyard: "a captive market" to sustain Brazil's industrial exports in the face of growing global competition.[16] However, the trade with its Mercosur partners has become deficitary since 1994. The main reason has been the overvalued exchange rate of the *real* against the dollar. In combination with increasing trade liberalization this has greatly stimulated imports in Brazil. These imports consist in large part of agricultural products and foodstuffs. Brazil also has become an important market for Argentina's industrial output, especially cars, agricultural machinery, textiles, dairy products, and fuels.[17]

The growing trade deficit forced the Brazilian economic policy makers to reintroduce import restrictions and to raise tariffs, also with respect to products from the other Mercosur countries. These measures took precedence over considering a devaluation of the *real*. Maintenance of monetary stability was the top priority of the first term of the Cardoso presidency and Mercosur considerations were temporarily relegated to second place. Such reversals of Mercosur's trade liberalization through unilateral decisions by Brazil are always preceded by consultation with the partner states. Maintaining economic stability in Brazil is in the interests of all. However, it is apparent that in the wake of the Asian crisis, Brazil will have difficulties upholding the value of the *real* by just muddling through. Further trade liberalization and regional integration may be put on hold in the light of the needed fiscal and budgetary reforms that are generally seen as the conditions for Brazil's long-term economic stability.

Regional Dynamics and World Economic Influences: The Case of Rio Grande do Sul

Rio Grande do Sul has traditionally been one of the most important regions in the nation. Since the early twentieth century, the state has occupied fourth place—in terms of the size of its economy as well as in terms of its political influence—after the triad of São Paulo, Rio de Janeiro, and Minas Gerais. At times, especially during the República Velha (1889–1930) and the Vargas era, the *gaúchos* (as the inhabitants of the state are called) have played a decisive role on the national political scene. The gaúcho economic strength traditionally has rested on the production for the domestic market and for export of agricultural commodities, such as rice, wheat, and soybeans. It has given the state the reputation of national *celeiro* (breadbasket) and has made it into one of the most prosperous of Brazilian regions.

Next to agriculture, industry has been taking part in the process of regional development. Industry originated in the trading centers or in the towns situated in the so-called *zona colonial:* the region of German, Italian, and Polish immigration and settlement. During the final decades of the nineteenth century and the beginning decades of this century, a process of "regional" import substituting industrialization had gained momentum, based on food processing and the production of other consumer non-durables but also on metalworking and machinery production. The industrial sector was closely linked to the expanding agricultural and commercial activities in the state. The leading industrialists were mostly of German or Italian origin.

From the 1930s onward, and especially during the 1950s and 1970s, this regional industrial sector went through cycles of expansion and recession. In the course of these years, Rio Grande do Sul's industry was progressively integrated into the national economy, although not always on equitable terms, which led to occasional outbursts of strong regionalist sentiment in Rio Grande do Sul against excessive intervention by the central government in the affairs of the state.[18]

Toward the end of the 1960s, industry assumed the leading role in a process of regional economic growth that would thoroughly change the gaúcho economy (see Table 10.2). While during the 1950s and 1960s Rio Grande do Sul had preserved its traditional status as an agricultural state, by the mid-1970s industry had replaced agriculture as the principal sector of production. Between 1970 and 1980 the real value of industrial output almost tripled. Employment in the industrial sector more than doubled in the same period (from 217,000 to 451,000), while the total number of industrial establishments increased only slightly (from 17,711 to 18,937), indicating the concentration of industrial production throughout the decade.[19] Advanced and dynamic branches of industry, producing on a greater scale and with relatively higher levels of capital intensity, became more pronounced within Rio Grande do Sul's industrial structure. In general, those branches of industry producing durable consumer goods, intermediary goods, and capital goods increased their share in regional industrial output.

The opportunities for industrial development in Rio Grande do Sul were heavily conditioned by the general dynamics of the regional and national economy and the interventions of the Brazilian state. On a regional level, primary sector activities had increased in importance. New forms of capitalist agriculture had been expanding, based on the cultivation of soybeans for the external market. The cultivation of staple crops like rice and wheat for the national market was equally increasing during those years. The dynamics of large-scale agriculture had important spin-offs toward the regional industrial sector. The production of agricultural products (mainly soybean derivates) and basic chemical inputs for agriculture increased rapidly. So did the manufacturing of agricultural machinery (including combines, harvesters, and tractors), turning Rio Grande do Sul into the principal producer of these capital goods in the country. Also part of this development was the production for export of other manufactured products: petrochemical products, leather goods, agricultural machines and equipment, handguns and ammunition, cellulose, cutlery, and other products. Most notable has been the case of the footwear industry. Shoe producing firms in the region made their first timid efforts at exporting in the late 1960s. During the 1970s, shoe exports from Rio Grande do Sul increased rapidly, reaching a value of US $ 175 million in 1975, and US $ 565.7 million in 1983. Sales on the national market remained still more important during this period.

The development of the regional chemical industry included the construction of a large petrochemical complex in Triunfo, near Pôrto Alegre. Agreed upon in the 1970s and completed by the mid-1980s, this so-called third Pólo Petroquímico (the other two complexes being in the São Paulo area and in the town of Camaçari near Salvador, Bahia) represented the gauchos' only success in attracting large-scale federal and foreign investments during the third stage of ISI. To some extent, it served to cushion the impact of the recession of the early 1980s and started to contribute significantly to the state's exports from the mid-1980s onward.

A final noteworthy industrial branch in Rio Grande do Sul was the electronics industry, which produces computers and computer-related

Table 10.2 Economic and Industrial Performance in Rio Grande do Sul, 1948–1997 (average annual growth rates)

Period	Total Production	Industrial Production	Characteristics
1948–1951	5.3	10.5	Accelerated regional import substitution
1952–1955	7.0	6.0	Diminishing productivity in agriculture
1956–1959	3.3	7.8	Recession in agriculture
1960–1963	5.3	5.2	Agricultural stagnation
1964–1967	2.7	1.0	General stagnation
1968–1971	10.6	13.3	Revitalization of regional economy
1972–1975	16.1	19.9	Boom in industry and capitalist agriculture
1976–1980	5.1	10.1	Continued industrial expansion; adverse cycles in agriculture
1981–1983	-3.4	-5.7	Economic crisis
1984–1989	3.6	0.0*	Recovery of primary and manufacturing exports; stagnation in other industries
1990–1997	2.3	2.4**	Alternation of growth and stagnation in both agriculture and industry

*1985–1990
**1990–1996

Source: Elaboration of data from Fundação de Economica e Estadística (FEE), *25 Anos de Economica Gaúcha,* vol. I, II, III, IV (Porto Alegre: FEE, 1976–1982); *A Produção Gaúcha na Economia Nacional* (Porto Alegre: FEE, 1983); FEE, "As Contas Regionais e o Desempentro da Economia Gaúcha," *Indicadores Econômicos* 25, no. 1 (1997): p. 14.

equipment. The development of this branch of industry in Brazil was a new phenomenon, resulting from federal policies dictated by the military governments with the objective of securing technological and industrial autonomy for Brazil. To this end, foreign-owned companies producing personal and mini-computers and additional equipment were excluded from the Brazilian market.[20] Rio Grande do Sul participated to a significant extent in the development of this new high-tech branch of industry.

Despite the spectacular success of exports and the establishment of new industries such as petrochemicals and informatics, the regional industrial sector as a whole did not manage to escape from the impact of the recession that hit Brazil during the first half of the 1980s. The structure of the regional economy appeared to be vulnerable, in large part because of the predominance of large-scale export agriculture, the weak regional financial sector, the declining share for Rio Grande do Sul in the nation's industry, and the fragile financial base of the regional state.

Thus, during the economic and political conjuncture marking the final years of authoritarian rule in Brazil, the euphoria over the rapid development of the 1970s was changing into a more critical reassessment of Rio Grande do Sul's economic position. The end of military rule and the increased importance of the electoral arena appeared to offer greater leverage to regional political forces. In effect, the heavily debated 1988 post-authoritarian constitution assigned greater financial and political resources to the state and municipal governments. Rio Grande do Sul, however, had not been able to profit fully from this partial realignment of power.

In fact, Rio Grande do Sul's economy continued to show the impact of the crisis and the general economic instability prevailing in Brazil until the early 1990s. The composition of the regional industrial sector basically had not changed from the one that had developed during the 1970s. Industries linked to the agricultural sector predominated, next to the footwear industry, bulk chemicals, and plastic manufacturers clustered around the now fully operational Pólo Petroquímico, in addition to car part manufacturing and tobacco processing. In essence, regional economic development by and large followed the vicissitudes of the national conjuncture: industries benefitted from the short-lived impact of the successive stabilization plans and were adversely affected by the posterior return of hyperinflation. Rio Grande do Sul's agricultural sector performed well during the second half of the 1980s, to enter a period of alternating good and bad years in the 1990s.

Economic liberalization began to affect Rio Grande do Sul's manufacturing sector negatively after 1990.[21] The state's non-durable consumer goods industries were facing increasing competition from abroad, notably from Argentina and Uruguay. The footwear industry was receiving competition from Chinese, Spanish, and Italian producers. Producing against imports became even more difficult as a result of the appreciation of the *real,* which was part of the government's anti-inflation strategy. A number of Rio Grande do Sul shoe producers had to lay off workers or close down altogether. Subcontracting and flexibilizing the workforce became increasingly important. A number of prominent gaúcho shoe manufacturers set up production facilities in Brazil's northeastern region, especially in the state of Ceará, where lower labor costs were accompanied by generous tax incentives from the state government. The necessary restructuring and modernization of this industry was undertaken after 1997 with help of federal funding, following pressure from the regional and national footwear industry organizations.[22] The manufacturing of agricultural machinery and implements, which had expanded considerably and had made Rio Grande do Sul the principal producer of this equipment in Brazil, was hit by the consequences of the anti-inflation package in 1994. For the agricultural sector, this package meant lower prices, limited credit, and higher interest rates. Many farmers and agro-industrialists postponed investments. The situation was aggravated by bad harvests in 1994 and 1996.[23]

Yet as a whole, Rio Grande do Sul's economic and industrial performance was not much different from that of other major industrial states, such as São Paulo and Minas Gerais. In fact, regional exports, especially those of manufactured goods, increased during the 1990s. Amidst such confusing and contradictory developments, the advent of Mercosur was widely welcomed as offering new possibilities to Rio Grande do Sul's industrial economy. In fact, the state's politicians and business representatives had for some time been pointing at the strategic location of Rio Grande do Sul, halfway between Rio de Janeiro–São Paulo and Buenos Aires and at the very center of the main urban-industrial axis of South America. In the second half of the 1980s, the state government had made modest attempts to strengthen commercial relationships with the neighboring countries of the River Plate basin through trade liberalization within the framework of existing Argentina-Brazil bilateral treaties.[24] Less than a decade later, Mercosur built on these relationships and added an important dimension to Rio Grande do Sul's integration into the global economy.

Rio Grande do Sul and Mercosur: Industrial Revitalization through Globalization?

The integration into Mercosur led to substantial changes in Rio Grande do Sul's political economy of industrialization. These changes resulted from an ambitious program of regional reform defined by the administration of governor Antônio Britto (1994–1998). These reforms led to an avalanche of new industrial and other investment projects, mainly organized by foreign capital. After they are implemented, these projects will significantly change the profile of Rio Grande do Sul's industry, not only in terms of its sectoral composition but also in terms of its regional private and public control. The favorable prospects offered by Mercosur have undoubtedly been decisive in bringing about reform and the subsequent wave of new investments.

For decades, Rio Grande do Sul's government had been unable to cover its own operation costs. The Britto government set out to solve this problem—to improve the efficiency and the financial situation of the regional public sector—in order to make funds available for public investment. Deficiencies in basic infrastructure (roads, ports, waterways, telecommunications, and electricity) in addition to the structural economic weakness of certain subregions (particularly in southern part of the state) and economic sectors (the consumer goods industry and small-scale family farms) were defined as the principal obstacles to regional economic development. The regional state, moreover, was burdened with the responsibility for employment in a large number of public companies that were unprofitable. The new regional development strategy emphasized administrative and fiscal reform, privatization, and contracting new loans and investment, especially from abroad. With the exception of the fiscal reform, the strategy appears to have succeeded.[25] A large number of state enterprises were privatized. Large loans from national and international agencies (the World Bank, IDB, Exim Bank, and private banks) have been contracted to finance the administrative reform program, to upgrade and expand the physical infrastructure, to implement environmental programs, and support the weak sectors in the rural areas. The privatization program has included not only a large number of smaller public companies, but also the important sea port of the town of Rio Grande, some 30 percent of the regional road system, and a sizable portion of the Companhia Riograndense de Telecomunicações (CRT). The latter company had been a symbol of regional economic independence since the nationalization of the local ITT network in 1961. Now 35 percent of its shares are owned by a consortium including Spanish and Chilean telecom corporations and a regional media group. The state-owned electricity company, with an estimated value of US$3 billion, was to be split up and sold in parts as well.

A large number of infrastructural projects were defined in support of the integration of Rio Grande do Sul into the Mercosur area, including the associated countries Bolivia and Chile. A large bridge over the Uruguay River will be completed in 1999 as part of a new transcontinental route linking Porto Alegre and Rio Grande to northern Argentina and Chile's northern Pacific ports. A new north-south highway will link

São Paulo with Buenos Aires, running through Paraná, Santa Catarina, Rio Grande do Sul, and Uruguay and crossing the River Plate estuary. Pipelines for natural gas will connect the gas-producing areas in Argentina and Bolivia with industries, thermal power plants, and private homes in Rio Grande do Sul. The economic integration engineered through Mercosur will solve Rio Grande do Sul's chronic energy shortage, linking the Rio Grande do Sul's electric energy system with the Uruguayan and Argentinan grids.

The most spectacular signs of a renewed economic dynamism are the industrial investment projects that have been initiated during the last few years. The total investment required amounts up to US$3.6 billion. The projects include expanding the capacity of Petrobrás oil refinery in Canoas, near Porto Alegre, to provide the inputs for the Central de Matérias Primas (the central basic input manufacturing facility) of Copesul at the Triunfo petrochemical complex. The capacity of the Copesul plant itself will be doubled. New investments are planned in plastics and PVC industries that form the so-called "third generation" firms of this complex. Some of the major agricultural machinery firms in the state will receive major foreign investment.

Most noteworthy among the new industrial investments are the car assembly plants being built by General Motors in Gravataí (near Porto Alegre) and by Ford in Guaíba (opposite Porto Alegre across the Guaíba estuary). Both car assembly plants will produce small-sized passenger cars for the national market but also for export, especially to the Mercosur area. General Motor's facility is part of a larger chain that includes factories in São Paulo (plating), Santa Catarina (engines), and Rosario, Argentina. The assembly plant was established at Gravataí because of its central location, the regional infrastructure, and the quality of its workforce. In addition, the state government intervened and offered important tax, financing, and facilities incentives.[26]

Rather than being perceived as a takeover of Rio Grande do Sul's most dynamic industrial activities by foreign interests—as would have been a probable viewpoint thirty years ago—these investments have been welcomed as proof of Rio Grande do Sul's potential as a high-quality growth region in the core of Mercosur, at least by the governing party. But the opposition, especially the Worker's Party (PT), maintained its resistance to the privatization and investment agenda and, through its control over the state after the October 1998 election, may attempt to intervene.

It still too soon to assess the wider impact of these investment projects on regional development apart from the sense of euphoria they generated among the economic and political elites within the state. For example, it has remained unclear whether the existing, well-developed car parts industry in the state will be able to produce inputs for the big car assembly plants or whether these multinationals will bring along their own "closed shop" trade with dependent suppliers.[27]

Still, the effects of Mercosur on Rio Grande do Sul's economy and industry are already positive. Exports from Rio Grande do Sul to the Mercosur countries have been growing rapidly since 1990 (see Table 10.3). More importantly, while the overall exports from the state have continued to be dominated by products from agriculture, agro-industry, and the footwear industry, exports to the Mercosur countries include mainly agricultural machinery, transportation equipment, and chemicals—precisely the areas in which new investments are being planned. In addition, an increasing number of gaúcho companies have been seeking to establish joint ventures with companies from Argentina and the other Mercosur states. The federation of Rio Grande do Sul industrialists has been developing a systematic support strategy for the Mercosur-related activities of its constituency and has become one of the more active entities within civil society supporting the process of regional integration.

Despite these export oriented activities, Rio Grande do Sul has been running an unusual trade deficit with the other Mercosur countries as a result of increasing imports of agricultural products and foodstuffs. These imports threaten the economic position of the rural areas of Rio Grande do Sul, especially in the southern part of the region. In these areas, the economy is based on relatively simple agriculture and livestock and on traditional food-processing industries. These have become the subject of a special regional development program set up by the state government.[28] In addition, a broad coalition of regional power holders proposed that the major regional bank—the Banco Meridional—not be privatized, but become instead an official investment bank for those sectors that should be strengthened in order to become more competitive within the context of Mercosur: textiles, wheat growing, dairy products, wine, canned food and vegetables, and leather. Their argument was that the Argentine and Uruguayan producers of these commodities are more productive and also receive considerable government support.[29] This proposition did not succeed; after much debate, the Banco Meridional was privatized in December 1997.

Yet any economic success of the industrial revitalization program will be only partial if it will lead to the economic and social exclusion of significant parts of Rio Grande's population. Although the average per capita income in Rio Grande do Sul has always been above the national average, and although the state takes pride in showing the highest Human Development Index of all Brazilian states, economic development still appears to be uneven. Next to the rural regions of the interior, urban labor may be another victim of the restructuring of the regional

Table 10.3 Exports from Rio Grande do Sur (RS) to Mercosur Member Countries in Selected Years

Year	Exports from RS (US$ million f.o.b)	Manufacturing Products Exported from RS (US$ million f.o.b)	Exports from RS to Mercosur (US$ million f.o.b.)	Exports from RS to Mercosur Countries as Percentage of Total Exports from RS	Exports from RS as Percentage of Total Exports from Brazil	Exports from RS to Mercosur as Percentage of Total Brazilian Exports to Mercosur	Imports to RS from Mercosur (US$ million c.i.f.)
1980	2,090	742			10		
1985	2,668	1,379			10		
1990	3,442	1,740	138	4	11	10	178
1994	5,027	2,873	704	14	12	12	919
1995	5,182	2,897	710	14	11	12	1,242
1997*	5,664	3,148	896	16	12	12	1,583

*January–October 1997

Source: Elaboration of data from Fundação de Economica e Estadistica, "As Contas Regionais e o Desempenho da Economia Gaúcha," Indicadores Econômicos 24, no. 1 (1996): p. 120; Fundação de Economia e Estadistica, "As Contas Regionais e o Desempenho da Economia Gaúcha," Indicadores Econômicos 25, no. 1 (1997): p. 130; Súmula Econômica 3, no. 6, p. 25; Indicadores Macroeconômico, on-line posting, available from www.riogrande.com.br/indicadores, September 16, 1998.

industrial sector under globalizing influences. Over the last few years, many jobs have disappeared from the formal labor market, especially in industry and the public sector. Recent surveys of the Porto Alegre Metropolitan Area show rising open unemployment, an increase in flexible labor arrangements, and an expansion of the informal sector.[30]

These phenomena are muffling the general euphoria surrounding Mercosur. The victory of the opposition candidate in the October 1998 gubernatorial elections is creating uncertainties about how the state government will deal with the economic and social changes initiated by the previous government. The privatization of the remaining regional state-owned companies and the incentives offered to new industries, particularly to the big car-assembly plants, are being debated.[31] These uncertainties are aggravated by the current turmoil suffered by the Brazilian economy under the impact of the "Asian crisis," especially since the "strategic political convergence" between the federal governmental coalition and the Rio Grande do Sul state government has (at least temporary) come to an end.

Conclusion

Brazil has been the last among the Latin American countries to give in to the pressures of adjustment and globalization that presented themselves forcefully after 1980. A first explanation for this can be found in the long-term characteristics of Brazil's ISI strategy. The country's large and highly diversified industrial economy was built on the basis of this strategy and appeared to weather successfully a first period of economic turmoil during the 1970s. However, the debt crisis of the 1980s made clear that the industrialization strategy that had been followed since the 1930s was no longer sustainable. It took several years, though, before the principal actors involved—the state and the private sector—were convinced that a strategy change was called for. A second explanation lies with the fact that short-term stabilization, that is, the fight against hyperinflation, received priority attention during the 1980s and early 1990s. Inflation became the key symbol for Brazil's economic problems, and the role of the state was evaluated on the basis of its capacity to deal with it. The third explanation is entirely political. The delicate agenda of democratic transition between 1985 and 1994, resulting in weakly performing governments of less than full legitimacy, precluded anything other than "muddling through." Only after a successful anti-inflation package was launched in 1994 was a broader political consensus built up through the alliance supporting Fernando Henrique Cardoso, allowing the government to initiate the necessary economic reforms and meet the challenges of globalization.

The formation of Mercosur served two major objectives. Initially, broadening the economic cooperation between Brazil and Argentina eased some of the problems connected with the ISI model in both countries. When the Mercosur integration process was speeded up after 1991, the regionalization strategy became at the same time the principal way toward the global insertion of the Brazilian industrial economy. Mercosur was creating progressive trade liberalization among the member states (Argentina, Brazil, Paraguay, and Uruguay) and associated countries (Bolivia and Chile) and also permitted the members to act as one in negotiations concerning the modus operandi of the global economic order. Brazil, however, has been reluctant to abandon "pragmatic nationalism" even when confronted with the Mercosur agenda. The management of domestic economic crises (including the recent effects of the Asia crisis) is taking precedence over strict adherence to the trade rules set for Mercosur. Within this regional dynamic, the southernmost Brazilian state of Rio Grande do Sul takes a special position. The state developed into an important industrial center as part of the Brazilian ISI process. In addition, a strong impetus to industrialization was encouraged by specific conditions at the regional level, such as a strong agricultural sector, stimulating the diversification of the agro-industrial complex; the salience of exports, especially of footwear; and the production of inputs for the durables industries of Brazil's industrial core. At the same time, however, this particular profile created a vulnerability to changes in the economic cycle, harvest problems, and other external constraints. The role of regional private capital in the process has been important. State support, either federal or regional, for advanced regional ISI was limited during the 1970s and the 1980s. The only important exception was the installation of the third national petrochemical complex, based on the seasoned ISI formula of the "triple alliance." The 1980s and early 1990s were years of crisis and regional economic instability.

In Rio Grande do Sul, the process of economic integration heralded by the Mercosur initiative was welcomed as a new opportunity. The gaúchos felt that their state was uniquely positioned to take advantage of the increase in economic exchange with the neighboring southern cone countries. In the 1980s, the state government had already made a short-lived attempt to define its own international strategy vis-à-vis these countries. After 1994, the regional government used the Mercosur challenge to realize—with federal support—an ambitious agenda of regional economic and administrative reforms. The privatization of important regional state-owned firms, the opening up of the regional economy, and the efforts to attract new (foreign) industrial investment were all part of a state strategy to participate successfully in supranational economic integration. This strategy has succeeded. The privatization program has progressed considerably. New policies were defined to attract industrial investments. The volume of trade with the Mercosur countries has increased considerably during the 1990s. This has offered new outlets to Rio Grande do Sul's manufacturing sector, especially agricultural machinery and petrochemicals. However, this trade integration does also bring certain risks to the regional economy given the important role of the agro-industrial complex, which is similar to—but less competitive than—neighboring regions in the other member states. The need for the reform of the small-scale rural sector and the small- and medium-sized agro-industries has some urgency.

The main obstacle to Rio Grande do Sul's continued active participation in the Mercosur integration process may, in the short term, prove to be political. The program of "economic modernization" and integration into the global economy has been put into question through the recent change in state government that brought the opposition PT to power. The argument of the admittedly considerable social costs of the adjustment efforts may (temporarily?) prevail over the inescapable exigencies of adjustment and participation in the process of regionalization.

Notes

1. Peter Evans, *Dependent Development: The Alliance of Multinational, State and Local Capital in Brazil* (Princeton, N.J.; Princeton University Press, 1979).
2. Jeffry A. Frieden, "The Brazilian Borrowing Experience: From Miracle to Debacle and Back," *Latin American Research Review* 22, no. 1 (1987): 95–131.
3. Ben Ross Schneider, *Politics Within the State. Elite Bureaucrats and Industrial Policy in Authoritarian Brazil* (Pittsburgh: University of Pittsburgh Press, 1991).
4. Robert R. Kaufmann, "How Societies Change Developmental Models or Keep Them: Reflections on the Latin American Experience in the 1930s and the Postwar World," in *Manufacturing Miracles. Paths of Industrialization in Latin America and East Asia*, ed. Gary Gereffi and Donald L. Wyman (Princeton: Princeton University Press, 1990), pp. 110–138.
5. Kees Koonings, *Industrialization, Industrialists, and Regional Development in Brazil* (Amsterdam: Thela Publicers, 1994).
6. Jörg Meyer-Stamer, "New Patterns of Governance for Industrial Change: Perspectives for Brazil," *Journal of Development Studies* 33, no. 3 (1997): 364–391; Maria Rocha, Geisa, "Redefining the Role of the Bourgeoisie in Dependent Capitalist Development. Privatization and Liberalization in Brazil," *Latin American Perspectives* 21, no. 1 (1994): 72–98; Lourdes Sola, "Heterodox Shock in Brazil: Técnicos, Politicians and Democracy," *Journal of Latin American Studies* 23, no. 2 (1991): 163–195.
7. Armando Castelar Pinheiro and Fabio Giambiagi, "Brazilian Privatization in the 1990s," *World Development* 22, no. 5 (1994): 739–740.

8. Jose Tavares de Araujo, Jr., "Concorrencia, Competitividade e Politica Eco-
    nomica," in *O Brasil e a Economia Global*, ed. Renato Baumann (Rio de
    Janeiro: Campus, 1996), pp. 75–86; Luciano G. Coutinho, "A Fragilidade do
    Brasil em Face da Globalização," in Baumann, *O Brasil e a Economia Global*,
    pp. 219–238; João Carlos Ferraz, David Kupfer and Lia Haguenauer, "The
    Competitive Challenge for Brazilian Industry," *CEPAL Review*, no. 58
    (1996): 145–174; Jörg Meyer-Stamer, "New Patterns of Governance for
    Industrial Change: Perspectives for Brazil," *Journal of Development Studies*
    33, no. 3 (1997): 364–391.
9. Amado Luiz Cervo and Clodoaldo Bueno, *História da Política Exterior do
    Brasil* (São Paulo: Ática, 1992); Gelson Fonseca, Jr. and Valdemar
    Carneiro Leão, ed., *Temas de Política Externa Brasileira* (Brasília:
    IPRI/Ática, 1989).
10. Monica Hirst and Maria Regina Soares de Lima, "Crisis y Toma de
    Decisión en la Política Exterior Brasileña: El Programa de Integración
    Argentina-Brasil y las Negociaciones Sobre la Informatica con Estados
    Unidos," *Sintesis* 12 (1990): 209–244.
11. Ademar Seabra de Cruz, Jr., Antonio Ricardo F. Cavalcante, and Luiz
    Pedone, "Brazil's Foreign Policy Under Collor," *Journal of Interamerican
    Studies and World Affairs* 35, no. 1 (1992): 119–144.
12. Jorge Grandi, "Le Mercosur en Période de Transition: Evaluation et Per-
    spectives," *Problèmes d'Amerique Latine*, no. 17 (1995): 73–87; Ricardo Seit-
    enfus, *Para Uma Nova Política Externa Brasileira* (Porto Alegre: Livraria do
    Advogado, 1994), pp. 102–103; Vera Thorstensen, Yoshiaki Nakano, Camila
    de Faria Lima, and Claudio Seiji Sato, *O Brasil Frente a Um Mundo Dividido
    em Blocos* (São Paulo: Nobel/Instituto Sul-Norte de Política Econômica e
    Relações Internacionais, 1994).
13. Grandi, "Le Mercosur en Période de Transition," pp. 73–87.
14. Luis Olavo Baptista, "As Instituições do MERCOSUL: Comparações e
    Prospectiva." in *O Mercosur em Movimento*, ed. Deisy de Freitas Lima Ven-
    tura (Porto Alegre: Livraria do Advogado, 1995), pp. 54–74.
15. Seitenfus, *Para Uma Nova Política Externa Brasileira*, p. 105.
16. Grandi, "Le Mercosur en Période de Transition," pp. 73–87.
17. Ricardo Seitenfus, "Washington Manoeuvre Contre le Mercosur," *Le Monde
    Diplomatique* 45, no. 527 (1998): 8.
18. Koonings, *Industrialization, Industrialists and Regional Development in Brazil*,
    passim.
19. Instituto Brasileiro de Geografia e Estatística, *Censo Industrial 1970*; *Censo
    Industrial 1975*; and *Censo Industrial 1980* (Rio de Janeiro: IEBG, 1975, 1980,
    and 1984).
20. Paulo Bastos Tigre, *Computadores Brasileiros. Indústria, Tecnologia e
    Dependência* (Rio de Janeiro: Campus, 1984); Peter Evans, "State, Capital,
    and the Transformation of Dependence: The Brazilian Computer Case,"
    World Development 14, no. 7 (1986): 791–808.
21. Maria Lucrécia Calandro, "Indústria: Desempenho no Ano de 1995," *Indi-
    cadores Econômicos* 24, no. 1 (1996): 37–52.

22. Maria Cristina Passos and Silvia Horst Campos, "O Desempenho da Indústria em 1996," *Indicadores Econômicos* 25, no. 1 (1997): 31–50.
23. Ibid., pp. 42–43.
24. Seitenfus, *Para Uma Nova Política Externa, Brasileira*, p. 87.
25. Alfredo Meneghetti Neto, "O Desempenho das Finanças Públicas Estaduais em 1995," *Indicadores Econômicos* 24, no. 1 (1996): 71–85; Alfredo Meneghetti Neto, "Finanças Públicas Estaduais: O Desempenho em 1996," *Indicadores Econômicos* 25, no. 1 (1997): 68–83.
26. *Gazeto Macantil Latino-American*, no. 9, December 1996, p. 20.
27. *Súmula Econômica* 2, no. 3 (1996): 23–28.
28. *Cone Sul/Cono Sur* 7, no. 49 (1996): 7.
29. *Revista do Mercosul*, no. 32 (1995): 60–62.
30. André Luis Leite Chaves, "Mercado de Trabalho na RMPA: Desempenho Ruim em 1996," *Indicadores Econômicos* 25, no. 1 (1997): 84–99.
31. *Zero Hora Digital*, on-line posting, available from *www.zh.com.br*, October 30, 1998.

11

Globalization and the Caribbean: Reconsidering the Options

Terry McCoy

It's the only thing we can sell to live on.
    —Banana farmer on the island of Dominica.

It's like a giant squashing an ant.
    —General manager of the Dominica Banana Marketing Association, commenting on the U.S. request that the World Trade Organization declare the EU's special marketing arrangements for bananas from the small islands of the Caribbean a violation of free trade.

Almost any crop you grow here could be outgrown by someone else.
    —Dominican Minister of Agriculture, regarding recommendation that farmers substitute other crops for bananas.[1]

Although the above interchange refers to the "Great Banana War" of 1997, it captures the more general challenge that globalization poses for the Caribbean. These small island territories, which have depended heavily on the export of one or two products for their economic and social well-being, appear to be incapable of competing in the emerging world economy, which is structured around free trade, large transnational corporations, and global finance. Their markets are too small and their costs of production are too high, either for traditional Caribbean exports like bananas and sugar or for nontraditional activities, from exotic fruits exports to tourism and financial services. And just as the Caribbean's economic viability is waning, the region has lost the strategic bargaining power that helped secure protected access to European and North American markets during the Cold War. The Caribbean has few, if any, options for coping with globalization, or so it seems.

This chapter analyzes the globalization challenge by, first, defining and characterizing the Caribbean as a region and globalization as a process. Then it discusses the shift from preferential trading arrangements to free trade regimes and reviews the history of regional integration in the Caribbean. The chapter concludes by examining several factors that further complicate globalization for the Caribbean and evaluating alternative approaches for reinserting it into the global economy. In this regard, it questions the view, widely held in the Caribbean, that regional integration is the key for successfully coping with globalization.

Background: The Caribbean as a Region

The focus of this chapter is on the Caribbean narrowly defined as the island territories of the Caribbean Sea plus Belize on the Caribbean coast of Central America and Guyana and Suriname on the northeast coast of South America (see Figure 11.1). This definition is to be distinguished from that of the Greater Caribbean or Caribbean Basin, composed of these territories plus the countries of Central America and sometimes including Colombia and Venezuela, both of which have territory bordering on the Caribbean Sea.[2] The justification for working with this more limited version is threefold: (1) Because of historical and cultural affinities as well as geographic proximity, this Caribbean is recognized as a distinct region of the Western hemisphere; (2) Caribbean leaders have consistently promoted regional identity for these small territories; and (3) globalization, by its very nature, poses different challenges for this region than for the larger Caribbean Basin.

As a region, the Caribbean is marked by three features relevant to globalization. The first is that the region is composed of small developing countries (see Table 11.1). In terms of surface, for example, Guyana and Suriname are as large as, say, Ecuador and Uruguay, but their populations and GDPs are equivalent to those of small cities. Cuba, the largest of the islands and historically the dominant Caribbean country, currently has a population of approximately 11 million people but registers a very modest GDP. The Dominican Republic, with a balance between territory, population, and economic output, is a small country by world standards while Haiti's extreme poverty undercuts its presence. The remaining countries of the region can only be characterized as mini-states. As a whole, the Caribbean has a population of slightly over 30 million, less than either Argentina or Colombia. The gross regional product of $78.3 billion is roughly one-tenth that of Mexico. The region's standard of living varies from Haiti's desperate poverty to the middle-income status of

Figure 11.1 Central America and the Caribbean

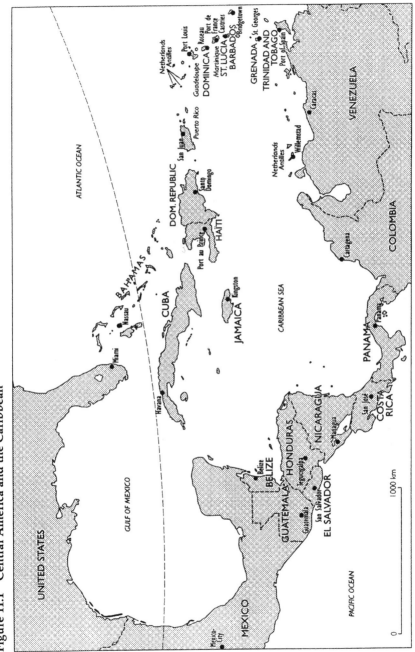

countries like the Bahamas and Trinidad and Tobago. On the basis of size and economic output, then, the Caribbean is on the periphery of the global scene. And, as Table 11.1 illustrates, the economies of the region are competitive—producing the same goods and services—rather than complementary. They are also highly trade dependent.[3]

The second feature defining the Caribbean is its strategic location in geopolitical terms. Astride major shipping lanes and at the confluence of the Americas, the region is an important crossroads for global commerce and international relations. Very early in the colonial period, it attracted the European powers and became the locus for competition among them in the New World. As a result, the pattern of "fragmented nationalism" and external domination became enduring features of the region by the mid-sixteenth century.[4] The strategic importance of the region grew during the nineteenth century as competition to build a transoceanic canal across the Central American isthmus intensified. With the Spanish American War of 1898 and the construction of the Panama Canal (1903–1913), the United States established itself as the regional hegemonic power, claiming the Caribbean as its core sphere of influence. The geopolitical significance of the region again increased with the introduction of the Cold War into the Western hemisphere when Fidel Castro guided Cuba into the Socialist bloc after 1959. With the end of the Cold War, the Caribbean has lost its geopolitical value, at least for the time being, but its location, next to the largest economy and most important market in the world, remains a potential economic asset.

The third distinguishing feature of the region is cultural diversity and political fragmentation. As a consequence of their struggles to establish a presence in the Americas through the Caribbean, Spain, England, France, the Netherlands, Denmark, and later the United States all established Caribbean colonies. This pattern of fragmented colonialism, overlaid with African slavery and then indentured labor, produced a region of complex racial, ethnic, linguistic, religious, and political cleavages. The most fundamental is between the Hispanic Caribbean—Cuba and the Dominican Republic—and the English, or Commonwealth, Caribbean, composed of the former English colonies that did not gain their independence until the 1960s. These "West Indian" countries, which constitute core membership of CARICOM (the Caribbean Community and Common Market), not only speak a different language than their Hispanic neighbors, but they are overwhelmingly Protestant societies with parliamentary political traditions. The Spanish-English cleavage leaves out the French Caribbean—Haiti, the second oldest republic in the Americas, as well as several overseas departments of France—the Dutch Caribbean— the independent country of Suriname, a CARICOM member, and several territories still linked to Holland—and the U.S. Caribbean—Puerto Rico and the U.S. Virgin Islands. Cultural and political differences have traditionally weakened the pull of a shared geography and the common status of small states with similar economic problems to render Caribbean-wide cooperation problematic. If the path to effective articulation with the global economy is through greater regional integration, these differences must be overcome.

Globalization and the Caribbean

Paul Hirst and Grahame Thompson argue that globalization is not new.[5] It is certainly not new to the Caribbean, where economies, societies, and political systems are the direct results of larger developments beyond local control. Ironically, the threat now is that the Caribbean will be left out of global developments.

Defining globalization as the integration of markets, trade, finance, information, and corporate ownership around the globe, Rubens Ricupero and Norman Gall date its historical origins to the fifteenth and sixteenth centuries with the expansion of mercantilist capitalism under the umbrella of European colonialism.[6] The Caribbean was an early and essential component of the emerging capitalist economy, incorporated through the exchange of sugar for slaves from Africa and consumer goods from the metropole. Subsequently the region was incorporated into the accelerated global economic integration that occurred from 1820 to 1914 (especially 1870–1914), propelled by the dramatic expansion of world trade. During this cycle, the economies of the Caribbean became important suppliers of tobacco and bananas, as well as sugar and, later, bauxite and petroleum, to the industrial markets of Europe and North America, from which they imported manufactured items. Following the interruption of the two World Wars and the Great Depression, economic globalization resumed in the 1950s, although trade as a share of world output did not recover to its 1913 level until the mid-1970s.[7]

Over the last decade, as the Cold War ended, world economic transformation has accelerated, propelled by three interrelated developments that, taken together, define and distinguish the current cycle of globalization. The first is the *rapid growth of trade*. Thanks to a combination of unilateral, bilateral, and multilateral reforms, global trade in goods and services is increasing faster than the world economy is growing. Intrafirm trade is increasingly even more rapidly. Two-thirds of all trade now takes place within or between transnational corporations. Second is the *expansion of international investment*. Foreign investment, especially direct investment by transnational corporations, is growing faster than trade. And third is the *surge in international financial transactions*, which have grown faster than either trade or investment. Technological advances in

Table 11.1 Nations of the Caribbean

Country	Total Area (sq. kms.)	Population 1995 estimate	GDP	GDP per capita in 1994 (US $)	Top Two Hard Currency Earners
Antigua/Barbuda	440	65,000	400m	6,000	Tourism/n.a.
Bahamas	13,940	256,000	4.4bn	15,000	Tourism/seafood
Barbados	430	256,000	2.4bn	9,200	Tourism/sugar
Belize	22,960	214,000	575m	2,750	Sugar/citrus con.
Cuba	110,860	10.9 mil.	14bn	1,260	Tourism/sugar
Dominica	750	82,000	200m	2,260	Bananas/tourism
Dominican Republic	48,730	7.5 mil.	24bn	3,070	Tourism/apparel
Grenada	340	94,000	258m	2,750	Tourism/spices
Guyana	214,970	723,000	1.4bn	1,950	Sugar/gold
Haiti	27,750	6.5 mil.	5.6bn	870	Remittances/n.a.
Jamaica	10,990	2.6 mil.	7.8bn	3,050	Tourism/bauxite
St. Kitts/Nevis	269	41,000	210m	5,300	Tourism/sugar
St. Lucia	620	156,000	610m	4,200	Tourism/bananas
St. Vincent/Gren	340	117,000	235	2,000	Tourism/bananas
Suriname	163,270	430,000	1.2bn	2,800	Bauxite/shirmp
Trinidad/Tobago	5,130	1.3 mil.	15bn	11,280	Petrol/chemicals

Source: Elaboration of data from *Caribbean Basin Commerical Profile* (1996), and *Economist Intelligence Unit Country Reports* (1997)

communication and transportation have facilitated these changes through electronic banking and high-volume trade in perishables. The most dramatic consequence of these developments is the emergence of a global economic system that is increasingly dispersing value-added production activities throughout the world according to the efficiency and cost criteria of transnational corporations and irrespective of national borders and policies.[8] The challenge for the Caribbean is to refashion itself as a recipient of these value-added activities or risk being left out of global economic expansion.

From Preferential Trade to Free Trade

Over the three decades since the Commonwealth countries gained their independence, the Caribbean's principal linkage with the international economic system has been through trade agreements granting preferential access to European and North American markets. The three major agreements—the Lomé Convention with the EU, the CBI with the United States, and the Caribbean-Canadian Trade Agreement—have also been sources of foreign assistance for the region. Now a variety of interests and forces are undermining these arrangements and confronting the Caribbean countries with hemispheric and global free trade regimes.

Preferential Arrangements

In 1975, the European Economic Community (now the European Union) negotiated the Lomé Convention in order to strengthen and formalize cooperation with developing countries that had colonial ties to Europe (the African, Caribbean, and Pacific—or ACP Group). The convention has been revised and renewed on three occasions, most recently in 1990, with Lomé IV remaining in force until 2000. The central component of the convention is trade. Through a combination of measures—nonreciprocity trade rules, guaranteed market access at a preferential price for commodities such as sugar and bananas, trade promotion, liberal rules of origin, a system for stabilizing export earnings, industrial cooperation and implementing institutions—Lomé gives sixteen Caribbean states (fourteen CARICOM members plus recently added Haiti and the Dominican Republic) favored access to EU markets.[9]

Because of Lomé, virtually all CARICOM trade with the EU over the past twenty-two years has been on concessionary terms. Lomé has also channeled European developmental assistance to the Caribbean, most recently in support of national structural adjustment programs and debt relief.[10] And at a general level, it also promotes ties between the Caribbean and the EU by sponsoring political, social, and cultural initiatives.

Although Lomé is criticized both because the EU is putting fewer resources into it and because it reinforces the Caribbean's dependence on traditional agricultural exports, there can be little doubt that it has been a significant determinant of Caribbean economic reality for nearly a quarter of a century, and its elimination, or serious restructuring, would be highly disruptive.[11]

The CBI, which took effect in 1984 with the enactment of the Caribbean Basin Recovery Act, is a U.S. trade and aid program for the greater Caribbean. The Reagan administration revived the Caribbean Basin as a geopolitical region of strategic value to the United States and conceived the CBI to stabilize it.[12] Washington viewed the Sandinista government in Nicaragua and guerrilla insurgents in neighboring El Salvador as extensions of the Soviet threat into Central America. Leftist governments in Jamaica, Guyana, and Grenada also reawakened U.S. concern about the spread of Cuban influence and communism in the island Caribbean. In addition to the military measures adopted to contain these threats—arming the Nicaraguan contras, supplying arms and advisors to the Salvadoran government, and sending U.S. troops to Grenada—Reagan and his advisors sought to stabilize the region by promoting economic development. In keeping with the administration's conservative free-market ideology, the CBI emphasized trade rather than aid, though foreign assistance, military and developmental, was an important part of the initial CBI package. Its centerpiece was a one-way free-trade arrangement granting duty-free access for Caribbean goods to the U.S. market.[13]

Originally authorized for twelve years, the U.S. Congress made the CBI permanent in 1990 just as the Cold War threat to U.S. security in the region was receding. No longer justifiable in terms of national defense, the foreign assistance element has all but disappeared. As a preferential trade arrangement, however, the CBI remains important to the Caribbean as the United States is its most leading trading partner, by far.[14] And even though major exports from the region are not covered, the consensus is that the CBI has helped offset the loss in revenue from traditional exports by granting nontraditional exports preferential access to the U.S. market.[15]

The Canadian government established the Caribbean-Canadian Development Program (CARIBCAN) in 1986 to promote trade and investment with the Commonwealth Caribbean countries. Unlike the CBI, its primary motivation was economic, not political, although the measure was adopted at a time when Canada was expanding its presence in the Americas.[16] Like CBI, CARIBCAN's centerpiece is duty-free access to the Canadian market for most but not all imports from the Commonwealth Caribbean. The Canadian government has also sponsored complementary measures to promote closer ties with the Caribbean and support its development. Although the impact of CARIBCAN is not comparable to that of either Lomé or CBI, since trade with Canada is much smaller, it is part of preferential trade regime that has structured the Caribbean's economic relations and development.[17]

The Free Trade Contagion

Over the past decade preferential trade has been giving way to free trade across the globe. With specific reference to the Caribbean, four forces are at work: national structural adjustment programs, the Uruguay Round of the GATT, regional integration, and the end of the Cold War. Together they place in serious jeopardy the special arrangements by which Caribbean economies have traded and received developmental assistance.

Trade liberalization is a core component of the structural adjustment programs adopted by less developed countries over the past decade. In Latin America and the Caribbean, economists and the international lending agencies promoted structural adjustment as essential for recovering from the debt crisis and the economic collapse of the 1980s, and the lending agencies conditioned their assistance on the adoption of prescribed programs. The "Washington consensus," as it came to be known, calls for comprehensive policy reform to restore macroeconomic stability (most importantly bringing inflation under control) and then to open the economy to market forces by freeing exchange rates, deregulating financial markets, liberalizing foreign investment regulations, privatizing state enterprises, and lowering trade barriers.[18] One of the central objectives of national structural adjustment programs is to increase the importance of trade to a country's economy, with special emphasis on developing nontraditional exports. Chile, which produced sustained economic growth by lowering trade barriers and promoting nontraditional exports, is held up as the model for the rest of Latin America to emulate. In the Caribbean, Trinidad and Tobago has been the leader in reforming its economy, reengineering its manufacturing plant and unilaterally opening its markets.[19]

Structural adjustment has not been carried out in concert with multilateral trade reform and regional integration. Despite difficulties and shortcomings, the Uruguay Round of the GATT produced major changes in the global trading regime. Its overall impact has been to deepen most-favored-nation ties and reciprocity as operating principles in international commerce and to reduce the GSP, which favors developing countries' access to developed markets.[20] The 1997 decision of the newly created WTO declaring the EU's preferential treatment of bananas imported under the Lomé Convention to be in violation of free trade has brought the reality of free trade home to the small banana exporting islands of the Eastern Caribbean while advancing the interests of their Caribbean Basin competitors in Central America.[21]

Hemispheric integration, though not entirely consistent with the global trade liberalization of the Uruguay Round, is the third ongoing process with implications for Caribbean trade and development. The Caribbean stands to suffer from the integration of markets in both Europe and the Americas. The EU is moving toward a single European market, and Lomé trading arrangements with the Caribbean are scheduled to expire. At this point, they may not be renewed, both because they violate the global free trade regime and, just as importantly, because the EU no longer has compelling political reasons to conduct concessionary trade with the Caribbean.[22]

Of greater potential impact is the process of regional integration taking place in the Western hemisphere. The countries of the Americas have embarked on the construction of an integrated regional market, initially triggered by the Enterprise for the Americas Initiative proposed by President Bush in 1990. The elements of this process are twofold: first, the commitment of hemispheric leaders at the December 1994 Miami Summit of the Americas to establish the Free Trade of the Area of the Americas (FTAA) by the year 2005 and second, the initiation and revival of subregional trade agreements (NAFTA, MERCOSUR, MCCA, etc.) that will, in some yet to be agreed upon fashion, link together to form the FTAA. As the smallest and most economically fragile region in the Americas, the Caribbean faces special challenges of integration.[23] Of immediate concern is NAFTA, launched in 1994. By giving Mexico duty-free access to the huge U.S. market and vice versa, NAFTA has thrown Mexican exports into direct competition with those from the smaller, higher-cost CBI countries. It also threatens to divert foreign investment and production from the Caribbean to Mexico: "From the apparel plants of Jamaica to the sugarcane fields of Trinidad, NAFTA has already resulted in the loss of jobs, markets and income for the vulnerable island nations of the region."[24]

The apparel industry is an important example of NAFTA's effects on the Caribbean. Responding to CBI and other U.S. trade incentives, the Jamaican apparel industry expanded rapidly, with exports growing from $US54 million in 1985 to $US530 million ten years later. However, since NAFTA, dozens of Jamaican apparel factories have shut down, and employment in the industry, in a country where about 16 percent of the labor force is unemployed, has dropped from 37,000 to 20,000.[25] The CARICOM countries have called for legislation, which the Clinton administration has sponsored, that would give the Caribbean NAFTA-parity. At the 1997 Barbados summit, President Clinton assured his Caribbean hosts that he would seek lower tariffs on Caribbean textiles and leather goods and continue pressing for NAFTA parity, but congressional approval of special exemptions for the Caribbean appears unlikely, for both economic and political reasons.[26]

With the end of the Cold War, the Caribbean has lost much of its strategic importance and with it the ability to leverage preferential trade arrangements and foreign assistance. As Jorge Domínguez argues, "Gone . . . is any appreciable strategic reason for the United States and other developed countries to assist the Caribbean."[27] Washington faces no significant military challenge in the region, and the EU is preoccupied with building a single European market and restructuring relations with Eastern Europe and Russia. Thus post–Cold War geopolitics combined with global economic reform and regional integration further marginalizes the Caribbean and erodes its preferential trading arrangements.

Regional Integration as a Response to Globalization

Regionalism has deep roots in the Caribbean. Historically, unification of the region's countries and peoples was seen as the only way to overcome their small size in dealing with the rest of the world. But the widely held regionalist credo has been easier to articulate (usually with great eloquence) than to achieve. Periodic and inevitably unfulfilled attempts at regional integration litter the post-independence history of the Commonwealth Caribbean. Yet despite its checkered past, regional integration has reappeared as the favored response to globalization.

The West Indies Federation, created by Great Britain in 1958 in anticipation of independence, was the first attempt at regional integration in the Caribbean. "The British pushed federation for the West Indies . . . thinking it a good solution for the small nonviable colonies they had created, in particular for their diseconomies of scale in government and administration."[28] But the logic of administrative efficiency and regional markets could not compete with "uncompromising insular interests," particularly those of Jamaica and Trinidad and Tobago, the federation's most important members. In 1962, the federation collapsed when these two islands "began the parade of Anglophone-Caribbean political independence."[29]

With the collapse of the federation, the Caribbean's political and intellectual leadership backed away from political unification in favor of integration patterned after the Western European model. The new approach had two dimensions. First, it sought to build Caribbean integration through functionalist cooperation on concrete issues that would eventually spill over into regional cooperation, resulting in the voluntary transfer of national sovereignty to regional authorities. Over the years, functionalism has had its successes: the multi-campus University of the West

Indies, the Caribbean Development Bank, the Caribbean Tourism Organization, and more recently, a regional airline.

Second, Commonwealth leaders committed themselves to building, in stepwise fashion, a regional economy. They have consistently reaffirmed support for this objective and just as consistently failed to meet their own self-imposed deadlines for achieving it. In 1968, they agreed to create the Caribbean Free Trade Association (CARIFTA). Although a free trade area is the lowest level of economic integration—calling only for the abolition of trade barriers among the members—and despite the objective and subjective factors that would seem to facilitate integration, CARIFTA failed. Caribbean leaders reacted to failure by calling for a deepening of the integration process through the creation in 1973 of the even more ambitious Caribbean Community and Common Market to replace CARIFTA. Today CARICOM exists as the highest level of Caribbean integration to date and its most visible manifestation. In 1981, leaders of the smaller, lesser developed English-speaking islands of the eastern Caribbean launched the Organization of Eastern Caribbean States under the CARICOM umbrella. The OECS entails political as well as economic commitments. For example, member states are committed to the harmonization of foreign policies and joint overseas representation.[30]

The Caribbean Community and Common Market

With the admission of Suriname in 1995 (the first non-English speaking member) and Haiti in 1997, CARICOM achieved its current membership of fifteen. There are also two associate members as well as nine observers. The Dominican Republic, currently an observer, has applied for full membership while a Cuba-CARICOM joint commission was created in 1993 to strengthen ties with the Caribbean's largest country. Loosely conceived, CARICOM thus encompasses all of the politically independent countries of the island Caribbean (and all of the countries in Table 11.1), although in actual practice it has been an instrument of the Commonwealth Caribbean. There is a permanent secretariat and final authority resides in the annual Heads of Government Conference.

CARICOM's central purposes include strengthening the Caribbean community of nations based on a shared identity and the progressive deepening of regional economic integration beyond the removal of internal barriers to trade. Never conceived as a classical common market in terms of a "fully integrated market for goods, totally free movement of capital and labor, and the unqualified right to establish and provide services," CARICOM instead stresses "coordination, cooperation and joint effort in production and development as on a common external tariff."[31] The organization has clearly had more success in building a sense of community than in deepening regional economic integration. The 1973 treaty included measures to harmonize both trade and developmental policies, but cooperation deteriorated almost immediately during the economic crises of the late 1970s and 1980s as the individual members again went their separate ways. Throughout the 1980s and into the early 1990s, the CARICOM Heads of Government worked on correcting the failure to meet agreed upon deadlines and sought to revive the integration process.

Implementation of the Common External Tariff (CET) proved to be especially elusive. In an effort to make the regional economy progressively more competitive in global and hemispheric markets, the Heads of Government decided in 1992 to lower the CET to the 5–20 percent range (with the rate varying by product) by 1998.[32] Progress in achieving this goal has been uneven—though better than it was before 1992. The same uneven record holds for the abolition of barriers to internal trade.[33] Beyond attempts to deepen CARICOM, the Heads of Government proposed widening the scope of regional integration.

Association of Caribbean States

At their 1989 meeting, the CARICOM Heads of Government issued the Grand Anse Declaration calling for the establishment of a single market for the Caribbean as quickly as possible and the appointment of a high level commission to make recommendations for preparing the peoples of the West Indies for the twenty-first century. They justified these steps in terms of the "need to work expeditiously together to deepen the integration process and strengthen the Caribbean Community in all of its dimensions to respond to the challenges and opportunities presented by changes in the global economy."[34]

Following two years of research and hearings throughout the region, the administrative body of CARICOM, the West Indian Commission, issued its report, *Time for Action,* in 1992. It recommended intensifying the commitment to build CARICOM into a single market and monetary union while at the same time establishing a new organization incorporating all nations of the Greater Caribbean. The Association of Caribbean States came into existence in July 1994 just as other subregional integration agreements were taking shape elsewhere in the Americas. ACS members include Mexico, the five Central American states, Panama, Colombia, and Venezuela, as well as Cuba, the Dominican Republic, and Haiti. France's overseas departments in the Caribbean are associate members and the British, Dutch, and U.S. territories are eligible for associate membership. The association is governed by a ministerial council and has a secretariat located in Port of Spain, Trinidad.

Viewed in terms of size, the ACS is impressive. It encompasses 200 million people with a combined GDP of US $ 500 billion, which would make it the fourth largest integrated regional market in the world.[35] But it is far from being an integrated market, nor does it have a vision to rival MERCOSUR or the Andean Pact, much less NAFTA or the EU. The goals and reality of the ACS are much more modest. In *Time for Action,* the West Indian Commission suggested that the association could be a vehicle for strengthening trade between CARICOM and the rest of the Caribbean Basin, for developing functional cooperation, and for building regional identity.[36] Put simply, the peoples of CARICOM and their governments must no longer think in narrow terms merely of "the Commonwealth Caribbean" but in wider terms of a "Caribbean Commonwealth"—and must work to fulfill this larger ambition."[37]

At this point, the ACS is no more than a forum on regional issues and not a very influential one at that, and it seems unlikely that it will ever evolve into a viable trading bloc. There is more competition than complementarity among ACS members—CARICOM and Central America are on opposite sides of the banana dispute—and all are already members of functioning trade blocs, including NAFTA, CARICOM, MCCA, the Andean Pact, and Group of 3. Given these conditions, the ACS will not displace CARICOM, much less play a role in incorporating the Caribbean into the regional FTAA and new global economy.[38]

The Caribbean, more than any other region of the Americas, has a long history of pursuing regional integration as the primary mode of articulation with the outside world. It is not surprising, therefore, that Caribbean leaders and scholars have reflexively embraced this tradition, calling for both a deepening and widening of integration in responding to the challenges posed to their region by the reconfiguration of the global economy and the international security system. However, given the repeated failure of Caribbean integration to fulfill expectations and given the character of contemporary globalization, the generation of Caribbean leaders who have risen to power in recent years might be advised to critically reconsider the regionalist orthodoxy of their elders.[39] Before discussing possible alternative strategies for securing the high-value-added activities now dispensed by transnational corporations, we will briefly consider additional factors complicating the Caribbean calculus.

Additional Complications to Regional Integration

The "Cuba question" is a major source of uncertainty for the region. CARICOM and the United States openly disagree about how to deal with Cuba. CARICOM has taken steps in recent years to reincorporate it into the Caribbean community—steps that Washington adamantly rejects. In

1993, the Heads of Government created the joint commission to oversee and strengthen CARICOM cooperation with Cuba across a range of issues. All CARICOM member states now have diplomatic and trade relations with Havana. Cuba is a full member of the Caribbean Tourism Organization and the ACS. At the May 1997 presidential summit in Barbados, CARICOM leaders publicly pressured Clinton to drop the embargo, and immediately following the meeting the Jamaican prime minister made a state visit to Cuba accompanied by a delegation of business leaders.[40] Beyond provoking criticism from Washington, CARICOM's conciliatory policy toward Cuba has placed congressional approval of NAFTA parity and other trade concessions for the Caribbean in jeopardy.[41]

Nor is the Cuba question defined only in terms of U.S. threats to punish Caribbean governments for improving relations with Cuba. In the longer run, there is the challenge that a post-embargo Cuba will present to the Caribbean. At some point, most likely after Fidel Castro is no longer on the scene, Washington will restore full diplomatic and economic relations with Cuba. When that day comes, U.S. investment, trade, tourism, and assistance will surely be diverted away from other Caribbean islands to the region's largest economy, and Cuba will become a serious competitor to its neighbors, especially in key sectors like tourism and sugar. On balance then, the CARICOM Caribbean currently profits from U.S. policy on Cuba, a situation that will change dramatically and, as things now stand, with little warning or opportunity for adjustment.

A second factor affecting the path of globalization in the Caribbean is continued U.S. hegemony in the region. Even though the security considerations that led to U.S. military intervention in the past have slipped into the background with the end of the Cold War, the Caribbean is otherwise overwhelmingly dependent on the United States. This relationship not only accounts for half of the region's trade, but through migration and circulation, or short-term, repeated visits, the Caribbean is socially bound to the United States.

The second or third largest urban concentrations of Dominicans, Haitians, or Jamaicans are found not on their home islands but in metropolitan New York City or Dade County, Florida. Caribbean dependence on the United States is not reciprocated. In fact, it could be argued that the Caribbean is less important to U.S. foreign and trade policies than any other region of the world, except perhaps Africa or South Asia. This extreme dependence makes the region vulnerable to the nuances of U.S. policy and politics—as the NAFTA parity issue demonstrates—and assures that the steps the Caribbean takes to come to grips with globalization will be mediated, if not dictated, by Washington.

Some observers have suggested that the special ties that exist between the Caribbean and the State of Florida constitute a channel for influencing U.S. policy. Florida has a significant economic and social stake in the Caribbean's future. Approximately half of all U.S. trade with the Caribbean flows through Florida's ports, and there are large Caribbean immigrant communities in south Florida. Miami serves as the de facto capital of the region.[42] Government and business leaders in Florida work to protect Florida's Caribbean interests at the federal level (although these concerns clearly take a back seat to the Cuba issue in Florida politics). So far, however, Caribbean leaders have been less willing or able to exploit the Florida relationship to influence U.S. policy in a favorable direction for their interests.[43]

Drug trafficking constitutes the third factor complicating the contemporary political economy of the Caribbean. Juxtaposed between the drug producers in the south and drug consumers in the north, the Caribbean is fully integrated into the burgeoning global commodity chain of illegal narcotics. The islands are major transshipment points for the cocaine, heroin, and marijuana going from South America to North America and Europe, and they are actively involved in the laundering of drug profits. While it could be argued that the Caribbean countries might use their vulnerability to the drug trade to leverage aid and trade concessions from Washington, the overriding risk is that the narcotics trade will distort, if not ultimately dominate, Caribbean articulation with the emerging global economy.

Open Regionalism and Globalism as Options for the Caribbean

There remains a role for region-wide collaboration. Additional integration along functional lines, such as building a regional sustainable development regime to protect the fragile marine environment, would certainly be beneficial for the Caribbean states. Nor should their common political heritage be ignored. Both Charles Skeete and Havelock Ross-Brewster argue that limited political unity among the CARICOM countries is worth pursing as an end it itself, given the identity shared by West Indian peoples, but they warn that production and trade be left to "integration on a global scale."[44]

Wider and deeper economic integration—despite its apparent logic for smaller economies—may not be the most productive path for the Caribbean countries to follow in responding to the challenges of globalization. The experiences of Trinidad and Tobago and Barbados suggest two intriguing alternatives.[45] A painful structural adjustment program and the reengineering of its manufacturing plant helped Trinidad develop comparative advantages in nontraditional exports for nontraditional markets. It is today a leading exporter of dentures (false teeth), linked to customers around the world through internet, fax, and overnight air freight. Trinidadian manufacturers are also competitive in disposable diapers, not in the U.S., but in developing markets like Ecuador, where they currently account for 30 percent of local sales. CARI-COM membership does little to advance either of these activities. In fact, CARICOM members are beginning to raise barriers to imports from Trinidad. Of greater benefit would be an *open regionalism* that facilitated Trinidad's access to the Andean Pact, MERCOSUR, or even Middle Eastern markets.

Barbados, recognizing that global economic integration is expanding faster than governments or regional organizations can react to it, much less control it, has adopted the strategy of focusing public resources on preparing its citizens to compete in the global marketplace. The government's primary responsibility is defined not in terms of making trade agreements or operating conventional job training programs, but rather in terms of educating Barbadians to operate in a virtual economy. Given practical computer literacy and electronic access to the global economy, workers and entrepreneurs can compete from their small island in the global economy. For Barbados, the evolving response suggested to globalization is *globalism*.

Regionalism has a long history in the Caribbean. However, the most effective way for the small countries of the region to attract the top end of the value-added activities currently dispersed by the transnational corporations of the global economy is not through a widening and deepening of Caribbean integration, but rather by devising more agile and innovative options. The future well-being of the displaced banana farmers of Dominica lies more in linking them directly to the global economy than in closer ties with neighboring islands.

Notes

The author wishes to thank Jean Carrière and Leann Brown, his colleague at the University of Florida, for their comments and Marcos Avellán for his assistance. He also recognizes the support of the Center for Latin American Studies at the University of Florida and the Department of Development Studies at Utrecht University.

1. Quoted in Susan Taylor Martin, "War of the Bananas," *St. Petersburg Times,* April 5, 1997, p. 1.
2. Terry L. McCoy and Timothy J. Power, "La cuenca del Caribe como subsistema regional," *Estudios Sociales Centroamericanos* 43 (January-April 1987): 13–25.
3. Imports account for over 50 percent of GDP for most countries in the Caribbean. Henry S. Gill, "CARICOM and Hemispheric Trade Liberaliza-

tion," in *Integrating the Hemisphere: Perspectives from Latin America and the Caribbean*, ed. Ana Julia Jatar and Sidney Weintraub (Washington, D.C.: Inter-American Dialogue, 1997), p. 91.

4. Franklin W. Knight, *The Caribbean: The Genesis of Fragmented Nationalism*, 2d ed. (New York: Oxford University Press, 1990).

5. Paul Hirst and Grahame Thompson, *Globalization in Question: The International Economy and the Possibilities of Governance* (Cambridge: Polity Press, 1996).

6. Rubens Ricupero and Norman Gall, "Globalism and Localism: What are the Limits of Competition and Security?" *Braudel Papers*, No. 16 (1997).

7. Ibid.

8. For example, the General Motors Corporation, long identified as a solidly U.S. corporation, is currently in the midst of a US$2.2 billion international expansion that will redefine GM. According to the president and managing director of GM Argentina, "We are talking about becoming a global corporation; that implies that the centers of expertise may reside anywhere they best reside." Rebecca Blumenstein, "GM is Building Plants in Developing Nations to Woo New Markets," *Wall Street Journal*, August 4, 1997, p. A1+.

9. Anthony P. González, "Europe and the Caribbean: Toward a Post-Lomé Strategy," in *The Caribbean; New Dynamics in Trade and Political Economy*, ed. Anthony T. Bryan (New Brunswick and London: Transaction Publishers, 1995), pp. 55–57.

10. Winston C. Dookeran, "Preferential Trade Agreements in the Caribbean: Issues and Approaches," in *Trade Liberalization in the Western Hemisphere* (Washington, D.C.: Inter-American Development Bank, 1995), p. 442.

11. For criticism from the Caribbean perspective, see González, "Europe and the Caribbean," pp.58–60. In a general study of Lomé, Carol Cosgrove, concludes that it has not promoted ACP trade as intended. Regardless of its shortcomings, Caribbean leaders are lobbying the EU to maintain Lomé intact. See Carol Cosgrove, "Has the Lome Convention Failed ACP Trade?" *Journal of International Affairs* 48, No. 1 (Summer 1994): 223–249.

12. McCoy and Power, "La cuenca del Caribe como subsistema regional."

13. Many products from the region were excluded, including sugar and leather goods to give two important examples, and political criteria were invoked to determine country eligibility. G. Pope Atkins, *Latin America in the International System*, 3rd ed. (Boulder: Westview Press, 1995), pp. 277–278.

14. Over 50 percent of CARICOM's trade is with the United States. Richard Bernal, "Influencing U.S. Policy Toward the Caribbean: A Post–Cold War Strategy," in Bryan, *The Caribbean*, p. 211.

15. Dookeran, "Preferential Trade Agreements in the Caribbean," pp. 439–440. According to Alexander F. Watson, Assistant Secretary for Inter-American Affairs of the U.S. Department of State, "To date [May 1995], the Caribbean Basin Initiative has been an unqualified success. The fundamental economic goal of the CBI—broadening and diversifying the economic base of the beneficiaries—is being realized. Since the CBI went into effect in 1984,

non-traditional exports from the region have grown at a rate of nearly 25% per year." Watson also stressed in his testimony before the U.S. Congress that the CBI had resulted in increased exports and jobs for the United States (Watson, "The Caribbean Basin Trade Security Act," *U.S. Department of State Dispatch* 6, No. 22 [May 29, 1995], pp. 460–462). The Caribbean benefits from another CBI-related U.S. law. Section 936 of the Tax Reform Act of 1986 grants tax write-offs for profits form U.S. corporations deposited in Puerto Rican financial institutions to promote economic development in Caribbean Basin Countries. *1996 Caribbean Basin Commercial Profile* (Miami: Caribbean Publishing Co. Ltd. and Caribbean Latin American Action, 1996), p. 44.

16. Gordon Mace and Jean-Philippe Thérien, "Canada in the Americas: The Impact of Regionalism on a New Foreign Policy," in *Foreign Policy and Regionalism in the Americas*, ed. Gordon Mace and Jean-Philippe Thérien (Boulder: Lynne Rienner Publishers, 1996), pp. 53–67.

17. According to Winston Dookeran, Canada's share of CARICOM exports varied between 3.7 and 6 percent in the 1984–1990 period. Dookeran, "Preferential Trade Agreements in the Caribbean," p. 441.

18. Terry L. McCoy, "Democratic Transition and Economic Reform in Latin America, 1982–1992," in *Comparison of Development Experiences: Latin America and Korea*, ed. Soo Keun Kim, Chul Hwan Dim and Yooshik Gong (Seoul: Ajou University Press, 1993), pp. 85–88.

19. Dookeran, "Preferential Trade Agreements in the Caribbean," pp. 461–465, and *1996 Caribbean Basin Commercial Profile*, p. 339.

20. González, "Europe and the Caribbean," p. 63.

21. At President Clinton's May 1997 summit with Caribbean leaders in Barbados, U.S. officials praised the WTO decision on bananas while assuring the Caribbean that Washington would seek other ways to protect its banana markets without specifying what these would be. *Miami Herald*, May 11, 1997, p. 17A.

22. Amos Tincani, "The European Union and the Caribbean: Challenges Ahead," in *Choices and Change: Reflections on the Caribbean*, ed. Winston C. Dookeran (Washington, D.C.: Inter-American Development Bank, 1996), pp. 188–196.

23. See Gill, "CARICOM and Hemispheric Liberalization."

24. *New York Times*, January 30, 1997.

25. *Miami Herald*, April 7, 1997.

26. *New York Times*, May 11, 1997, p. 8. The *Wall Street Journal* reported in an editorial ("President Farley," August 8, 1997, p. A12) that the Senate Finance Committee removed NAFTA parity from the 1997 balanced budget compromise bill in the face of heavy lobbying by Fruit of the Loom corporation. In November, the House of Representatives defeated the NAFTA parity bill. (On-line posting at *HeraldLink*, available from *www.herald.com*, November 6, 1997). Later that same month, facing defeat in the House, Clinton withdrew his request for "fast-track" authority to negotiate trade agreements.

27. Jorge I. Domínguez, "The Caribbean in a New International Context: Are Freedom and Peace a Threat to its Prosperity," in Bryan, *The Caribbean*, pp. 2–4.

28. Havelock R. H. Ross-Brewster, "The Future of the Caribbean Community," in Dookeran, *Choices and Change*, p. 36.

29. Knight, *The Caribbean*, p. 302.

30. *1996 Caribbean Commercial Profile*, p. 47.

31. Charles A. T. Skeete, "Caribbean Identity and Survival in a Global Economy," in Dookeran, *Choices and Change*, p. 29.

32. Dookeran, "Preferential Trade Agreements in the Caribbean," p. 450.

33. According to Nancy Zaretsky, total intra-CARICOM trade fell from 12.6 percent of regional trade in 1990 to 11.5 percent in 1993. See Nancy Zaretsky, *Caribbean Integration: The Association of Caribbean States and its Economic Impact on Florida* (Miami: Florida Caribbean Institute, Florida International University, 1997), p. 6.

34. "Grand Anse Declaration," in *Time for Action: Report of the West Indian Commission*, 2d. ed., ed. West Indian Commission (Largo, Md: International Development Options, 1994), p. 525.

35. Zaretsky, *Caribbean Integration*, p. 5.

36. Trade among ACS countries was only 7.3 percent of total regional trade in 1997. Ibid.

37. West Indian Commission, *Time for Action*, p. 449.

38. The ACS secretariat is a one-person operation with the secretary spending most of his time going from capital to capital in an attempt to convince the member governments to fund his operation. A minister of state from Barbados characterized the ACS as the "spruce goose" of regional integration, and he described CARICOM as a "debating society" that was not significant in shaping his government's policies. An official of the U.S. government who participated in preparatory meetings for 1997 Trade Ministerial in Belo Horizonte, Brazil, remarked that the Caribbean contingent was very ineffectual, even disruptive, arguing for a special role in the FTAA process but unable to agree among themselves about what that role should be. In November 1997, the secretaries general of CARICOM and ACS announced that they had signed an agreement "eliminating duplication of work by the two organizations" and promoting closer collaboration. "Caribbean Report," on-line posting at *HeraldLink*, available from www.herald.com, November 20, 1997.

39. The deaths of Michael Manley of Jamaica and Cheddi Jagan of Guyana within a month of one another in early 1997 is a reminder that the torch of leadership is passing in the Caribbean. The new leaders, with their more technical training, are referred to as the "doctors" or the "numbers boys."

40. *Miami Herald*, May 30, 1997.

41. Domínguez, "The Caribbean in a New International Context," pp. 8–9. Miami representative Ileana Ros-Lehtinen introduced a bill into the U.S. House of Representatives that would sanction Caribbean countries if they "engage Cuba as an economic partner." Rep. Ros-Lehtinen lectured a

group of Caribbean leaders about the consequences of close ties with Cuba. "Caribbean Report," on-line posting at *HeraldLink*, available from www.herald.com, August 14, 1997.

42. Zaretsky, *Caribbean Integration*, p. 3.
43. David E. Lewis, "Intra-Caribbean Relations: A Review and Projections," in Bryan, pp. 91–92.
44. Skeete, "Caribbean Identity and Survival in a Global Economy," pp. 2534; Havelock R. H. Ross-Brewster, "The Future of the Caribbean Community," in Dookeran, *Choices and Change*, pp. 35–40.
45. These alternatives were suggested in conversations with the minister of International Trade and Business of Barbados and the vice president of the Tourism and Industrial Development Company of Trinidad & Tobago at the May 1997 Business Forum of the Americas meeting in Belo Horizonte, Brazil.

PART FOUR

Europe

12

Globalization and the Changes in Europe's Economic Landscape

Egbert Wever

International economic developments in western Europe have resulted in confusing images of the effects of globalization. We have witnessed shifts in the location of industry and developments in foreign direct investment that, at first sight, appeared to operate contrary to the expectations or the logic of the international division of labor as indicated by neoclassical theory. We have seen west European companies relocating in eastern Europe; Russian, Malaysian, and Korean companies manifesting their interest in a takeover of the now defunct Dutch aircraft-producer Fokker; Japanese and Korean companies investing in Great Britain; and even a Taiwanese company establishing in the Netherlands to produce bicycles!

The dynamics of these processes are impressive, fuelled as they are by the rapid changes in the strategies of large firms. It has not always been easy to make sense of these developments in terms of the locational choices or changes in the structure and functioning of the firms involved. The avalanche of new concepts that have been introduced in the literature in an effort at interpretation may, in itself, be an indication of a certain lack of direction.[1]

In the absence of a clear insight into the nature of these processes, their direction and long-term effects, negative perceptions prevail. A similar situation occurred in the United States and Mexico when the ratification of the NAFTA treaty was being discussed. In both cases these processes of economic restructuring were interpreted as resulting from uncontrolled globalizing tendencies, leading—as Philippe Naert formulated—to "a merciless, nobody respecting, cut-throating hyper competition" that will threaten economic growth in many a region.[2] The efforts to attract firms through an improvement of the investment climate will—in this view—result in sharp competition between regions, with possible negative effects for income and for the social conditions of the working population.

The Heckscher-Ohlin-Samuelson (HOS) variant of Ricardo's theory of comparative advantages does teach us that the reduction or abolition of trade barriers will create the opportunity for firms to produce at those locations where their needs for specific production factors (labor, capital, resources) coincide optimally with the supply of these factors. The globalizing trends, in addition to the various projects of regional integration, are making it easier for firms to restructure the location configuration of their plants on a global scale, making use of these comparative advantages. The ultimate result—as the HOS model does indicate—will be regional specialization and the balancing out of factor prices.

Interregional Competition

The European regions are being affected by these processes through the relocation of economic activities to countries outside the EU, as well as through shifts in activities between regions within the Union itself. In particular, those companies involved in standardized, labor-intensive production have been relocating. For them, eastern Europe has become an attractive destination. Within the Union, a region like Ireland has become a preferred location for various types of labor-intensive manufacturing. These new opportunities are enabling the large firms to develop a productive structure that is better adapted to competition in a global market. The previous situation, in which the large European firms had a presence in many individual national markets, gave way to a process of concentration and the establishment of large plants that would be able to profit optimally from economies of scale while producing for one unified European market. In this manner, European integration paved the way for a more efficient configuration of plants. In other sectors a similar development has taken place. In distribution and logistics, the small, nationally based distribution centers are increasingly being replaced by large centers serving the European market.

Interregional competition has intensified now that manufacturing companies, distribution centers, and sales offices or call centers can choose between many acceptable alternative locations. The quality of relevant location factors has improved considerably in many regions, including some that within the EU used to be considered peripheral and economically backward. Those marked differences between regions as to the quality of their physical infrastructure, telecommunications structure, educational facilities, and general living conditions are gradually becoming less prevalent. The competition for jobs has been the main factor behind this process. In many countries development agencies have been created to attract foreign investment and alleviate interregional socioeconomic differences. They may operate on a national level, like the successful Irish Development Agency (IDA) or on a regional level like the Northern Development Agency (NOM) in the Netherlands.

The relocation and concentration of activities within the EU has become more feasible for large firms, with economies of scale leading to reduced production costs, while transport costs are also decreasing as a result of new developments in the areas of distribution and logistics. The establishment of European Distribution Centers and the introduction of route planning and consolidation procedures has increased the spatial scale on which firms are operating and has facilitated the move onto an international market. The crucial question is, To what extent have these changes altered the European economic landscape in a substantial way? To what extent are the neoclassical arguments on comparative advantages being reflected in actual developments?

The Logic of Location and Relocation

An analysis of the general restructuring and relocation processes within the EU shows us that the dynamics of these processes, the frantic activity of firms locating and relocating, do not translate into radical changes in the general European economic landscape as we know it. The economically strong areas of the past have remained strong and will probably maintain their strength in the future. The main European corridor in manufacturing and related services still runs from northern Italy, through the southern and western part of Germany, the eastern and northern part of France, Flanders and the western part of the Netherlands, to England (see Figure 12.1). It appears that changes in these patterns will occur much more gradually than might have been expected given the growing number of alternative locations that offer themselves to investors. Future relocation may take place along the international corridors that are branching out from the main corridor, but these developments are very slow and it will be a long time before they will produce the changes that globalization adepts predict. Apparently, as Gunnar Hallin and Anders Malmberg stated: "Political regime may be overthrown overnight, and institutional systems may shift dramatically in a fairly short time, which we have learnt, if not before, from recent developments in Eastern Europe. The real economy, the production and trade of goods and services, changes in a much more inert way, however."[3]

Consequently, the feared negative effects of industrial restructuring and relocation as a result of processes of globalization or economic internationalization have been greatly exaggerated. As in the NAFTA discussions, it should be emphasized that these are seldom processes producing zero-sum situations. Outgoing investments resulting in job losses are often compensated for by incoming investments and new employment opportunities. Firms like Samsung, Nissan, Hyundai, Toyota, Daewoo, Compaq, Eastman Kodak, and others, have invested heavily in member countries of the EU, and this process of foreign direct investment will undoubtedly continue in the future.

In addition, the opportunity to produce goods or buy components in far away, low labor-cost locations is not always a decisive factor for producers that have to operate in close contact with the European market. This has to do with the changing organizational structure of international manufacturing firms' activities. Especially in those sectors using components or modules, many activities outside the basic production process that traditionally were realized at the plant site may now take place at separate locations. They do not necessarily accompany a plant

Figure 12.1   The Main European Corridors in Manufacturing andRelated Services in the 1990's

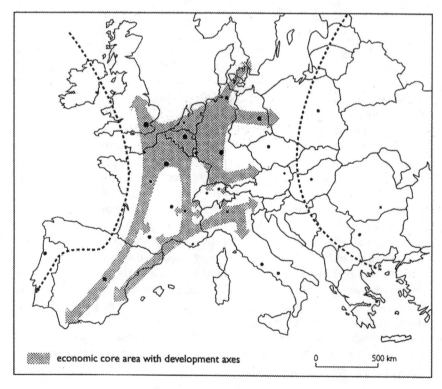

economic core area with development axes   0   500 km

that is to be relocated, but may be organized in distribution centers that are established close to the market. This results from the need to coordinate these "value-added activities" or "postponed manufacturing activities"——like repacking, labeling, customizing, quality control, assembly, testing, and repair—with the wishes of individual clients. At the same time, these activities represent the most valuable portion of value added in the total value chain. Finally, the employment effects of relocation are often mitigated by the growing tertiarization in the traditional manufacturing regions and the concentration of employment in the urban agglomerations.

We can conclude that the HOS model of comparative advantages is of limited use in explaining the spatial behavior of large firms in a changing international business environment. Apparently, entrepreneurs do not behave according to the kind of economic rationality that neoclassical theorems assume. In international trade, the model has been shown to explain some 50 percent of trade flows. Its explanatory value with regard to trade in the western industrial world or interregional trade will be even less.[4] This failure to model behavior according to neoclassical prescriptions and to (re)structure investments following existing comparative advantages must be caused by certain inertia factors that have no place in neoclassical theory.

We find an explanation of these factors in the body of ideas that form part of evolutionary economics.[5] The behavioral approach in location theory has advanced the idea that the concept of "satisficer" is a more appropriate description of the role of the entrepreneur than that of the "optimizer" who prominently figures in neoclassical analysis. In the former, entrepreneurs operate within a framework of "bounded rationality," implying that their knowledge about potentially new, more advantageous locations for the productive activity they are engaged in is limited and "colored" by regional identifications and prejudices. Large organizations as well as individual entrepreneurs will be subject to the influence of these inertia factors. As long as the current profit rate is acceptable, moving production activities will normally not be considered. And even if profit rates are declining, they will have to be part of a structural problem before radical decisions will be made. Even such situations may not always lead to relocation but may result in product or process innovations.[6]

A second source of inertia may be connected with the accumulation of so-called tacit knowledge, which is not documented, only transferable at high transaction cost, and forms part of the industrial and business tradition of specific regions, industrial districts, or urban agglomerations.[7]

A third strong inertia factor deals with the effects of agglomeration economies. It is common knowledge that economic activities tend to cluster spatially, a trend that gains momentum with the supply of highly-skilled personnel, the availability of special inputs and services, and the presence of externalities in the form of (technological) spill-over effects.[8] Economies of scale can be more easily realized in an agglomeration where these developments are taking place. One may even assume that transaction costs will be lower here, given the proximity between firms and other relevant actors.[9] The clustering of economic activities will result in a business environment in which the individual firms will be well-integrated or embedded, making it difficult for them to locate elsewhere.[10]

Europe's Economic Landscape

The argument about the importance of inertia factors does not suggest an absence of change in Europe's economic landscape. On the contrary, economic change is experienced in the considerable dynamics in several peripheral areas, including Catalonia and Ireland. However, the central part of the EU remains the more important area of activity. In this part of Europe, the interregional differences in business environment are gradually diminishing. The opportunities for regions to promote their own competitive position vis-à-vis other regions in the European heartland have increased.[11] The role of comparative advantages is becoming less adequate as an explanation for the shifts in economic activity in and between regions.[12] Other factors must be introduced into the analysis. Michael Porter supplements the traditional neoclassical factor conditions with other variables like market structure, company strategies, competition between firms, market demand, the presence of networks between firms and policy, and even chance.[13] The theses of endogenous growth theory and institutional economics go even further to include social, political, and cultural factors like the quality and motivation of labor, entrepreneurial spirit, managerial competencies built up over time, cooperation or networking between large and small firms, the quality of the administrative infrastructure, regional state policies, and networking between firms and knowledge centers. As Paul Cheshire has noted: "Regions which develop more successful territorial competitive policies will grow at the expense of those that do not."[14] In this context Roberto Camagni defined the concept of "innovative regional milieus" to denote the "winners" in the processes of economic restructuring and relocation that are generated by projects of supranational economic integration and the impact of globalization. Their "winner status" is attributed to a conglomerate of factors to which the above mentioned variables belong.[15]

The image (Figure 12.1) of the overall situation in manufacturing and related services should not lead us to simplify developments. Within the core area that this image illustrates, we find regions of dynamic growth

Table 12.1 Europe's Top Ten Regions for Investors by Investment Priority, 1993

Rank	Manufacturing	Distribution & Logistics	Communication
1	Ireland	Limburg (Netherlands)	Zürich (Switzerland)
2	Andalusia (Spain)	Limburg (Belgium)	Oberbayern (Germany)
3	North (Portugal)	Navarra (Spain)	Ile-de-France (France)
4	Lorraine (France)	Champagne-Ardenne (France)	Lombardy (Italy)
5	Basse-Normandie (France)	Lombardy (Italy)	E.-Romagna (Italy)
6	Overijssel (Netherlands)	Zealand (Netherlands)	Hannover (Germany)
7	Basilicata (Italy)	Franche-Comté (France)	N-Holland (Netherlands)
8	Puglia (Italy)	Emilia-Romagna (Italy)	Piedmont (Italy)
9	Canary Islands (Spain)	Hannover (Germany)	Geneva (Switzerland)
10	Highland & Islands (UK)	Veneto (Italy)	Darmstadt (Germany)

Source: Elaboration of data from Roberto Camagni, "The Concept of Innovative Milieu and Its Relevance for European Lagging Nations," *Papers in Regional Science* 74: 317–340.

Table 12.2   Europe's Top Ten Regions for Wealth and Growth

Rank	GDP, 1993	Economic Growth, 1983–1993
1	Northrhein-Westfalia (Germany)	East Anglia (UK)
2	Ile-de-France (France)	South-West (UK)
3	Bavaria (Germany)	Lazio (Italy)
4	Baden-Württemberg (Germany)	Campania (Italy)
5	South-East (UK)	South-East (UK)
6	Paris Basin (France)	Abruzzi-Molise (Italy)
7	Hesse (Germany)	East Midlands (UK)
8	Lower Saxony (Germany)	Wales (UK)
9	East (Spain)	North East (Italy)
10	West-Netherlands (Netherlands)	Sardinia (Italy)

Source: Elaboration of data from Eurostat (Brussels: European Commission, 1993)

next to regions that are stagnating and not performing optimally. In addition, several regions peripheral to the core area have booming economies. The European economic landscape does show, in fact, a complex mosaic of dynamic and stagnating regions that raise doubts as to the meaning of the labels *center* or *periphery*. The information in Tables 12.1 and 12.2 underlines the complexity of this regional picture.[16] The rank order of the top ten regions in the areas of manufacturing, distribution, logistics, and communications does not exactly coincide with the rank order of the top ten in terms of GDP and rate of economic growth. This is clearly a very diverse situation. Within the EU, individual regions will be increasingly in a position to realize a unique and path-dependent development, to intensify interregional competition, and in some cases to promote their interest directly at the supranational level, bypassing the national state. The "Europe of the regions" may be on the horizon.

Notes

1. Note the great number of new terms coined to conceptualize the locational choices and functioning of modern firms. Just to mention a few at random: *back-to-core-business, core-competence, co-supplier, co-maker, just-in-time-delivery, zero-stock, holistic management, network-organization, post-fordist production, team organization, job-rotation, flexible workforce.*
2. Philippe Naert, "Hoge Werkloosheid Eigen Schuld van Europese Unie," in *NRC Handelsblad*, April 18, 1997, p. 14.
3. Gunnar Hallin and Anders Malmberg, "Attraction, Competition, and Regional Development in Europe," in *European Urban and Regional Studies* 3, no. 4 (1996): 334.

4. Steven Brakman and Charles van Marrewijk, "De Beperkingen van de Handelstheorie," in *Economisch-Statistische Berichten,* January 22, 1996, p. 628.

5. See Ronald Boschma, "Evolutionaire Theorie," in *Economisch-Statistische Berichten,* April 16, 1997, pp. 313–316.

6. A good example concerns the oldest wool mill in the Netherlands, AaBe in Tilburg. The mill went bankrupt in 1996. However, a short time thereafter it made a new start and managed to secure a niche in the market (clothing and carpet for aircraft) that put the plant on a new path of growth.

7. Bart Nooteboom, "Innoveren, Globaliseren," in *Economisch-Statistische Berichten,* October 9, 1996, pp. 828–831.

8. The agglomeration economies associated with this spatial clustering of economic activities were analyzed long ago in the works of the classic economists Alfred Marshall, Alfred Weber, and Walter Christaller. See also Charles van Marrewijk, "Agglomeratie-Effekten," in *Economisch-Statistische Berichten,* May 1, 1996, p. 410.

9. Walter J. J. Manshanden, *Zakelijke Diensten en Regionaal-Economische Ontwikkeling: De Economie van Nabijheid* (Ph.D. diss., University of Amsterdam, 1996).

10. Boschma, "Evolutionaire Theorie," pp. 313–316.

11. See Paul Krugman, *Development, Geography, and Economic Theory* (Cambridge, Mass.: M.I.T. Press, 1995).

12. Paul Cheshire, "The Spatial Impact of European Integration," (paper presented at the *36th Congress of the European Regional Science Association,* Zürich, Switzerland, 1996), pp. 1–2.

13. Michael E. Porter, *The Comparative Advantage of Nations* (New York: Free Press, 1990).

14. Cheshire, "The Spatial Impact of European Integration," p. 2.

15. Roberto Camagni, "The Concept of Innovative Milieu and Its Relevance for European Lagging Regions," *Papers in Regional Science* 74: 317–340.

16. The original research underlying the report on the most attractive regions for investment in Europe was done by the German consultant firm Empirica. See Empirica, *Zukunftstandorte in Westeuropa; Ein Regionalführer für Investoren in EG und EFTA* (Bonn: Wirtschafts- und Sozialwissenschaftliches Forschungs- und Beratungsgesellschaft GmbH, 1993). Regions were ranked on a wide range of criteria, including physical infrastructural factors (e.g., accessibility), economic variables, the quantity and quality of the workforce, the presence of knowledge centers, the support of public policies, and facilities for new investments. The information was systematized by Hallin and Malmberg, "Attraction, Competition, and Regional Development in Europe," p. 62.

Fov

Rll

13

Globalization, National State Policies, and Regional Differentiation: The Case of the United Kingdom

Ray Hudson

There is widespread agreement that the character of contemporary capitalism has shifted in significant ways, but there is much less agreement about the theoretical and political significance of these changes. This is registered in the number of competing scenarios, such as those claiming a transition to late capitalism,[1] late modernity,[2] reflexive modernity,[3] or postmodernity.[4] A common thread running through these competing accounts, however, is a recognition of the dramatic reduction in the tyranny of distance, of a world in which time-space has shrunk dramatically (albeit very unevenly) as a result of technological innovations in transport and communications, especially information technologies. This in turn has been associated with related claims about the transition to a global political economy and processes of globalization, and these claims implicitly or explicitly relate to debates about changes in the regulatory capacities of national states and debates about the "hollowing out" of national states—upwards, downwards, and sideways.[5] The collapse of the Bretton Woods system of fixed exchange rates between national currencies is seen as a particularly critical moment in the transition toward a global economy, since this had profound implications for the national regulation of national economies. One of the particularly important aspects of the "upward" move by the regulatory powers of national states has been the creation of macroregions, such as NAFTA and the EU, as a result of agreements between national states. These have been critical formative moments in the emerging macrogeography of globalization.

Globalization is a hotly contested concept, not least in terms of the relationship between the local, the national, and the global and the degree to which national states are seen as having been hollowed out. Beyond that, however, there is debate about the extent to which globalization encompasses more than just a shifting geography of regulation as the local and the global interpenetrate and influence one another in new and novel ways. At the risk of some oversimplification, four broad analytic positions can be identified, although those who subscribe to any one of them often draw very different political implications.[6]

Perspectives of Globalization

First, there are those who claim that in fact little has changed at all, and that the economy remains essentially international, based on links between national economies regulated by national states. There has been no transition to a radically different global economy, but "business as usual" via the expansion of the capitalist economy on an international level, with national states behaving much as before, as regulators of national economies. The emphasis is upon apparent quantitative continuities rather than qualitative discontinuities in the organization and regulation of the economy. As Paul Hirst and Grahame Thompson put it, "the notion of globalisation is just plainly wrong. The idea of a new, highly internationalised, virtually uncontrollable economy based on world market forces. . . . is wide of the mark."[7]

A second position is diametrically opposed to such a view, and its proponents see the global economy as one in which transnational capital scours the globe in search of profit, with virtually no constraint on its activities. National states are fatally weakened and deprived of regulatory capacity as one facet of a radical process of their "hollowing out," which shifts power decisively to "footloose" transnationals, thus facilitating the emergence of that "borderless world" for which commentators such as Kenichi Ohmae yearn.[8] Others recognize the emergence of such a world but are much less sanguine about it. As William Robinson puts it: "Capitalist globalisation denotes a world war. This war has proceeded with transnational capital being liberated from *any* constraint on its global activity," not least those constraints "that could earlier be imposed on it [transnational capital] through the nation state."[9]

A third view accepts that there has been some weakening of the national states but argues that they nonetheless continue to have considerable significance, albeit with important alterations to their mode of operation.[10] Such analysts accept that there have been fundamental shifts in the organization of the global political economy, and that globalization does indeed register a qualitative change in the character of the political economy of contemporary capitalism. This does not, however, entail the emasculation of the national state; announcements of the death of the national state are premature.[11] Although the mode of national state regulation has altered (for example, with a growing emphasis on the enabling role of the state), it certainly has not been ended.

Finally, a fourth view accepts that there are qualitative processes of change that can be caught in the concept of globalization, but argues that these processes permeate the crevices of everyday life and individual experience of contemporary capitalism. It thus emphasizes that globalization leads to a redefinition of relations not only between a global economy and national states but between a global economy and national and local civil societies. David Held, drawing on Anthony Giddens' concept of time-space distanciation, suggests that "globalisation can be taken to denote the stretching and deepening of social relations and institutions across space and time such that, on the one hand, day-to-day activities are increasingly influenced by events happening on the other side of the globe and, on the other hand, the practices and decisions of local groups can have significant global reverberations."[12] Giddens makes the point with a slightly different emphasis: "Globalisation is not just an 'out there' phenomenon. . . . It is an 'in here phenomenon,' affecting the intimacies of personal identity . . . Globalisation invades local contexts of action but does not destroy them; on the contrary, new forms of local cultural identity and self-expression are causally bound up with globalising processes."[13]

The perspective that I wish to defend combines elements of the third and fourth of these positions. As Ash Amin puts it, it is a view of globalization "as a process of linkage and inter-dependence between territories and of 'in here–out there' connectivity."[14] It certainly acknowledges the hollowing out of the national state—upward (for example in the EU), downward (to the regional and local levels), and outward (into a variety of organizations within civil society at subnational, national, and supranational levels)—and that there have been significant changes in the mode of regulatory activities of national states. Yet it also strongly insists on the continuing salience of the national state. National states are active subjects in shaping processes of globalization rather than simply passive objects and victims of these processes. Consequently, globalization should not be conceptualized as a process somehow external to economy, society, and state, for national states have played a key role in bringing about regulatory and other changes that have facilitated the emergence of the processes and agencies of globalization. A further corollary is that national states remain key sites of power in mediating the relations between processes of globalization and territorial patterns of socioeconomic change within national spaces, although decentralization of state power to local and regional levels has altered the forms of this mediation. While there are reciprocal relationships between changes at local, regional, and global levels, the impacts of globalization have been deeply uneven, both between and within national territories.

Globalization and the Political-Economic Consequences of Thatcherism

For some three decades after 1945, the political economy of the UK can be characterized as cast in a "One Nation" mold, with a specific mode of regulation involving the transition from a liberal to an interventionist state,[15] Keynesian economic management to sustain "full employment" and a commitment to a welfare state. This constituted the UK's version of Fordism, but it differed in critical respects from the canonical Fordist model. It did so precisely because of the legacies of empire within the UK and the related considerable and long-established involvement of UK capital in the international economy. As Alain Lipietz puts it, "Britain, because of the resistant strength of its working class and the weight of finance capital, which is too internationalised to be given over to this internal revolution [of intensive accumulation], has partially missed the boat of Fordism."[16] In fact, Lipietz partly misses the point, since manufacturing, as well as banking and financial capital based in the UK, had long been internationalized to a greater extent than in other national states. There were attempts to restrain internationalization tendencies within limits—not least via the Exchange Control regulations limiting capital export, introduced in 1947. Nevertheless, even these limits allowed capital to maneuver enough to undermine the central premise of a Fordist regime of accumulation, which is based on intensive accumulation within the national territory with state policies mediating the links between productivity growth and rising mass consumption norms.

It was therefore certainly the case that the UK economy was relatively open over the post-war period, in comparison with other major advanced capitalist economies, and so was particularly susceptible to the pressures transmitted from international and, in due course, globalizing markets. It was precisely these growing pressures that helped pull the rug from beneath the Keynesian mode of regulation that was integral to the Fordism of the One Nation project and initiated a shift to a very different "Two Nations" strategy. Indeed, the Two Nations strategy can be seen as a response to the accelerating decline of the UK economy precipitated by the transition from an international to a global economy. This change in political strategy began in 1975 but reached its fullest expression after 1979 and the election of Margaret Thatcher as prime minister.

The resultant restructuring of the UK state that followed from this shift in political strategy can be related to the "hollowing out" thesis, but several aspects of state restructuring as part of the Two Nations project sit uneasily with the canonical model of hollowing out. While there was some transfer of state power upward to the EU, within the UK the dominant tendency was not decentralization to regional and local levels but centralization of state power at the national level. The most significant shift was in the boundary between state and market and in the regulation of markets. The political economy of Thatcherism sought to create more space for market forces as the primary mechanism for steering and restructuring the national economy, giving particular prominence to the role of global markets. Processes of globalization were clearly emerging in the 1970s prior to the ascendancy of Thatcherism, but they were given a massive boost after 1979. Equally, while in some respects a response to the deteriorating position of the UK economy in the context of emerging globalization tendencies, the Two Nation strategy also became an attempt to influence the sectoral and spatial shape and form of globalization, both within and outside the UK.

After 1979, the UK national government deliberately created space allowing global political-economic forces greater influence in shaping the sectoral and spatial patterning of the UK economy and in so doing generated more support for neoliberal policies in other national states and space for globalization tendencies to flourish. The dismantling of exchange controls in 1979 was a crucial moment and the proximate cause of a greatly accelerated de-industrialization and much smaller inflow of FDI. Between 1979 and 1986 the UK's forty largest manufacturing firms cut employment by 290,000, with a growth outside the UK of 125,000 but a domestic reduction of 415,000. Over the same period there was a great increase in foreign investment by UK-based banks and finance houses.[17]

The privatization program was another crucial moment in reining in the scope of state involvement in the economy and opening up significant sectors of the economy to global influences. But perhaps of greatest import were the regulatory changes to enhance the competitive position of the City of London as a financial center and global city, one of the key command and control nodes in the globalizing economy. All of these specific changes shared a general intent: to create space for globalization processes by developing a national political strategy that would alter the sectoral and spatial balance of the national economy in pursuit of enhanced global competitiveness. The UK economy and polity were not merely passive victims of external globalization processes, for dominant political forces within the UK played a decisive role in the emerging shape of the globalizing economy.

These varied deregulatory and reregulatory policies—for it is a great mistake to equate Thatcherism simply with market deregulation—significantly affected the sectoral and spatial composition of the national economy. The effects differed widely between and within regions and cities, resulting in a complex pattern of sectoral and spatial change within the UK: a mosaic of "winners" and "losers." In broad terms, the switch from an economy based on production to one based on services, consumption, and leisure in a post-industrial heritage park resulted in further expansion in the Southeast based around financial and business services and decline in the remaining regions associated with deindustrialization.

But in fact, superimposed on this mosaic was a much more finely grained map of winners and losers associated with change in the major conurbations, their suburbs, and the adjoining hinterlands of small towns and villages in rural areas. This map was also related to a changing conception of territorial development in the new global context and heightened competition between places, both within and outside the UK. Spatial policy within the UK became cast in an increasingly competitive mold. The terms of this competition were shaped, in large part, by the central government as it cut back regional policy while expanding urban policy, imposing severe restrictions on the budgets and competencies of elected local authorities while creating powerful but nonelected regeneration agencies, notably the Urban Development Corporations.[18]

In the rest of this chapter these differentiating effects will be exemplified with reference to changes in two regions: first, the changes in the Southeast associated with the promotion of London as a global financial center, and second, the changes in the Northeast associated with deindustrialization—resulting from cutting back the state sector—and with a much more muted re-industrialization—resulting from inward investment and the restructuring of manufacturing within the UK.

Mapping Sectoral and Spatial Change: Two Contrasting Examples

The "Big Bang": The Growth of London as a Financial and Business Center and Its Regional Impact

The collapse of the "old order" of Bretton Woods and the debt crisis of the latter part of the 1970s and early 1980s, resulting from the recycling of petro-dollars to Third World governments,[19] inspired the emergence of a new international financial system in the 1980s. This development posed major challenges that threatened the viability of major banks, Third World states, and existing financial centers in the late capitalist world. A combination of the further internationalization of capital, securitization, and new technology rendered counterproductive any attempts to impose stringent national controls on international financial institutions and flows of capital, repelling rather than attracting companies and capital. As a result, the 1980s saw a dismantling of domestic financial restrictions in many of the advanced capitalist states. The City of London was the site of the most radical response to the new market conditions, as the Thatcher Government enforced a drastic overhaul of practices within the domestic securities markets. The restructuring of the equities and gilts market in turn was used as a catalyst to set in motion a more generalized restructuring of financial institutions and markets.[20]

During the 1970s the City of London began to lose market share in emerging global financial markets. In part, this reflected the cozy, self-regulating system then prevalent in the City, based on tacit understandings and a strong "old boy" network of noneconomic relationships between the main actors. Competitiveness declined also in part as a consequence of the tightening of financial regulation by the UK government, which was trying to revive the domestic manufacturing sector.[21] At the same time, the dominance of the United States in defining the "knowledge structure"[22] relevant to financial regulation created strong pressures on other states, including the UK, to imitate its regulatory systems in order to remain competitive in global financial markets. The restructuring of the City of London was a process set in motion by state action in 1976 in the wake of the national economic crisis that forced the UK government to seek the support of the IMF. It was not, however, until 1983 that the stock exchange agreed to change, and it was not until October 27, 1986, and the enactment of the financial services legislation that the "Big Bang" finally occurred. The Big Bang is often identified with the deregulation of financial markets. It was, however, not so much deregulation as a new form of reregulation that privileged the interests of banks and financial organizations operating in global markets. The aim was to effect a social and political reconstruction of the City's place as a global financial center and to revive its global competitiveness. Even so, it was not so much a response *to* globalization as a defining moment *in* the creation of global financial markets. It led to a spurt of mergers and acquisitions among UK financial institutions, with the winners emerging both bigger and internationally more competitive than before, operating across a wider spectrum of financial activities. More significantly, it strengthened the City's position in the global economy and as a result, attracted considerable flows of investment by foreign banks and financial houses. Some influx of foreign banks and finance houses had already been associated with the rise of the Eurodollar market in the late 1960s and the growth of the Eurobond market in the late 1970s. As a result, between

1968 and 1986, the number of foreign banks represented in London increased from 135 to 144.[23] With the certain expectation of the Big Bang, this process accelerated markedly after 1983. As Michael Moran put it, referring to the subsequent growth of globally oriented financial services in the City, "London's comparative advantage as a world centre is due, above all, *to regulatory policy.*"[24]

The changes leading up and encapsulated in the Big Bang had numerous effects on labor and property markets and on class structures, both producing enhanced differences among localities within the Southeast region and further differentiating the region from the rest of the UK space economy. It further reinforced processes through which the Southeast was increasingly linked to globalized sectors. An obvious manifestation of the enhanced position of the City in global financial markets was the boom in office rents and office building construction in the City and elsewhere (although this became problematic after the crash of 1987, especially in the new Docklands developments).

Perhaps the most significant effect of the changes of the 1980s was the expansion and thorough integration of the labor market in the City of London into the global labor market for highly qualified workers in financial services. The growing demands for skilled labor, along with the redefinition of skills associated with the creation of new financial products and instruments, pulled international skilled migrants into the City.[25] These flows assumed growing importance with a sharp increase in the pace of investment coming into the City from foreign banks and finance houses. In 1986 alone, the number of employees in foreign banks in the City rose by over 25 percent, from 42,800 to 53,800, while between 1984 and 1987 overall employment in the City grew by 75 percent.

As a consequence of this simultaneous expansion and integration, salaries began to rise rapidly, from their previous relatively low levels to internationally comparable ones. By 1986 more than half of the City workforce was in the top 10 percent of wage earners nationally. Or to put it another way, in 1986 people working in the City accounted for between 12 and 14 percent of all incomes in the UK between £20,000 and £50,000, between 23 and 24 percent of all incomes between £50,000 and £100,000, and 50 percent of all salaries over £100,000.[26] Most of these people were men. Many possessed great wealth—especially those earning very high incomes—were drawn from a particular upper and upper-middle-class background, and used their money to help reproduce that class structure, not least by investing in the private education of their children.[27]

On the other hand, many employees, most of whom were women, received much lower levels of pay in clerical and personal services occupations. The City's labor market remained deeply segmented, by both occupation and gender, and remained resistant, though not completely impervious, to change.[28] One effect of these labor market changes was the emergence of new and more complicated commuting patterns to and from the City. More generally, deepening labor market segmentation within the Southeast was linked to a strong tendency for intraregional income inequalities to increase there.[29]

The generation of income and wealth within certain sectors of the City—and more widely throughout the Southeast, which by the early 1990s had over half of all UK employment in business (or producer) services—in turn had wider effects within the rest of London and the Southeast region. It increased demand for domestic and personal services among the professional workers who worked in the City. These services comprised, in large part, poorly paid occupations mainly filled by women.[30] Further, growing wealth generated demand for a range of services associated with consumption and leisure outside the home, such as restaurants and leisure clubs, many of which were supplied by multinational companies as part of their evolving global strategies. The resultant jobs were often characterized by low pay and poor, often precarious, conditions of work and employment.[31]

Perhaps most significantly, growth in the City led to a spiralling escalation of housing prices within the Southeast and above all in London. House prices rose by 66 percent between 1983 and 1986 in London,[32] but increases were especially concentrated within certain parts of the City, especially where foreign banks and finance houses were purchasing housing for key employees. City employees were particularly prominent among buyers of country houses in the Southeast, where over half of the homes sold were purchased for cash, and they spent heavily on associated status and positional goods (Range Rovers, fine art, antique furniture, and so on).[33] This conspicuous consumption, this emulation of the lifestyle of the landed upper classes by seeking to demonstrate "taste,"[34] was strongly reminiscent of the behavior of both successful nineteenth-century industrial capitalists and late-twentieth-century property developers and speculators.[35] At the risk of oversimplification,[36] it can be concluded that an important, more general consequence of differential house price inflation was that, in effect, two spatially discrete housing markets emerged within the UK: the Southeast and the rest of the country.[37] This had profound consequences in that it virtually ended the possibilities of migrating to the Southeast for the vast majority of the population of the rest of the UK.

It must be noted that after 1987 there were significant and largely unprecedented problems in the Southeast, as its economy proved to be vulnerable to recession, resulting in significant reductions in service sector employment, salaries in financial services, and property prices. Nonetheless, these were largely conjunctural rather than structural phenomena, as the spatially uneven recovery of the 1990s revealed. The Southeast remained a prosperous region largely articulated to the international economy around the pivotal hinge of London's position as a global city. It is important to point out, however, that the City's role as a global command and control center and, more generally, the greater level of prosperity, affluence, and material well-being in the Southeast were also strongly underpinned by public expenditure. Public expenditure per capita comfortably *exceeded* the national average in the 1980s, as it had done over the preceding decades.[38] It would therefore be a profound mistake to interpret the City's role as a global financial center and Southeast's dominant position in the UK as a simple outcome of global market forces.

The relationships between the Southeast and the rest of the national economy (if the latter had not indeed become a Keynesian myth)[39] were styled by the Southeast's characteristics as a political and economic command and control center. Nevertheless, the key decisions affecting investment and employment in much of the rest of the UK were not made in the City, nor indeed within the UK. Not least, this was because other strands of the political economy of Thatcherism had sought to create linkages between the processes of globalization and peripheral regional economies in the UK. As a result, the control over development in many regional economies at the UK periphery lay in New York, Tokyo, and other major economic and financial centers outside the UK. The Northeast of England represents an example of such development.

Reforming a Former Workshop of the World: England's Northeast

Two related aspects of the process of rolling back the boundaries of the state are of particular relevance in understanding the changing pattern of production, work, and inequality in the Northeast. The first is the increasing and deliberate reliance upon the global market as the arbiter of the fate of national and regional economies. This has involved a growing emphasis on free market forces and especially on global market forces as the prime economic steering mechanism within the UK. The high exchange rate and counterinflationary policies of the early 1980s had particularly severe effects on the economy of the Northeast, as did the 1979 deregulation of outward FDI. The latter resulted in a massive outflow of capital from the UK in the first half of the 1980s, intensifying deindustrialization both nationally and regionally. Manufacturing employment in the Northeast fell by 15 percent between 1978 and 1993. This phenomena affected both private and public sector industries. Intensified competitive pressures on private sector manufacturing in traditional enterprises—

such as heavy engineering and chemicals—and in many new consumer goods industries that had previously located in the region[40] led to widespread capacity closures and substantial job cutbacks in those plants that had managed to remain open. The more typical phenomena, however, involved the migration of investment, production, and jobs to countries outside the UK, in addition to capacity closures, net capacity reductions or bankruptcies, and the subsequent closure of companies.[41] The second aspect of rolling back the state relates to the rationalization and privatization of the formerly nationalized industries. This had draconian impacts on coal mining, the manufacturing of steel and ships, and public sector services alike, leading to massive capacity closures and job losses. A central element in the political strategy of Thatcherism was the destruction of the nationalized industries, which were central to the "old" industrial economies of regions such as the Northeast. These regions were seen as core areas of support for the Labour Party (equated with socialism) and symbolic of post-war Keynesian economic management within a One Nation consensus politics.[42]

The rationalization of these industries within the public sector, however, had already begun in the One Nation era. Efficiency and pseudo-profitability criteria were introduced to the nationalized industries, starting in the coal industry, from the late 1950s on, in response to growing pressures on international markets.[43] As a result these industries had experienced capacity closure and job loss in the Northeast for almost two decades prior to the emergence of the Two Nations strategy. The pace of decline accelerated in the 1980s as the Two Nations strategy took root, when further rationalization in search of profitability was a prelude to privatization in increasingly global markets. This development was associated with the introduction of new terms and conditions of work. However, concerns about poorer quality jobs were soon replaced by fears about an absence of any jobs whatsoever in these industries.

Privatization led to the virtual elimination of coal mining, iron and steel production, and shipbuilding from the economy of the Northeast. By the early 1990s, these industries, which had formed the historic core of the regional production system, had been reduced to one colliery (although there was still a considerable amount of privatized and environmentally destructive opencast coal mining in the region), one steel works, and some sporadic ship repair activity—in all, fewer than 10,000 jobs, compared to almost 300,000 in the mid-1950s. In the workplaces that remained, drastically new methods of working had been introduced as massive job loss left employers in a very powerful position to impose new terms and conditions of work on their residual workforces.[44] The links between the existing mass unemployment in the region, new forms of work introduced into the residue of the old industrial economy, and the terms and conditions under which work was offered in the factories as a result of new inward investment, especially from Southeast Asia, were very clear.

While pursuing policies that resulted in the destruction of the old industrial economy of the region, Mrs. Thatcher's government actively encouraged inward FDI, especially from Japan. This strategy was designed to restructure manufacturing industry and labor relations in the UK while addressing some of the unemployment problems of deindustrialized regions.[45] New FDI was seen as a crucial element in the creation of a "new" regional economy in the era of globalization of the 1980s.[46] This strategy was not without precedent in the region; it had been tried in the 1960s. In a situation of low regional unemployment rates and high demand for male labor in the region's traditional coal mining and manufacturing industries, inward investment into the region was sharply discouraged at first, in order to damp down competition between companies for male labor.[47] As a result, there were only 8,500 people employed in foreign-owned factories in the region by 1963.[48]

The accelerating decline of the old industrial economy in the 1960s forced a radical shift in attitudes and policies. Attracting inward FDI came to be seen as critically important in the construction of a diversified regional economy, able to provide employment in a range of modern industries. This goal was pursued through a combination of strengthening the central government's regional policy and encouraging institutional innovation and social change within the region itself, both being elements of a program of regional modernization.[49] Consequently, in the late 1960s and early 1970s inward FDI increased, as did the number of transnational branch plants, especially from the United States. By 1978, employment in foreign-owned plants had risen to 53,000, or 12.9 percent of total regional employment in manufacturing.[50] However, the FDI by transnational corporations produced ambivalent reaction within the region. The investments did help to diversify the range of industries present there. At the same time, however, it led to a greater degree of homogeneity in the industrial structure. The Northeast became characterized by routine assembly or component production operations across a range of industries. The limitation to a particular stage in the overall spatial\technical division of labor led to concern about the quality and stability of branch plant employment. Fears were expressed about deskilled and unstable jobs in the "global outposts," situated at the extremities of corporate hierarchies and far removed from the key centers of command, control, and strategic decisionmaking, in a dependent, externally controlled, and vulnerable regional economy.[51] The renewed decline of the region's industrial economy in the early 1980s initially seemed to confirm these fears. The deflationary impacts of national economic policies and more competitive global markets led to disinvestment from the Northeast. Multinationals that, little over a decade earlier, had been heralded as the key to a new modern regional manufacturing economy either shed labor or closed completely. Fears about the quality of jobs in a branch plant economy were replaced by fears about an absence of any jobs in industry in a region that had ceased to be attractive to industrial capital.

The successful attraction and retention of a new round of inward FDI in manufacturing in the late 1980s was therefore seen as of great significance in the region. In sharp contrast to the Southeast, some 95 percent of new jobs resulting from FDI in the Northeast were in manufacturing.[52] The first Japanese automobile assembly plant in the UK was a Nissan plant in Washington New Town, a choice that was deeply symbolic and had momentous consequences both within the Northeast and within the automobile industry in the UK.[53] It was to be the harbinger of a broader wave of inward investment from Southeast Asia, bringing 11,000 new manufacturing jobs to the Northeast between 1985 and 1993, over 50 percent of the total increase of jobs in foreign-owned plants over this period. This surge of FDI from Southeast Asia was heavily concentrated sectorally. Among the new jobs brought in after 1985, 23 percent were in electrical and electronic engineering (for example, jobs associated with investment by companies such as Fujitsu, Goldstar, Samsung, and Sanyo) while 34 percent were in the automobile industry, primarily jobs associated with investments by Nissan and some component suppliers. Inward investment from Southeast Asia encompassed both greenfield factories and, unusually for Japanese companies, significant takeovers (notably the takeover of Dunlop's Washington tire factory by Sumitomo and Caterpillar's Birtley factory by Komatsu).

Despite an acceleration in the pace of inward FDI, the stock of employment in foreign-owned factories remained at 53,000 in 1989, although this by then amounted to 20 percent of total manufacturing employment. Stagnation in absolute levels of multinational employment both reflected and concealed variations at the company level. Acquisitions of UK companies added to the stock of employment in foreign-owned factories, while fresh jobs were created in new factories and existing ones lost because of plant closure or in situ restructuring in pursuit of enhanced labor productivity. However, employment and investment in foreign-owned factories increased spectacularly from the second half of the 1980s on with significant inflows from Germany (for example, by Siemens, both via acquisition and new greenfield investment) and the United States— which together continued to dominate the overall stock of FDI—as well as from Southeast Asia. By 1993 almost 370 foreign companies, employing over 80,000 people, were established in the region.[54] Nevertheless, at the same time total employment in manufacturing fell further while the jobs in coal mining disappeared completely.

In the course of the 1980s, however, it appeared that inward FDI should not simply be evaluated in a quantitative way because it also had qualitatively different impacts on the Northeast, as corporate strategies were changing in significant ways in an era of globalization. No longer was inward FDI necessarily associated with the creation of "global outposts"; transnational companies were pursuing more "regionalized" or "glocalized" versions of their global strategies—with R&D, production, distribution, and sales organized on, say, a European rather than a worldwide basis.[55] There is no doubt that the surge of inward FDI into the Northeast in the late 1980s and early 1990s (£3 billion between 1985 and 1993[56]) reflected corporate responses to the immanent completion of the Single European Market. Many of the new plants were established in Northeast England specifically to penetrate the EU market, to locate productive capacity within the Common External Tariff barrier before the completion of the Single European Market. This suggests that the regionalization of the global market and the Europeanization of production were of greater significance than globalization per se. Moreover, Europeanizing production in this way also involved a degree of localization of production and spatial clustering associated with just-in-time production strategies. Component companies located adjacent to Nissan's plant to allow synchronous production.[57] Similar groups of suppliers are building up around other new plants, such as the Samsung plant. These input-output relations between spatially adjacent plants may reflect a greater degree of embeddedness within the region, with potentially more positive developmental implications for the Northeast than the previously disarticulated branch plants. To a degree, it would seem that the regional economy is being reconstructed around spatially agglomerated complexes of companies linked into just-in-time production systems.[58]

There are clear risks connected with the creation of an economy that is particularly vulnerable to the decisions of "lead" companies operating globally in the automobile and electronics sectors. In the short term, however, such investments do create jobs, again with concerns about their quality and quantity. While inward FDI has been instrumental in bringing new forms of work organization to the Northeast, there are conflicting opinions about the extent that it has actually done so and, insofar as it has, whether this represents a regressive or progressive change. As F. Peck and I. Stone note, there was considerable heterogeneity in labor requirements, recruitment strategies, forms of work organization, and regimes of labor process control in relation to the new Japanese factories of the 1980s. Consequently, while "some inward investment projects can be regarded as 'best practice' plants, . . . others do not appear to differ greatly from the traditional branch factory."[59] The debate about the quality of new jobs may be exemplified by the case of Nissan. The company projects an image of work at its Washington factory as empowering production workers, offering considerable job security (if no longer a job for life) and an enriching form of work for multiskilled workers, and built around themes of flexibility, quality, and teamwork. In contrast, its critics see it as disempowering and disabling, characterized by control, exploitation, and surveillance, and bound together into a single union factory with low levels of union activity.[60]

Perhaps the most fundamental point, however, is that the employment brought by inward FDI has had little impact on overall unemployment levels in the Northeast. Although individual factories may employ a considerable number of people, many more have been lost as a result of the closure of coal mines, steel works, shipyards, and factories in other sectors of manufacturing. There are clear *limits* to inward investment as a solution to the contemporary problems of regional unemployment—as opposed to those of output growth or industrial diversification. Indeed, a continuing substantial pool of unemployed people was a significant and necessary attraction for such inward investment. By the second half of the 1980s and early 1990s, the Northeast had become a low wage region relative to the core economies of the EU, characterized by high unemployment rates and large reservoirs of malleable labor. In such a context, transnational companies can exercise great selectivity in labor recruitment in order to create particular forms of work organization and workplace relations. Work*place* relations decisively influence and shape those of *work*place.[61] While in some ways exceptional, the 33,000 applications that Nissan received within six weeks in 1992 for 600 new job openings are instructive and revealing. Because they can exercise a marked degree of selectivity in recruitment, often preferring to recruit from the ranks of the employed rather than the ranks of the unemployed, such companies effectively exclude the vast majority of people in the region from consideration as part of their potential workforces. The net result is that the Northeast has become a region of permanent mass unemployment and associated poverty. The "North-South" gap in employment and unemployment has widened further in the 1990s, a phenomenon severely understated in the official government data.[62]

Conclusion

The combined effects of globalization and national state policy strategies in the UK have enhanced the position of London as a global city, with economic and social effects that have penetrated the rest of England's Southeast. The socio-spatial and cultural differences within the Southeast have increased, although the region as a whole shows a growing prosperity in relation to the rest of the UK. In the other regions, the impact of the same combination of processes and policies, along with enhanced interregional and interlocality competition for investment and jobs, resulted in a significant and spatially uneven expansion of poverty and unemployment and a rearticulation of the links between regions and the global economy. The geography of deindustrialization and reindustrialization resulting from the redefinition of the relationship between state and market has been quite uneven. In the Northeast the "rolling back of the state" was intimately related to the destruction of the "old" industrial economy, which originated in the UK's former role as a center of manufacturing in an international economy. At the same time, it was pivotal in the creation of a "new" industrial economy, shaped by a different state policy agenda and influenced by the UK's changed position in an emergent global economy.

The processes of globalization clearly have profoundly affected the UK economy and society. It is equally obvious that the strategies of the UK state have not simply responded to the increased importance of globalization tendencies but have encouraged and helped shape them. In some respects it could be argued that this engagement between national state strategy and the processes of globalization has not been without positive effects. It has undeniably led to new forms of production and work as a result of the influence of inward FDI from Germany, Japan, and the United States. It has revived or enhanced the competitiveness of a range of companies and sectors within the UK, although the overall productivity of manufacturing in the UK continues to lag behind that of France, Germany, Japan, and the United States.[63] There have undoubtedly been "winners" within the UK, not in the least many of those involved with the City of London, which has reinforced its competitive position in global financial markets, with a wider effect on the economy of the Southeast.

Nonetheless, there have been "losers" in the Southeast, both manufacturing companies and places that depended on them for jobs. Conversely, while there have been winners in the rest of the UK, both in terms of companies and places, they have been much less in evidence than the losers. Large swathes of the UK outside of the Southeast have been blighted by mass unemployment and poverty as a consequence of heightened exposure to the pressures of global markets, which have led to deindustrialization and job loss. In this sense, there is no doubt that globalization has enhanced socio-spatial inequality and heightened the contrast in the map and mosaic of winners and losers within the UK, raising questions as to the adequacy of local modes of regulation.[64]

The increased role of global market forces within the UK did reflect a definite political choice. There was nothing natural or inevitable about the drastic changes in the mode of regulation that created more room for global market forces to determine the trajectory of economic change. In addition, state strategies were intimately involved in heightening inequality in another key respect. It is important to remember that the changes in the political-economic strategy of the UK state involved an increase in per capita public expenditure in the already well-treated Southeast while it cut public expenditure over much of the rest of the national territory, with an important direct impact on the map of uneven development.

The knowledge that globalization does not necessarily have to be embraced and promoted as the arbiter of the structure, content, and geography of the economy within the national territory suggests the presence of alternatives. Those who interpret the national economy as a "Keynesian myth"[65] are answered by those who regard the resurgence of national economies and states as both desirable and unavoidable. As Manfred Bienefeld puts it: "A return to stronger nation states is not Utopian but inevitable. The only question is the *form* these states will take."[66] Deliberately creating space for global market pressures to reshape the sectoral and spatial structure of economic activity was integral to the Two Nations political strategy of Thatcherism. Reversing such a strategy and its impacts within the UK will be much more difficult, but not necessarily impossible. The form of a revivified national state in the UK may be the only question—as Bienefeld asserts—but the answer will be of pivotal importance in seeking to reconstruct relationships between the local, national, and global that will combat burgeoning spatial inequality and produce a more inclusive and equitable developmental trajectory within the UK.

Notes

1. Ernest Mandel, *Late Capitalism* (London: New Left Books, 1975).
2. Anthony Giddens, *The Consequences of Modernity* (London: Polity Press, 1990).
3. Ulrich Beck, *Risk Society: Towards a New Modernity* (London: Sage, 1992).
4. David Harvey, *The Condition of Postmodernity* (Oxford: Blackwell, 1989).
5. B. Jessop, "Post-Fordism and the State," in *Post-Fordism: A Reader*, ed. Ash Amin (Oxford: Blackwell, 1994), pp. 57–58.
6. Ash Amin, "Placing Globalisation," *Theory, Culture, and Society* (Durham: University of Durham, 1997), 14, no. 2: 125–137.
7. Paul Hirst and Grahame Thompson, "Globalisation: Ten Frequently Asked Questions and Some Surprising Answers," *Soundings* 4 (1996): 47–66; Paul Hirst and Grahame Thompson, *Globalization in Question* (London: Polity Press, 1996).

8.   Kenichi Ohmae, *The Borderless World* (New York: Harper Collins, 1995); Kenichi Ohmae, *The End of the Nation State* (Glencoe, Ill.: Free Press, 1995).
9.   W. Robinson, "Globalisation: Nine Theses on Our Epoch," *Race and Class* 38, no. 2 (1996): 13–31. Emphasis added.
10. Robert Boyer and Daniel Drache, eds., *States Against Markets: The Limits of Globalisation* (London: Routledge, 1995).
11. James Anderson, "The Exaggerated Death of the Nation State," in *A Global World?* ed. James Anderson, Clirês Brook, and Allen Cochrane (Oxford: Oxford University Press, 1995), pp. 65–112.
12. David Held, *Democracy and the Global Order* (London: Polity Press, 1995).
13. Anthony Giddens, "Affluence, Poverty, and the Idea of a Post-Scarcity Society," *Development and Change* 27 (1996): 365–377.
14. Ash Amin, "Globalisation and Regional Development: A Relational Perspective" (Durham, England: University of Durham, 1997).
15. Jurgen Habermas, *Legitimation Crisis* (London: Heinemann, 1975).
16. Alain Lipietz, "New Tendencies in the International Division of Labour: Regimes of Accumulation and Modes of Regulation," in *Production, Territory, Work,* ed. Allen Scott and Michael Storper (New York: Unwin Hyman, 1986), pp. 16–40.
17. Ray Hudson and Allen Williams, *Divided Britain,* 2d ed. (London: Wiley, 1995).
18. Ibid.
19. Alain Lipietz, *The Enchanted World: Inflation, Credit, and the World Crisis* (London: Verso, 1985).
20. Nigel Thrift, "Doing Regional Geography in a Global System: The New International Financial System, the City of London, and the South-East of England," in *Regional Geography: Current Developments and Future Prospects,* ed. R. Johnston, Joost Hauer, and Gerard Hoekveld (London: Routledge, 1990), pp. 180–207.
21. Ron Martin, "Stateless Monies, Global Financial Integration, and National Economic Autonomy: The End of Geography?" in *Money, Power and Space,* ed. Steward Corbridge, Ron Martin, and Nigel Thrift (Oxford: Blackwell, 1994), pp. 253–278.
22. Susan Strange, *States and Markets* (London: Pinter, 1988).
23. Andrew Leyshon, Nigel Thrift, and P. Daniels, "The Urban and Social Consequences of the Restructuring of World Financial Centres: The Case of the City of London," *Working Papers on Producer Services,* Number 16 (Bristol: University of Bristol, 1987).
24. Michael Moran, *The Politics of the Financial Services Revolution* (London: Macmillan, 1991). Emphasis added.
25. J. V. Beaverstock and J. Smith, "Lending Jobs to Global Cities: Skilled International Labour Migration, Investment Banking, and the City of London," *Urban Studies* 33, no. 8 (1996): 1357–1377.
26. Nigel Thrift, "Serious Money: Class, Consumption, and Culture in Late Twentieth-Century Britain" (paper presented at the IBG Conference on New Directions in Cultural Geography, London, 1987).

27. Hudson and Williams, *Divided Britain*.
28. L. McDowell and G. Court, "Missing Subjects: Gender, Power, and Sexuality in Merchant Banking," *Economic Geography* 70 (1994): 229–251.
29. Hudson and Williams, *Divided Britain*.
30. Nicky Gregson and Michelle Lowe, *Servicing the Middle Classes: Class, Gender, and Waged Domestic Labour in Contemporary Britain* (London: Routledge, 1994).
31. Huw Beynon, "The Changing Experience of Work: Britain in the 1990s" (paper presented at the Conference on Education and Training for the Future Labour Markets of Europe, Durham, England, September 21–24, 1995).
32. Chris Hamnett, "The Political Geography of Housing in Contemporary Britain." in *A Political Geography of Britain*, ed. J. Mohan (London: Macmillan, 1989).
33. Thrift, *Serious Money*.
34. Pierre Bourdieux, *Distinction: A Social Critique of the Judgement of Taste* (London: Routledge and Kegan Paul, 1984).
35. Hudson and Williams, *Divided Britain*.
36. For a more detailed discussion of real estate price inflation, see Paul Balchin, *Regional Policy in Britain* (London: Paul Chapman, 1990).
37. Hudson and Williams, *Divided Britain*.
38. Ray Hudson and Allen Williams, *The United Kingdom* (London: Paul Chapman, 1986); Hudson and Williams, *Divided Britain*.
39. H. Radice, "The National Economy—a Keynesian Myth?" *Capital and Class* 22 (1984): 111–140.
40. Ray Hudson, "Producing an Industrial Wasteland: Capital, Labour, and the State in North East England," in *The Geography of Deindustrialization*, ed. Ron Martin and R. Rowthorne (London: Macmillan, 1986), pp. 169–213.
41. Hudson, "Producing an Industrial Wasteland."
42. Hudson and Williams, *Divided Britain*.
43. Ray Hudson, *Wrecking a Region: State Policies, Party Politics, and Regional Change in North East England* (London: Pion, 1989).
44. Ray Hudson and David Sadler, "Manufacturing Success? Reindustrialisation Policies in Derwentside in the 1980s," *Occasional Publication* No. 25 (Durham, England: Department of Geography, University of Durham, 1991); Huw Beynon, Ray Hudson, and David Sadler, *A Tale of Two Industries* (Plaats: Open University Press, 1991); Huw Beynon, Ray Hudson, and David Sadler, *A Place Called Teesside* (Edinburgh: Edinburgh University Press, 1991).
45. Ray Hudson, "The Japanese, the European Market, and the Automobile Industry in the United Kingdom," in *Towards a New Map of Automobile Manufacturing in Europe?* ed. Ray Hudson and Eike Schamp (Hamburg: Springer, 1995), pp. 63–92.
46. Ray Hudson, "Institutional Change, Cultural Transformation, and Economic Regeneration: Myths and Realities from Europe's Old Industrial Regions," in *Globalization, Institutions, and Regional Development in Europe*,

ed. Ash Amin and Nigel Thrift (Oxford: Oxford University Press, 1994), pp. 331–345.

47. Ray Hudson, *Wrecking a Region: State Policies, Party Politics and Regional Change in North East England* (London: Pion, 1989).

48. Ray Hudson, "The Role of Foreign Investment," in *Northern Region Economy: Progress and Prospects,* ed. L. Evans, P. Johnson, and B. Thomas (London: Cassell, 1995), pp. 79–95.

49. Hudson, *Wrecking a Region.*

50. I. Smith and I. Stone, "Foreign Investment in the North: Distinguishing Fact from Hype," *Northern Economic Review* 18 (1989): 50–61.

51. T. Austrin and Huw Beynon, *Global Outpost: The Working Class Experience of Big Business in North East England* (Durham, England: University of Durham, 1979); J. Firn, "External Control and Regional Development; the Case of Scotland," *Environment and Planning A,* 7 (1975): 393–414.

52. L. Bussel, "Inward Investment: Impact on the Northern Region," *Business Review North* 2 (1990): 24–31.

53. Ray Hudson, "The Japanese, the European Market and the Automobile Industry in the United Kingdom," in Hudson and Schamp, *Towards a New Map of Automobile Manufacturing in Europe?* pp. 63–92; Ray Hudson, "The Role of Foreign Investment," in Evans, Johnson and Thomas, *Northern Region Economy,* pp. 79–95.

54. J. Bridge, "The Regional Impacts of Inward Investment in Europe: A Study of the North of England," *Regional Prospects in Europe* 3 (1993): 33–57.

55. Roland van Tulder and Wilfried Ruigrok, "Regionalisation, Globalisation, or Glocalisation: The Case of the World Car Industry," in *The Impact of Globalisation on Europe's Firms and Industries,* ed. Marc Humbert (London: Pinter, 1993), pp. 22–33.

56. Bridge, "The Regional Impacts of Inward Investment in Europe," pp. 53–57.

57. David Sadler and Ash Amin, "'Europeanisation'" in the Automotive Components Sector and Its Implications for State and Locality," in Hudson and Schamp, *Towards a New Map of Automobile Manufacturing in Europe?,* pp. 39–62.

58. Ray Hudson, "Regional Futures: Industrial Restructuring, New Production Concepts, and Spatial Development Strategies in Europe," *Regional Studies,* 1997: 76–128.

59. F. Peck and I. Stone, "Japanese Inward Investment in the North-East of England; Reassessing Japanization," *Environment and Planning C,* 11 (1993): 56–67.

60. Philip Garrahan and Paul Stewart, *The Nissan Enigma: Flexibility at Work in a Local Economy* (plaats: Mansell, 1992).

61. Jamie Peck, *Workplace* (London: Guilford, 1996).

62. C. Beattie, S. Fothergill, T. Gore, and A. Herrington, *The Real Level of Unemployment* (Sheffield, England: Sheffield Hallam University, 1997).

63. Organization for Economic Co-operation and Development, *Labour Productivity Levels in OECD Countries* (Paris: OECD, 1997).

64. Jamie Peck and A. Tickell, "Local Modes of Social Regulation? Regulation Theory, Thatcherism, and Uneven Development," *Geoforum* 23 (1992): 347–363.

65. H. Radice, "The National Economy—a Keynesian Myth?" *Capital and Class* 22 (1984): 111–140.

66. M. Bienefeld, "Is a Strong National Economy a Utopian Goal at the End of the Twentieth Century?" in *States Against Markets: The Limits of Globalisation*, ed. R. Boyer and D. Drache (London: Routledge, 1995), pp. 415–441. Emphasis added.

14

Globalization, the European Market, and the Urban Regions: The Case of Southern Germany

Eike Schamp

Globalization: this one word evokes the far-reaching anticipation of change, the feelings of uncertainty, fear, and, sometimes, hope for future well-being that are so common in old industrialized regions and countries. In public debate, globalization seems responsible for a variety of very different changes currently taking place. This might seem to make it easy for scholars to dismiss the concept. However, it has gained significance as transnational corporations skip over national boundaries in their strategic organization of functions, sites, and flows, producing an increasing tertiarization in all highly developed countries.[1] In addition, global financial markets have emerged, defying national regulations and financial policies. Both processes were facilitated by new technologies that resulted in substantial reductions in the transport costs of goods, personnel, and information.

In economic terms, globalization can be interpreted roughly as an extension of markets. Since Adam Smith, scholars have agreed on the idea that the division of labor is dependent on the extent of the market. In consequence, globalization means a fast-growing specialization of economic activities among sectors, firms, and regions. This, in turn, makes the presence of nodes increasingly necessary to further the exchange of commodities, personnel, and information and to coordinate and control production—in short, to govern the contemporary capitalist system. The current debate on world cities and global cities makes it obvious that scholars see the urban system as enabling the emergence of globalization while at the same time being affected by it.[2]

Figure 14.1   The Pattern of Agglomerating in Germany in the 1990's

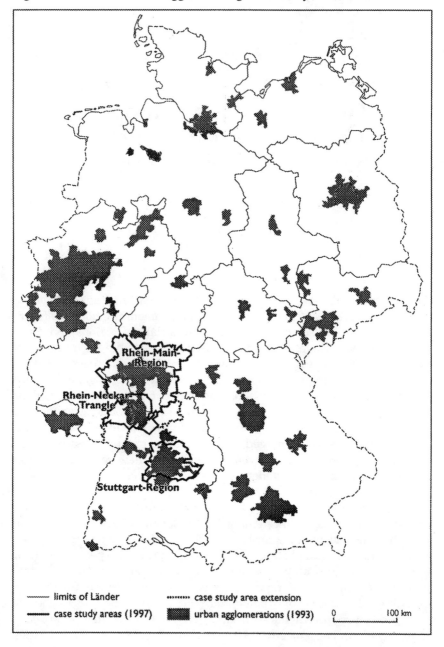

How a particular city performs under globalization—that is, whether it will be a "winner" or "loser" in the process—is often seen as a question of local resources, local heritage and knowledge base, and local action. But what does *local* mean here?

For some time, administrative reorganization has not followed economic suburbanization. Furthermore, the traditional concept of an urban core, dominating a dependent suburbia, is no longer valid. Now economic actors form regional networks across the entire space of the urban agglomeration area. In consequence, core cities increasingly are obliged to look for cooperation with suburban municipalities and firms if they want to improve their competitive position. As a result, they are driven to take advantage of networking as well.

In my view, however, there is no *direct* link between processes of globalization and economic changes in a particular city. What affects the urban economic base is rather an interwoven system of expanding markets, new (international) economic competitors, changing state regulation (i.e., deregulation and reregulation), increasing social pressures, and various attempts to foster the local political base. Increasing suburbanization in recent decades suggests that the appropriate administrative level for economic political response is not the core city alone but a wider urban agglomeration area or urban region. Although the tension between the urban core and suburbia is not new and the debate about a political and administrative reorganization was sharp and controversial in Germany during the 1960s and 1970s, it is the current economic crisis that has given a major push to new political action. "Old" solutions are newly discussed, such as the incorporation of suburban municipalities into a larger city and the establishment of a regional district. But it is obvious that new solutions that are less hierarchical and more cooperative in scope gain more impetus in the public debate. Networking matters more, particularly if the membership of a network will include economic institutions as well as the various planning authorities.

In this chapter I will analyze some attempts to cope with the changes in the economic structure of cities, especially those that master increasing regional competition through cooperative relationships between core cities and surrounding communities. I will focus on three urban agglomeration areas in southern Germany. When comparing these with similar processes in other countries we have to bear in mind the particular decentralized urban system in Germany, in which cities are subject to global competition according to their economic specialization. In addition, we have to take into account Germany's political system, which produces the diversified relationships between different state actors who set the framework for "local" action: first, a federal state losing competencies in favor of the European Commission but, nevertheless, disposing of powerful means to intervene in local (urban) trajectories; second, the unfocused intervention of the states (*Länder*) whose role is strengthened by the European Commission; and third, different local capabilities for the concerted action of communal administration and other local institutions, such as chambers of commerce and firms. Within this framework, the chapter will deal with current economic trends and the response of regional actors, such as political institutions, economic intermediaries (in particular, chambers of commerce[3]), economic associations, and those large firms that pursue strategies that have a major impact on the urban economy.

Three urban agglomeration areas in southern Germany will be considered: the Region Rhein Main, the Region Stuttgart, and the Rhine Neckar Triangle. They differ in size of population (4.3 million, 2.6 million, and 1.9 million, respectively), in economic base and economic strength (their 1992 annual gross value added amounted to 220 billion DM, 125 billion DM, and 85 billion DM, respectively), and in their ability to build a new urban region. It is argued that historically grown characteristics, including the economic base of the urban agglomeration area, have a major impact on the process of region building and its outcome.

Following Michael Porter and Dieter Läpple,[4] I will analyze the regional economy in terms of its structure of *clusters*, or interrelated economic activities around a key sector. These clusters are a major factor determining the rise (and decline) of regional economies. Present globalizing tendencies may affect the competitiveness of the key sector and related activities, making a regional response necessary. Before analyzing these issues I will briefly discuss two factors that play a major role in present urban region building in Germany: the role of the European Commission and the current crisis of local labor markets in Germany.

The Role of the European Commission in Region Building

In the process leading to the consolidation of a single European market, the region has become increasingly significant—both in the Commission's policies and in the public debate about a "Europe of the Regions."[5] But what constitutes "the region" in this debate? The organization of a federal state in Germany gave the Länder a high degree of autonomy, making them among the first to establish "embassies" in Brussels for regional lobbying. The Commission was soon convinced that the Länder were the appropriate regions in Germany.[6] The Maastricht Treaty, however, did not strengthen the role of urban agglomerations in the European integration process.[7] Large cities are only represented in Brussels through their *Land* government.[8]

Some urban agglomeration areas in Germany had accumulated considerable experience in regional cooperation, in particular in the area of physical planning. However, the privatization and/or regionalization of public facilities have recently reduced the cities' significance in this respect. Thus, organizations such as the Siedlungsverband Ruhrkohlenbezirk, Grossraum Hannover, or Umlandverband Frankfurt have either failed or have remained restricted to a limited number of local activities. The attempt to create a regional district as a way to integrate municipalities on a larger scale also failed, partly because municipalities at the suburban fringe resisted the effort.

In recent times, the economic pressures generated by increasing unemployment in the core cities and conflicts about land utilization at the urban fringes have brought new actors into play. Economic interest organizations, such as the chambers of commerce and local decision makers, have combined their efforts to create new regional institutions for business development—leading to the emergence of a new type of urban region. This development may foster the economic base of the *Land* while undermining its political power.

The German Labor Markets in Crisis

Regional economies still belong to a national economy, and the long-term development of this economy, combined with the political and social responses at the level of the nation state, does matter.[9] In spring 1997, unemployment in Germany officially reached the level of 4.7 million people. The rate had been increasing very gradually to this extreme level for more than two decades, but it appeared that the public became aware of it now rather suddenly.

Since the end of the Second World War, Germany's economic success was identified mainly with the particular structure of its manufacturing industry and the societal organization of the production system. The strength of Germany's manufacturing resided in capital goods production: chemical industries, automobile production, mechanical engineering, and electro-technical industries. These are the sectors that dominate manufacturing in the regions discussed in this chapter. This development of the German economy was supported by a particular societal model that has emerged gradually since the 1950s and is referred to as *Rhenanian capitalism*.

Previously, Germany had a corporatist system through which the large manufacturing firms and the banks cooperated closely and the *Mittelstand* or middle class occupied a position of great importance.[10] Trade unions were integrated into the system after the Second World War, an integration that was consolidated by the 1972 workers participation law. Problem solving under this system was done by consensus rather than conflict.

After the Second World War, the Korean crisis created new possibilities and helped economic recovery. In the 1970s the oil crisis was successfully managed and major problems were averted. Growth continued uninterrupted through the 1980s. There were no pressures to change the societal system, despite increasing unemployment. According to Frieder Naschold, there was little awareness among leading decision makers that the world economic system had changed fundamentally during the late 1980s and early 1990s.[11] First, the Japanese were conquering those markets that were most important for the German capital goods industries, particularly in car and machine tool manufacturing. Japan's flexible ("lean") production models proved to be more efficient, and it was only after the publication of analyses like James Womack's[12] that this fact reached public consciousness. Second, new competitors, particularly in electronics, mechanical engineering, and the production of standard goods, emerged from Southeast Asian countries. Only the chemical industries were not that much affected by increasing global competition. Third, the growth of a Single European Market forced strategy changes upon German firms that still mainly depended on a European import-export market. Finally, the opening up of Eastern Europe and the transformation of post-socialist societies brought serious competition from nearby low-cost production localities.

Societal response to these challenges was hesitant. Among the major European nations, Germany had the lowest average productivity increases. The necessary modernization of the production apparatus and its organization was slow in coming. The unexpected unification of West and Eastern Germany produced a short economic boom that hid the structural crisis from society. The socioeconomic system had lost its flexibility, leading some experts to conclude that, as a result of its long-standing economic success, the German model appeared to have lost the ability to react to crises and learn from them. This holds particularly true for the regulatory and institutional systems. The current public discussion on deregulation and changes in the tax structure and the social security system are an example of the continuing resistance to change.

In 1992–1993, the crisis became apparent to everyone. The demand boom created by the unification process had been fed both by a transfer of purchasing power from West to East and an increase in the federal state's deficit spending, a strategy that could not be sustained. When demand broke down, the cumulative effects of both short-term and long-term weaknesses contributed to a crisis of the German economy.

This situation was made worse by the growing influence of the European Commission in structural matters of economic policy, particularly in the areas of regional policy and competition. Increasingly, the commission has seen reason to intervene in the subsidies that have been granted by the federal state and the different Länder to large companies, enabling them to make huge investments.[13] The rising capital needs of the state in financing the unification and making the preparations for entering the European Monetary Union resulted at times in an overvaluation of the national currency, harming the international competitiveness of the German manufacturing sector.

This was the socioeconomic environment in which the different urban agglomeration areas were embedded. In these areas, which shared a history of early industrialization, increasing unemployment led to serious financial problems as a result of rising social expenditures.[14] Even the prosperous urban agglomeration areas of southern Germany began to suffer from the labor market crisis. The next sections will analyze their response, conditioned by their economic history, the effects of globalizing influences, the social fragmentation between core and suburbia, and the impact of newly emerging political institutions.

I will review the different strategies designed to cope with the crisis, including, first, the modernization of the urban fabric through large projects in infrastructure that required financial support from outside sources (such as the Land, the federal state, or the private sector), and second, the coordination of the different communal economic policies through the building of an urban region. I will conclude with more general evaluative remarks on the process of urban region building in Germany.

The Region Rhein Main

The Region Rhein Main (RRM) is one of the most important urban agglomeration areas in Germany and even in Europe. It has more than 4 million inhabitants and in 1992 produced a gross value added of approximately 220 billion DM, more than some smaller European countries. The region is multipolar, with Frankfurt am Main as its core city. Its territory goes beyond the borders of the Land of Hesse into the Länder of Rhineland-Palatinate and Bavaria and has two Land capitals within its borders, Wiesbaden and Mainz, capitals of the states of Hesse and Rhineland-Palatinate. The competition between these cities located in different Länder has complicated the region building process.

The development of the region in recent decades has been quite spectacular. The original industrial structure dates back to the second half of the nineteenth century, when the citizens of Frankfurt refused the establishment of manufacturing industries within the city boundaries and forced then to settle in neighboring municipalities, such as Hoechst (chemical plants), Offenbach (mechanical engineering), Darmstadt (pharmaceuticals and cosmetics), Rüsselsheim (automobile production), and Aschaffenburg (clothing industries).

The integration of these heterogeneous structures into one urban agglomeration area was the result of the growth of the city of Frankfurt after the Second World War. Like Munich,[15] Frankfurt profited from the division of Germany, although in a different way. Domestic traffic flows turned from West-East (from the Ruhr Area to Berlin) to South-North (from Munich and Stuttgart to Hamburg), making Frankfurt the central node in car and rail traffic. The airport was expanded to become one of the leading European airports in passenger traffic and cargo. Both developments made Frankfurt into a major center for distribution and business services. In addition, national state institutions had relocated from Berlin and Leipzig to Frankfurt after the partition of Germany. The new federal organization of the national state resulted in the establishment of the two Land capitals, Wiesbaden and Mainz, increasing the importance of the public sector within the RRM. Finally, the establishment of the American headquarters in Frankfurt after the Second World War led to the organization in Frankfurt of the Bank Deutscher Länder, the predecessor of the Bundesbank, and contributed to Frankfurt becoming a financial center. It followed that the first foreign firms coming to Frankfurt were American.

Tertiarization of the regional economy advanced rapidly, particularly during the 1980s. The inflow of foreign firms increased spectacularly in the 1990s, and now Frankfurt has emerged as a European distribution node, if not a global node controlling the German economy and articulating it with the global economy.[16] At first sight, the region looks like a winner within the context of globalizing tendencies.

A Heterogeneous System of Economic Clusters

In the course of this regional development process, a very heterogeneous economic structure has emerged in the RRM, consisting of the following clusters:

1. different industrial clusters in the chemical, automobile, and mechanical engineering sectors that form the traditional manufacturing base of the RRM and have been facing increasing competition for quite some time;
2. a financial cluster that gained importance during the 1980s, leading to an emerging global role of Frankfurt ("Bankfurt");[17]
3. a heterogeneous cluster of business services, mainly composed of control functions such as auditing, consultancy, and so on, as well as distribution functions such as communication, advertising, and distribution proper.

First we will deal with the industrial clusters. The deindustrialization in the traditional manufacturing clusters continued through the 1980s, causing rising unemployment and a narrowing tax base. The impetus for deindustrialization has taken different forms, including relocation, crisis, and bankruptcies, as well as automation and rationalization combined with specialization of production. Another major cause of deindustrialization is the increasing tertiarization of manufacturing firms, particularly through the shifts from production to services and R&D. The RRM emerged as one of the leading industrial research regions in Germany, besides Munich and Stuttgart. The Opel research labs are now the central labs for General Motors outside the United States. Some Japanese car manufacturers, namely, Honda, Mazda, and Mitsubishi, also founded R&D labs in the region that mainly produce modern "European" design. Next to the large R&D labs of local firms (such as Hoechst Corporation), many small development departments of foreign firms were established in the RRM region, changing it into a market-driven, design-oriented knowledge center.[18]

The only "pure" manufacturing sector remained the cluster of chemical industries driven by leading global firms. According to a 1995 study on production in the German chemical industry, this sector has not joined the worldwide trend toward productivity increases through the adoption of lean management strategies.[19] What would happen to the region if the sector caught up? At this point, though still a leading cluster in the region, manufacturing has become more a part of the regional labor market problem than its solution.

The financial cluster is often considered to be the main growth sector of the urban economy of Frankfurt. Frankfurt has a long history as a center for banks and fairs.[20] Today, its importance in this area is inseparably bound to the location of the central bank (Deutsche Bundesbank) and the success of the German economy after the Second World War. Frankfurt emerged as a major financial center in several phases. After the war, the Bank Deutscher Länder (later Bundesbank) was obliged to locate near the American headquarters. When the Federal Republic of Germany regained monetary sovereignty in 1957, the large German private banks began relocating in Frankfurt. The city developed into Germany's leading banking center and stock exchange at the expense of other cities, such as Düsseldorf. These financial activities internationalized during the 1980s and 1990s (see Table 15.1), when leading foreign banks established in the city. In the meantime, the financial cluster of Frankfurt has been developing activities in the region, either through back offices in neighboring municipalities, such as Eschborn and Offenbach, or through the establishment of specialized financial institutions, including leasing companies and insurance companies, in surrounding towns like Mainz, Bad Homburg, and Wiesbaden.

Frankfurt was threatened with the loss of the central bank in the wake of Germany's reunification in 1990. A change of law was necessary to prevent the bank from moving to the new capital, Berlin. The creation of a European Monetary Union diminished the importance of national central banks. The establishment of the European Central Bank in Frankfurt may compensate for this loss, although it remains quite uncertain to what extent this will help maintain Frankfurt's role as a leading financial center in Europe.

In terms of employment, the financial sector is not the leading growth sector of the regional economy, employing only 14.4 percent the workforce in the city of Frankfurt in 1994.[21] Manufacturing is still more important, but the cluster of diversified business services is of still greater importance. Control and consultancy activities are increasing as Frankfurt has developed into a major center for accountancy and legal services. In addition, a marketing subcluster is emerging, formed by activities such as communication, advertisement, logistical services, and marketing. In the subcluster of business services, foreign firms have played a major role already for quite some time; the influx of foreign firms into the subcluster of distribution appears to be a rather recent phenomenon. Frankfurt and the RRM are now emerging as a major distribution node for the German market and neighboring countries, including Eastern Europe. This cluster's success is based on steady reinvestment in transport infrastructure, such as the international airport, the metropolitan area information networks, and road and railway infrastructure.

Table 14.1　Banking at Frankfurt, 1953–1996

Type of Bank	1953	1970	1982	1993	1996
Headquarters of German banks	69	73	74	71	68
Subsidiaries of German banks	11	35	56	51	76
Foreign banks	—	8	39	84	95
Branches of foreign banks	3	13	46	43	48
Representation of foreign banks	—	14	90	128	105
Other banks	2	14	2	—	—

Source: Elaboration of data from Ruth Bördlein, "Frankgurt als Zentrum hochrangiger Diestleistungen: Das Beispiel des Finanzbereichs," in *Das Rhein-Main-Gebiet: Aktuelle Strukturen und Entwicklungsprobleme,* ed. Günter Meyer (mainz, Germany: Geogr. Insitut der Johann Gutenberg Universität, 1995); *LBZ 1996.*

Joint Strategy of Cluster Protection and Region Building

What motivates the new efforts to build an urban region? Apart from Munich, the RRM is the only urban agglomeration area in Germany where during the last two decades employment levels were maintained. According to recent estimates employment will even slightly increase, by 0.6 percent per year, until the year 2000.[22] Nevertheless, in the city of Frankfurt itself unemployment has risen. Increasing immigration, particularly from foreign countries,[23] and the outmigration of middle-class and upper-class families from the city to the suburban fringes have caused a social fragmentation of the population and have generated a certain uneasiness about the social and economic future of the RRM.[24] In the political arena, local political parties clash with economic actors who demand policies that will improve the international competitiveness of the urban agglomeration area.

The investments to maintain and develop the economic base of the RRM, however, cannot be made through efforts of the city government alone. Support from other political institutions or economic actors will be necessary. To support the financial cluster, in 1996 the city promoted the creation of the first private metropolitan area network in Germany.[25] In addition, the government of the state of Hesse urged the university and private banks to improve the knowledge base of the financial sector through a newly created Center for Financial Studies and donated professorships in banking to the university. As for the business services cluster, investment into a new "Cargo City South" recently strengthened the airport's role as the leading European cargo node, using those areas that were formerly occupied by the American airbase. Whether the manufacturing cluster could play a new role in regional development, for example through new industrial technologies in the field of environmental protection,[26] is a major concern of the Umlandverband Frankfurt.

The Umlandverband Frankfurt is the result of earlier attempts at the intermunicipal coordination of activities. It was created in 1975 and given the responsibility for planning and public facilities. However, the organization never managed to cover the total economic area of Rhein Main, nor was it given sufficient decisionmaking power to have an impact on economic development in the region.[27] There are even questions about its survival today. The increasing competition among cities would require more efficient forms of regional cooperation.

Frankfurt's political elites, however, lack consensus about the future economic trajectory of the city. As a result, new institutions serving the integration of the urban region are still rather scarce. The regional chambers of commerce joined efforts in 1990 to try to stimulate regional initiatives, but they had little success. In 1995, local actors, including the

Umlandverband, more than sixty-five municipalities, chambers of commerce, and large infrastructure providers (such as the airport company), established a registered society for business development—Verein Wirtschaftsförderung Frankfurt/Rhein-Main e.V. The Rhein Main area was not totally covered by this society, as the cities of Wiesbaden and Mainz and the Bavarian districts were excluded. The head office was allocated to the Umlandverband, in effect identifying the effort as a local administrative initiative. Its activities included an improvement of local site management, local and regional marketing, and the organization of information services. In 1996, several large firms established the Wirtschaftsinitiative Frankfurt Rhein-Main e.V. as a registered society, with the objective of fostering regional economic projects and supporting the business development society. However, the financial sector did not participate. In all, these efforts still meet with rather limited participation and operate with different regional settings in mind.

The Region Stuttgart

The characteristics of Baden-Württemberg as an "industrial district" are extensively debated. On the one hand, scholars present Baden-Württemberg as a region characterized by new, flexible, post-Fordist forms of industrial organization. Others prefer to see the Land as a particularly successful example of Fordist organization of production.[28] The Stuttgart region is only one of the industrial regions of the state, although it is the most important one.[29] It has 2.5 million inhabitants and produces a gross value added of 125 billion DM, slightly over half of what RRM produces. The region ranks second among Germany's manufacturing regions, surpassed only by the Ruhr area.[30] Manufacturing is dominated by labor-intensive production of capital goods and is heavily oriented toward exports. Stuttgart represents one of Europe's most prosperous and competitive industrial regions. It is an example of late industrialization, although efforts at industrial and technological development date back to the nineteenth century.[31] The great economic success, however, came after the Second World War, when the regional economy showed such fast and consistent growth that the region was considered safe from crisis.[32]

A Unique Industrial Cluster

The most important industrial activities in the region are taking place in three different sectors: first, car manufacturing, with Mercedes-Benz in a dominant position; second, the electrical industry, with world-renowned firms like Bosch, Hewlett-Packard, and IBM; and third, mechanical engineering, with a major presence of small and medium-sized firms. Combined, these sectors contribute 46 percent to regional GDP. They form a unique cluster around one core: Mercedes-Benz. This firm is by far the largest employer of the region and has the biggest plant. Actually, together with its suppliers—among them many companies of the electrical industry and mechanical engineering—the firm represents a regional production complex. In 1992, Mercedes bought more than 90 percent of its inputs within the region.[33]

The industrial apparatus consists of a cluster of large plants surrounded by a great number of small and medium-sized firms. There are eighteen such plants with more than one thousand employees in Stuttgart.[34] They employ three-quarters of the manufacturing workforce in the city. Production is mostly labor-intensive but the skill levels of the workforce are not as high as is often assumed; according to Hans Braczyk and his colleagues,[35] they are even below the German average. In addition, there has been a considerable tertiarization of jobs within those manufacturing firms headquartered in the region. The number of R&D jobs in particular has increased; 42 percent of R&D jobs in the Land Baden-Württemberg are now found in the Region Stuttgart.[36]

In the 1990s, the region entered into a crisis already foreseen in a 1988 study predicting that it would become "the Ruhr Area of the 1990s."[37] The region's industrial products are now considered to be "overengineered" and captured in a high price trap.[38] Employment in the manufacturing sectors decreased by almost one hundred thousand between 1991 and 1994.[39] Workforce reduction continued through subsequent years.[40]

The segments of the local labor market that were dominated by Mercedes-Benz have shown above average unemployment rates as the auto industry dismissed about one-quarter of its workforce within five years.[41] The electrical industry and mechanical engineering followed at about the same pace, resulting in the current situation, in which the three sectors employ together fewer people than they did in 1980.

Judging on the basis of these developments, the firms have quickly learned to translate strategies of lean management into action, particularly in the automobile and electronics industries.[42] In car manufacturing, the strategy of lean production as a means to cut costs had been supported by an unexpected depreciation of the German mark against the U.S. dollar in 1996 and 1997, enabling firms like Mercedes-Benz and Porsche to regain profitability. The sector of mechanical engineering, however, had not yet found an adequate answer to global competition.[43] Its position was weakened by the growing importance of global sourcing in the automobile industry and the disappearance of supplier and machine tool firms, which further reduced opportunities to source regionally.[44]

Efforts to Improve the Economic Base

The answer to the crisis was sought in collective entrepreneurship, a close cooperation between the public and private sectors that might, according to some authors, even lead to the emergence of a new "Model Baden-Württemberg."[45] This strategy produced several initiatives, including the following:

1. After long negotiations with the workers council, Mercedes-Benz decided to invest in a new plant for a new generation of high-powered engines (six and eight cylinders) at Cannstadt. Production costs were drastically reduced, both by changing the design of the engines and by integrating the plant into a worldwide production network. Approximately 2 billion DM have been invested, but no employment has been created. Instead, the workers council accepted changes that implemented wage controls and made the work organization more flexible.

2. The Land Baden-Württemberg reinforced the traditional instruments of its technology-oriented policy. It established an academy for technology assessment in 1992, created the Zukunftsmission Wirtschaft 2000 (Commission for the Future Economy 2000), and organized a council for innovations. These organizations advise both firms and political decision makers.

3. In 1994, the Land parliament passed a law creating the Verband Region Stuttgart, a new regional political organization with its own regional parliament. The main objective of this initiative was to foster regional cooperation. Actions included the establishment of a Business Development Society Region Stuttgart (1995) with the participation of different interest groups such as municipalities, chambers of commerce, unions, and the central bank of the Land Baden-Württemberg. Initiatives included the organization of an employment program for the long-term unemployed, regional marketing, tourism, sports, and culture.

4. Both the federal and the Land governments have financed large infrastructural projects in roads, railways, and airports.

5. Finally, politicians and entrepreneurs together have undertaken initiatives to diversify the economy and to reduce dependency on the dominating industrial cluster. The publishing and printing houses of the region and other media institutions, such as public television, joined in a multimedia project with the participation of the major electronics firms.

However, these projects also demonstrate the vulnerability of "collective entrepreneurship" and of cooperation between private firms and the state where the strategies of the region and the strategies of the dominating firm do not coincide.

The Rhein Neckar Triangle

The Rhein Neckar Triangle (RNT) is the smallest urban agglomeration area of the three discussed here. It has about 1.9 million inhabitants and produced a gross value added of 85 billion DM in 1992. The RNT ranks sixth among the urban agglomerations in Germany, but it differs from others in that its urban structure is polycentric; moreover, the region covers territory in three different Länder (Baden-Württemberg, Rhineland-Palatinate, and Hesse). Mannheim, with its three hundred thousand inhabitants, is presently too small to fulfill the role of a core city that could dominate the region, but it was the place where industrialization began in the nineteenth century, much earlier than in the Kingdom of Württemberg or in the city of Stuttgart. In Mannheim the early chemical industry and mechanical engineering firms were founded, followed by the early automobile industry, based on Carl Benz's invention. The chemical industry, led by the giant firm BASF, later relocated to Ludwigshafen on the opposite bank of the Rhein River.[46]

The RNT has remained a highly industrialized region, relatively untouched by the strong trend toward deindustrialization that is found elsewhere. Among the total workforce, 47 percent are still employed in manufacturing; in Ludwigshafen, as much as 66 percent.[47] Large plants had already emerged at the beginning of this century. Now there are mainly branch plants or subsidiaries of large companies. Tertiarization has been developing rather slowly.

A Fragmented Economy Without Clusters

The manufacturing sector of the RNT largely consists of isolated industries with separate locations, creating local specialization and dominance. The chemical industry, with its main location in Ludwigshafen (BASF), forms Europe's largest single industrial complex, employing forty-five thousand workers (1996). The city of Ludwigshafen has become a company town, fully dependent on BASF. The chemical industry has refrained from implementing strategies of lean production and flexibilization.[48] Surprisingly enough, this has not affected its performance, not even in difficult economic times. The firms in this sector have internationalized their activities but have kept their industrial core at the old sites, which is also where their research capacity is located.

The electronics industry is of principal importance in the city of Mannheim, employing 28 percent of the industrial workforce.[49] The largest employer is ABB, Asea Brown Boveri, a company occupying about 70 percent of this branch of industry.[50] The company emerged from a merger between the Swedish Asea and the Swiss Brown Boveri in 1988.

Mercedes-Benz is the largest employer in the engineering sector with ten thousand workers, or 60 percent of the employment in this sector in the region. Employment at Mercedes-Benz is under pressure because of intense competition within the market segment they occupy. The company has invested heavily in a production network involving different locations outside the region (Kassel, Gaggenau, Wörth) and—with cooperation from the workers councils—in the reorganization of production in the Mannheim and Stuttgart plants, leading to higher flexibility and lower wage costs, while preventing job loss.

The dominating presence of large firms in most industrial branches has given them a greater ability to weather the storms of international competition. In contrast, the branch of mechanical engineering—historically the leading branch in Mannheim—had been dominated by medium-sized firms, which has made it vulnerable. It has suffered closures and bankruptcies and presently ranks third.[51] The growth of regional gross value added has remained below average in recent years, and unemployment in Mannheim has become the highest of Baden-Württemberg.[52] This is undoubtedly also a result of the insufficient tertiarization of the regional economy.

The RNT—In What Sense a Region?

Given the needs and problems of industrial development in the region, one might have expected an early emphasis on political coordination in the RNT. In practice, however, regional initiatives have remained weak. Several factors contribute to this development. First, the location of the region within the territory of three different Länder has reduced political support.[53] Second, the absence of a dominating urban core leads to political fragmentation and makes regional initiatives difficult. The heterogeneity of industrial structures and local specialization cause further complications. Finally, the political milieu of an old industrialized city, Mannheim, characterized by the close cooperation between social democratic local government and the trade union movement, has contributed to political stagnation that in turn has hampered the implementation of much needed economic changes.[54]

Nevertheless, new movements have emerged to create a region. In August 1989, the three cities, the chambers of commerce, and the regional planning agency established the Rhein Neckar Triangle as a registered society. The society was joined by municipalities, districts, and almost a hundred private firms and institutions, including the largest of the region.

The society proved so successful that other districts joined in, leading to an expansion of the region to the French-German border in 1997.

The different administrative, political, and economic actors in the region were successfully brought together for a number of different projects:

1. Activities in different fields of action (such as culture, sports, the formation of a regional image, and public relations) were designed to make the region part of public consciousness.
2. Activities aimed at structural change through technological change; the region succeeded—on the basis again of public-private partnerships—in attracting federal funds to support further developments in the field of biotechnology.[55]
3. Activities intended to attract business from outside the region. In 1996, a private company for regional marketing was founded that will take care of all activities related to regional business development.

Conclusions

Global competition has increasingly influenced the dynamics of the local labor market and has affected the economic base of cities. The attempts to build urban regions in a cooperative and collaborative way should be considered as a strategy to respond to these developments. This chapter has examined the experience of three urban agglomeration areas in Southern Germany. To these experiences, we could easily add those of Munich and Hannover.[56] European cities are increasingly competing with each other in their efforts to build urban regions. The more prosperous urban agglomeration areas in Germany are at the forefront of this kind of cooperative urban region building.

This strategy requires cooperation between the administration of core cities and urban fringes, economic institutions and private firms. Obviously, there are different methods and different degrees of cooperation. Problems of coordination and cooperation are not easily settled within local administrations (core and suburbia), or between administrations, chambers of commerce, and private firms. In RNT, the "region" has taken the form of a registered society, with administrations, chambers, and private firms as members. The Region Stuttgart has been pursuing other strategies of region building, and appears to be the most successful case at present. I suggest the following explanation:

1. the long and successful presence of institutions fostering technological change and entrepreneurial activities;[57]

2. the strong interest that the different governments of the Land Baden-Württemberg have always manifest in the well-being of the region as the core of its territory with the City of Stuttgart as its dominating center;

3. the presence of only one dominating cluster in the region consisting of core firms with headquarters and core plants.

In contrast to earlier attempts at regional cooperation, which were mainly oriented toward coordination of physical planning, the new forms of cooperative urban region building are meant to promote economic development and regional competitiveness. Naturally, the first decisions made in the new urban region concern the organization of a regional business development agency. In the process they may integrate the earlier initiatives in physical planning, but they go far beyond the scope of these efforts in creating a movement of public-private partnerships directed toward regional development. The presence of large companies is essential in urban region building; although they may be under competitive squeeze, most will not easily disinvest and withdraw from the region. Their interest in R&D and the modernization of production will facilitate the structural changes in the regional economies that are forced upon them by projects of supranational integration and the effects of economic internationalization.[58]

The cooperative management in the new urban regions has similar strategies: first, to create a business development agency; then, to foster the development of modern technologies, such as biotechnology or media technology; and third, to support economic targets through a broad range of activities in support of "soft" location factors such as culture, leisure, and sports. In addition, there is also an important role for the nation state in determining economic management in urban regions. Most large-scale investment in infrastructure has remained the responsibility of the federal government or of national public institutions, such as the federal railway corporation. Federal technological policies favor some urban regions over others, as is also the case with financial policies (the example of Frankfurt is instructive here). In addition there are other, more general effects of federal influence: the revaluation of the German currency several years ago caused a crisis in many export-oriented sectors, but the current depreciation of the currency has created new export perspectives for the mechanical engineering sector and the automobile and chemical industries. National policies are defined primarily to maintain the economic strength of the national economy. They influence the debate on a common EU currency and on technology policies. In this respect, they may still have a greater impact on future regional economic development than the new institutions involved in urban region building and may prove to increase the competitiveness and economic success of the large urban agglomeration areas in Europe.

Notes

1. Eike W. Schamp, "Globalisierung von Produktionsnetzen," *Geographische Zeitschrift*, no. 84 (1996): 205–219.

2. Jan Lambooy, "The European City: From Carrefour to Organisational Nexus," *TESG*, no. 84 (Winter 1993): 258–268; Paul L. Knox and Peter J. Taylor, eds., *World Cities in a World System* (Cambridge: Cambridge University Press, 1995).

3. German Chambers of Industry and Commerce are compulsory associations of firms in both sectors.

4. Michael Porter, *Competitive Advantage of Nations* (Basingstoke, England: McMillan, 1994); Dieter Läpple, "Die Teilökonomien einer Großstadt in einer Phase strukturellen Umbruchs: Das Beispiel Hamburg," in *Regionalentwicklung und regionale Arbeitspolitik*, ed. Uwe Blien, Hayo Herrmann, and Martin Koller (Nuremberg: Institut für Arbeitsmarkt- und Berufsforschung der Bundesanstalt für Arbeit, 1994), pp. 106–139.

5. Ute Bauer, *Europa der Regionen-swischen Anspruch und Wirklichkeit* (Vienna: Österreichische Akademie der Wissenschaften, 1994).

6. Michael Chapman, "Le role de L'Union Europeenne dans le developpement economique local," in *Du local au global: Les initiative locales pour le developpement economique en Europe et en Amerique*, ed. Christophe Demaziere (Paris: L'Harmattan, 1996), pp. 191–209.

7. In fact, it was Jacques Delors who encouraged the Länder when he was president of the European Commission.

8. New forms of city networks are arising that may slightly change this situation; see, for example, the Eurocities network.

9. Paul Hirst and Grahame Thompson, *Globalization in Question: The International Economy and the Possibilities of Governance* (Cambridge: Polity Press, 1996).

10. Werner Abelshauser, *Wirtschaftsgeschichte der Bundesrepublik Deutschland, 1945–1980* (Frankfurt/Main: Suhrkamp, 1983).

11. Frieder Naschold, "Jenseits des baden-württembergischen 'Exceptionalism': Strukturprobleme der deutsche Industrie," in *Kurswechsel in der Industrie: Lean production in Baden-Württemberg*, ed. Hans-Joachim Braczyk and Gerd Schienstock (Stuttgart: Kohlhammer, 1996), pp. 184–212.

12. James Womack, Daniel Jones, and Daniel Ross, *The Machine that Changed the World* (New York: Maxwell MacMillan International, 1990).

13. Läpple, "Die Teilökonomien einer Großstadt in einer Phase strukturellen Umbruchs: Das Beispiel Hamburg."

14. Helmut Seitz, "Die Städte in Baden-Württemberg: Beschaftigung, Infrastruktur, und kommunale Finanzen," *ZEW Wirtschaftanalysen*, no. 2 (1994): 5–34.

15. Bodo Freund, "Die Entwicklung von Wirtschaftund Bevölkerung im Rhein-Main-Gebiet," in *Rhein-Main, Die Region: Vorträge zu Wirtschaft,*

Verkeht, Umwelt, und Bevölkerung, ed. Stadt Mainz (Mainz, Germany: Amt für Stadtentwicklung und Statistik, 1993).

16. Klaus Ronneberger and Roger Keil, "Ausser Atem—Frankfurt nach der Postmoderne," in *Capitales Fatales: Urbanisierung und Politik in den Finanzmetropolen Frankfurt und Zürich,* ed. Hitz et al. (Zürich: Rotpunktverlag, 1995), pp. 284–353.

17. Ruth Bördlein, "Das Rhein-Main-Gebiet als Standort hochrangiger Dienstleistungen: Stand und Perspektiven des Internationalisierungsprozesses einer Region," *Rhein-Mainische Forschungen,* no. 110 (1993); and Ronneberger and Keil, "Ausser Atem-Frankfurt nach der Postmoderne," pp. 284–353.

18. See, for example, Andrew Mair, *Honda, a Global Local Corporation* (Basingstoke, England: Macmillan, 1994).

19. Harald Bathelt, "Global Competition, International Trade, and Regional Concentration: The Case of the German Chemical Industry During the 1980's," *Environment and Planning C: Government and Policy,* no. 13 (1995): 395–424; Harald Bathelt, *Technologischer Wandel, Arbeitsteilung, und Standortstruktur in der Chemischen Industrie der Bundesrepublik Deutschland: Ein Bietrag zur Erforschung neuer Produktions- und Raumstrukturen in einem nachfordistischen Entwicklungszusammenhang* (Gießen, Habilitations, Thesis, 1997).

20. Ruth Bördlein, "Frankfurt als Zentrum hochrangiger Dienstleistungen: Das Beispiel des Finanzbereichs," in *Das Rhein-Main-Gebiet: Aktuelle Strukturen und Entwicklungsprobleme,* ed. Günter Meyer (Mainz, Germany: Geogr. Institut der Johann Gutenberg Universität, 1995).

21. Ibid.

22. Wolfgang Klems and Alfons Schmid, "Arbeitsmarkt Rhein-Main 2000," in *Rhein-Main 2000: Perspektiven einer regionalen Raumordnungs- und Strukturpolitik,* ed. Alfons Schmid and Klaus Wolf (Frankfurt/Main: Umlandverband Frankfurt, 1996).

23. The percentage of foreign inhabitants figures highest in Frankfurt (33%) among German cities. Michael Chapman, "Le role de L'Union Europeenne dans le developpement economique local," in Demaziere, ed., *Du local au global* pp. 191–209.

24. Freund, "Die Entwicklung von Wirtschaftund Bevölkerung im Rhein-Main-Gebiet"; Wolf Schriever, "Impulse, Perspektiven, Probleme der regionalen Entwicklung des Frankfurtere Raumes," in *Agglomerationsräume in Deutschland: Ansichten, Einsichten, Aussichten,* ed. Akademie für Raumforschung und Landesplanung (Hanover: Akademie für Raumforschung und Landesplanung, 1996), pp. 218–233.

25. Ibid.

26. Knut Koschatzky, et al., *Technologieprofil der Region Rhein-Main* (Frankfurt/Main: Umlandverband Frankfurt, 1993).

27. Martin Wentz, "Frankfurt am Main und die Region: Herausforderungen und Gestaltfähigkeiten," in *Region. Frankfurt/Main,* ed. Martin Wentz (New York: Campus, 1994), pp. 35–62.

28. Hans Joachim Braczyk, Gerd Schienstock, and Bernd Steffensen, "The Region of Baden-Württemberg: A Post-Fordist Success Story?" in *Industrial Transformation in Europe*, ed. Eckhard J. Dittrich, Gert Schmidt, and Richard Whitley (London: Sage, 1995), pp. 203–233.

29. Wolf Gaebe, *Stärken und Schwächen der Region Stuttgart im interregionalen Vergleich* (manuscript, 1997).

30. Reinhold Grotz, "Die Industrie im Wirstschaftsraum Stuttgart," in *Industriegeographie der Bundesrepublik Deutschland und Frankreichs in den 1980er Jahren*, ed. Wolfgang Brüchner, Reinhold Grotz, and Alfred Pletsch (Frankfurt/Main: Moritz Diesterweg, 1991), pp. 143–174.

31. Ibid., p. 143.

32. Udo Staber, "Accounting for Variations in the Performance of Industrial Districts: The Case of Baden-Württemberg," *International Journal of Urban and Regional Research*, no. 20. (1996): 299–316

33. Grotz, "Die Industrie im Wirtschaftsraum Stuttgart," pp. 143–174; Braczyk et al., "The Region of Baden-Württemberg," pp. 203–233.

34. Grotz, "Die Industrie im Wirtschaftraum Stuttgart," pp. 143–174.

35. Braczyk et al., "The Region of Baden-Württemberg," pp. 203–233.

36. Werner Abelshauser, *Wirtschaftsgeschichte der Bundesrepublik Deutschland, 1945–1980* (Frankfurt/Main: Suhrkamp, 1983).

37. Gerhard Richter, *Stuttgart—Problemregion der 90er Jahre?* (Munich: IMU-Institut für Medienforschung und Urbanistik, 1988).

38. Philip Cooke, "Der Baden-Württembergische Werkzeugmaschinenbau: Regionale Antworten auf globale Bedrohungen," in Braczyk and Schienstock, *Kurswechsel in der Industrie*, pp. 52–68.

39. Naschold, "Jenseits des baden-württembergischen 'Exceptionalism'."

40. Alran Fischer et al., *Krise als Normalität: Wirtschaft und beschäftigungspolitische Lage der Region Stuttgart* (Munich: IMU-Institut für Medienforschung und Urbanistik, 1996).

41. Ibid.

42. Braczyk and Schienstock, *Kurswechsel in der Industrie*.

43. Cooke, "Der Baden-Württembergische Werkzeugmachinenbau," pp. 52–68.

44. Heike Bertram and Eike W. Schamp, "Flexible Production and Linkages in the German Machine Tool Industry," in *Complexes, Formations, and Networks*, ed. Marc de Smidt and Egbert Wever, Netherlands Geographical Studies, no. 132 (Utrecht: Faculteit der Ruimteljke Wetenschappen, 1991), pp. 69–80.

45. Philip Cooke and Kevin Morgan, "Growth Regions under Duress: Renewal Strategies in Baden-Württemberg and Emilia Romagna," in *Globalization, Institutions, and Regional Development in Europe*, ed. Ash Amin and Nigel Thrift (Oxford: Oxford University Press, 1994), pp. 91–117.

46. Werner Mikus, "Struktur und Entwicklungsprobleme der Industrie im Rhein-Neckar-Raum," in *Mannheim und der Rhein-Neckar-Raum*, Festschrift zum 43, *Deutschen Geographentag in Mannheim 1981*, ed. Ingrid Dörrer

(Mannheim, Germany: Geographisches Institut der Universität Mannheim, 1981), pp. 229–244.

47. Jürgen Egeln, Manfred Erbsland, Annette Hügel, Peter Schmidt, and Helmut Seitz. *Der Wirtschaftsstandort 'Rhein-Neckar-Dreieck,' Standortprofil und Unternehmensdynamik* (Baden-Baden, Germany: Nomos, 1996).

48. Bathelt, *Technologischer Wandel.*

49. Wolfgang Moidek and Elizabeth Müller-Neumann, *Entwicklung von Wirstschaftsstruktur und Arbeitsmarkt in Mannheim 1970–1990* (Mannheim, Germany: Stadt Mannheim, 1992).

50. In 1996, 13,300 employees. Läpple, "Die Teilökonomien einer Großstadt in einer Phase strukturellen Umbruchs: Das Beispiel Hamburg."

51. Hans Skarke, *Die Entwicklung des Industriestandortes Mannheim* (Mannheim, Germany: Geographisches Institut der Universität, 1987).

52. In 1996, 12.7 percent of the economically active population.

53. Wolf Gaebe and Hans Skarke, "Strukturwandel im Rhein-Neckar-Raum," *Zeitschrift für Wirstschaftsgeographie*, no. 33: 113–123.

54. Hans-Arthur Haasis, *Industriestädte im Wandel: Der Fall Mannheim* (Baden-Baden, Germany: Nomos Verlagsgesellschaft, 1990).

55. Ibid., pp. 113–123.

56. Sabine Weck, *Neue Kooperationsformen in Stadtregionen—Eine regulationstheoretische Einordnung. Dortmunder Beiträge zur Raumplanung 74* (Dortmund, Germany: Irpud, Universität Dortmund).

57. Cooke and Morgan, "Growth Regions under Duress"; Cooke, "Der Baden-Württembergische Werkzeugmaschinenbau," pp. 52–68.

58. Gaebe, *Stärken und Schwächen der Region Stuttgart im interregionalen Vergleich.*

PART FIVE

Conclusion

(global) For

15

Epilogue: Toward an Actor-Oriented Approach in the Study of the Globalization Process

Menno Vellinga

The notion that modern economic activity is becoming "globalized," that contemporary economics is not territorially rooted but that it functions through flows of resources managed by large corporations with a truly global reach, has become very popular, at least as indicated by the avalanche of books and articles that are being published on the theme. It should not surprise anybody familiar with academic debates that such extreme positions are receiving equally massive comments. This publication is a participant to this debate.

In the discussion on the nature and direction of globalization we find many elements that remind us of the earlier debates in economics and the social sciences on economic internationalization, modernization, and the rise and fall of geopolitical orders.[1] In each of these debates there was the notion of a development toward global homogenization resulting from the workings of strong unifying forces of an economic, social, and political nature. The counterarguments inevitably included an emphasis on the role of counter-movements and on the importance of the regional and/or local context in giving direction to the development process—very similar to what we are witnessing in the present globalization debate. In these debates the various disciplines tended to follow a slightly different course. Generally, economists have been inclined to underline the impact of global forces and to view economic development as becoming deterritorialized. Social scientists, on the other hand, have tended to defend the territorial specificity of development patterns. Within the realm of political economy, with its attention to economics in relation to the political and social process, these contradictions can be avoided and a more balanced approach can be presented, taking a middle road between the two positions. It is this approach that has guided the various contributions in this volume.

It has become clear from globalization analyses that a pure flow economy—in which territorial factors play a minor role and individual locations, with their available factors of production, can be easily substituted by others—is a phenomenon still very much limited to the financial sector and to "footloose" industries in the low-wage, low-skill segment.[2]

Figure 15.1 Regional Production Systems and the Impact of Globalization: The Actors Involved

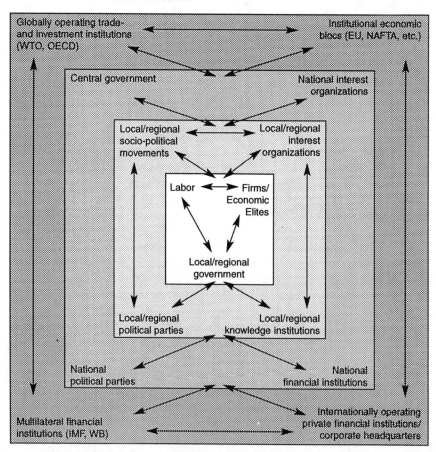

Some additional developments in the organization of other sectors of manufacturing and in consumer services can be noted that also tend toward the creation of economies that are no longer territorially rooted.[3] However, there is increasing evidence of the dependence of productive activity on resources and supporting factors that are strongly tied to a territorial context and that create an embeddedness in a local and/or regional economic, socio-political and socio-cultural environment that is not substitutable.

Comparative Perspectives

Comparative studies of industrialization processes have shown the importance of the factors leading to such embeddedness. In an earlier comparative study of eight cases of regional industrialization—four from Latin America (Monterrey, Medellín, Arequipa, and São Paulo) and three from Europe (Catalonia, Northern Italy, and Basque Country)—we investigated the role of territorially rooted processes and institutions that gave rise to specific regional production systems.[4] Such processes of regional industrialization have fascinated economists, social scientists, and historians for a long time. How does regional industrial growth begin, take off, and consolidate? Which conditions have a positive influence on such developments? Where does the necessary capital come from? What motivates regional entrepreneurs to take part in the organization of industrial enterprise and by which factors are these motives conditioned? In any individual case of regional industrialization, it is often difficult to systematize the conglomerate of often interdependent factors that intervene in the process and to establish an order of causality. This could also be seen in the analysis of the eight cases mentioned above. To get a clear view of all the factors involved in the formation of these regions and the rise of the regional production systems was not easy. "Regions," says Eric Van Young, "are like love, difficult to describe, but we know them when we see them."[5] This is also what happens when attempting to explain the regional embeddedness of productive activity.

The explanatory factors that are most obvious, like capital, labor, resources, and the like, move on a macro-structural level and—in combination—constitute necessary but not sufficient conditions for the rise and consolidation of regional production systems.[6] These processes involve complex decisionmaking based on motives that go beyond these macro-factors and will only be well understood through an actor-orientated approach. The entrepreneurial class is involved in decisionmaking that forms part of a process leading to the establishment and consolidation of capitalist relations of production. In the course of this process they will develop into an economic, social, and political force which—on the basis

of their definition of interests—will lead and support capitalist modernization. In a parallel way, the other actors—labor being the most prominent—will also develop into distinct economic, social, and political categories that will participate in the formation of a regional production
system. In this respect, industrialization is also a social process giving
form and content to the region with its specific territorial connotation. We
note again that—in our perspective—regions are historical constructs,
projects arising from interaction and negotiation between the various
local actors. In the case of industrial regions, industrialization will contribute the material base for the interests that struggle and negotiate
while establishing the region's sphere of influence and in the course of
these processes forge a regional identity.[7] These identities are strong and
persistent and may condition firm decisionmaking beyond the logic of a
flow-substitution economy. The various factor complexes involved in the
formation of regional production systems—the economic, the social, the
political and the cultural—tend to reinforce each other and cast this system in a particular mold that is hard to change.

The studies from Asia, Latin America and Europe dealt with in this volume, exemplify the importance of this phenomenon. In all cases the
effects of a growing integration across national borders has been experienced. However, at the same time—and paradoxically enough—these
processes coincide with the affirmation of regional identities among the
participating production systems. Historical and/or political-decisional
factors, ethnicity and/or religious and linguistic differences play an
important role in shaping the region's identity, in addition—of course—
to the very basic variables concerning levels of economic and socio-economic development and the ways in which the regional economy has
been participating in the international economy. With regard to these latter variables, Latin America, Asia and Europe present differing images.
The general development paths that have been followed and that dominated in either one of the macro regions since the 1950s have been quite
different and have led to dissimilar outcomes. The Latinamerican
economies opted for an expansion of the import substituting industrialization strategy. The Asian countries, however, changed from import substitution to export-oriented industrialization.[8] The development path of
Western Europe has taken a different route, conditioned by the expansion
of the services sector, and initial de-industrialization—resulting from the
relocation of labor-intensive production toward newly industrializing
countries—followed by re-industrialization, export-oriented and based
on advances in modern technology. These decisions on development
strategy had radical consequences for the growth pattern of the respective macro regions. Those Southeast and East Asian countries that had
adopted a growth strategy based on industrial exports were able to profit

from the rapid expansion in world trade in the subsequent decades. In those same years, most Latin American countries were confronted with stagnating growth when import substitution met its limits on their small domestic markets.

The performance of these strategies with regard to the social dimensions of development; e.g., poverty alleviation, equity and social exclusion, has been very different. These differences followed in part from the respective development model and the policies that were functional for either import substitution or exports. To a great extent, however, and certainly in Latin America, they resulted from decisions within the sociopolitical structure, the accommodation of the various social classes and their interests, and the ensuing public policies on distribution and welfare.

The East Asian countries have performed consistently better in the area of income distribution and redistribution.[9] This performance has resulted, above all, from the export model's superior achievement in job creation. Labor-intensive and semi-skilled export production has been more successful in absorbing labor than capital-intensive and more skilled production under import-substituting industrialization. In this manner, the Asian model has been able to realize growth with considerable equity, although substantial pockets of inequality have remained, particularly in the labor-intensive export industries. Official policies have mostly been unfriendly toward income redistribution and the labor movement has been too weak and too repressed to be an effective agent for change in this area. In Latin America, the populist regimes implementing the import substitution strategy had an important dimension of redistribution with—in many countries—a key role for a labor movement integrated into corporatist structures. These were also present in East Asia, but there corporatism served primarily objectives of security and strict political control. Under these conditions, the labor movement has not been able to develop organizational strength and become a politically significant force.

A basic difference affecting these social dimensions of the development path followed by these macro-regions concerns the distribution of access to resources prior to industrial take-off. At that stage, East Asian countries had relatively egalitarian social structures, in particular in the area of landownership and the distribution of wealth. Latin America's socioeconomic structures were less egalitarian in these areas and this heritage has remained a significant factor in obstructing the definition of more equitable growth strategies. Most countries continue to show income distributions that are highly skewed toward the small societal elites. The savings resulting from this concentration of income have—through the years—disproportionately found their way toward speculative investment and foreign bank accounts. Long-term, internationally competitive investment has been slow. The willingness among the elites to invest in such projects has not been as pronounced as in East Asia where industrialists have responded with considerable enthusiasm to the possibilities offered by the expansion of international trade. In the countries of Central America, but also in the smaller countries of South America, it has been even more difficult to develop a production milieu that will support participation in the international economy on the basis of economic undertakings other than simple, externally inspired *maquiladora*-type assembly activities and traditional agro exports. The European experience has shown the development of innovative production milieus to be a complicated long-term process with—next to the economic dimensions—important historical, social, political and cultural factors involved. In particular the larger, internationally-oriented firms tend to develop strong regional roots, and in the course of this process, "mold" the region in their own image while establishing a global-local nexus.

Under export industrialization, the impact from globalizing processes had to be mediated towards domestic society. The state took control in this area already at an early stage.[10] Contrary to Latin America, where these policy terrains were continuously being invaded by private interests, the Asian countries had a bureaucratic and executive elite which maintained a certain degree of insulation from civil society while pursuing long-term development goals. While managing their strategy, they did not experience the invasion by private interests to the degree as has happened in Latinamerican countries.[11] At each level of society in those countries, private interests have infiltrated public institutions to such an extent that— as William Glade describes in his discussion of privatization of public enterprises as part of the structural adjustment process in the 1980s—the issue became rather one of privatization of the private sector.[12]

The changes in the pattern of relations between state, market and civil society since the 1980s have created a "window of opportunity" for those groups and classes identified with the modernization of the economy and their insertion in the international economic system. The recent trend toward decentralization of the public sector in Latin America and the shift of responsibilities toward the sub-national regional and local levels has created additional opportunities for regional elites, especially in those (yet scarce) cases where this trend has been accompanied by a substantial decentralization of the public budget. They have responded to these challenges in differing ways, depending on whether they opted for participation in intra (macro)-regional integration schemes (such as Mercosur) or inter (macro)-regional arrangements (such as NAFTA), or whether they found other ways to participate in the global economy.

In East Asia, experience with international trade has been accumulated since the 1960s, when industrialists were first mobilized in support of national development goals. Learning to produce on competitive terms within an international economy, however, has been a relatively recent experience for many industrial entrepreneurs in Latin America, including those in the larger economies of Mexico, Argentina and, to a lesser extent, Brazil. Previous experience on international markets among entrepreneurs in the smaller economies had remained limited to an involvement with traditional exports of minerals and agricultural products. Those regions presently showing greater ability than others to produce successfully in a globalizing environment, appear to be those with an industrial tradition, including the presence of an innovative entrepreurial class, activity involved in the formation of a regional production system. We discussed these cases earlier in this chapter. A similar development has occured in the traditional industrial areas in Western Europe.

The polarizing effects of economic internationalization have sharpened the socioeconomic differences between regions that have been able to anticipate globalizing trends and those that have not. These differences will mostly probably increase as a result of the multipliers present within the regional growth process and may produce interregional disparities, such as we find in Europe between "winner" Northern and "loser" Southern Italy. In Latin America, Northern Mexico and Southern Brazil appear to have started imitating Northern Italy's role.

Counterpoints to Globalization

Globalization does not imply economic, nor does it create sociocultural hegemony. The processes that are being labelled as such are not as unidirectional. Processes of standardization and diversification, unification and fragmentation are often occurring simultaneously and account for a rather chaotic and contradictory picture. Globalizing tendencies interact constantly with localizing processes. On the sociocultural level these tendencies and processes will produce a complex synthesis of universalistic and particularistic values. Local cultures in non-Western countries often show a remarkable ability to adapt to global processes emanating from the industrialized West, integrating "foreign" elements into their cultural framework while maintaining a strong cultural identity. At the same time, however, this process may provide the basis for the articulation of oppositional social and political claims and may lead to the emergence of pockets of resistance against what is experienced as a totalizing or homogenizing globalization process that eventually will destroy regional/local cultures.

The global system at the end of the 20th century is not synonymous with global capitalism, but the dominant forces of global capitalism are the dominant forces in the global system.[13] Within this system, the concept of modern technology has an almost automatic connection with modernization in a socio-cultural sense and with the overpowering impact of a western-oriented consumer culture. These are processes that are organized on a global scale. Counterpoints, however, tend to present themselves locally.[14] They may develop into movements that oppose capitalism and/or the culture-ideology of consumerism. These often originate from a counter trend toward fundamentalism in beliefs and lifestyle and oppose the blending of traditional attitudes and behaviour with "Western ways."[15] Environmental movements have organized similar counter currents.[16]

More often, however, the activation of regional identities—and, in general, the cultural dynamics at the sub-national regional level resulting from the citizenry's reaction to globalization's homogenizing drives— will take a different turn. These processes may lead to significant, regionally-specific social and socio-cultural practices and purposive politically significant action directed toward the regional development potential and the possibilities of its realization within an international context.[17] The mobilizations in support of this regional project are often community oriented and operate across class-lines with collective self-other representations based on ethnic, linguistic or historical factors added to a territorial reference. Rather than opposing global capitalism, these movements—inspired, guided and often manipulated by regional/local powerholders—help mobilize the various sectors of society, especially labor, in support of actions undertaken to increase international competitiveness and to insert the regions successfully into the international economy, often bypassing the national government. In Europe, examples of this phenomenon can be seen, as we mentioned before, in Northern Italy, Catalonia and Basque Country, but there are, of course many similar cases.[18]

In Latin America, where strong regionalist tendencies are present in virtually all countries, this phenomenon is very common. All through history, back to colonial times, the continent has known strong regionalist movements that have mobilized in support of a regional project of development, often defined in opposition toward the capital-center of the country.[19] In present times, these movements have remained a potentially powerful factor in the formation of regional production systems, their insertion in the global economy and in the international division of labor.

In Southeast and East Asia as well, regionalisms and localisms abound, although the link with movements supporting regionally embedded projects of development does not appear to be a generalised phenomenon yet. The emphasis on export-oriented industrialization has subjected the larger region to powerful global economic pressures and modernizing influences. Resistance against these influences has been voiced by fundamentalist groups, environmental agencies (often led by NGO's) and consumer associations (Malaysia, Japan).[20] However, neither one of these appears even remotely likely to challenge global capitalist consumerism or the fundamental institutional supports of global capitalism. This challenge cannot even be found in Vietnam or China where the emphasis on political control and the preservation of the national cultural identity has led to campaigns against "Western ways" and efforts to participate in a globalizing economy on their own terms.

Conclusion

The developments analysed in this volume show clearly that the theses of the radical globalizers should be amended. The formation of global capitalism is taking place through the interaction between flow economies—and their political, social, and cultural correlates—and territorial economies. Strong globalizing tendencies meet with equally strong tendencies toward the regional embeddedness of production systems.[21] In a dialectical way, the contradiction between a globally operating economic system and a territorial economic organization is giving rise to the new and qualitatively different process of glocalization. In the study of glocalization, the sub-national region is the context of analysis. On these regional and local levels the role of "agency" has to be taken into account when analyzing the ebbs and flows of international competition and the resulting changes in regional production systems and their products. Regional industrialization is not only an economic process; it is above all a social process. A considerable number of actors are involved: corporations, entrepreneurs, labor, local/regional government, regional movements, and pressure groups—all pursuing their particular interests within the context of the parameters set by international economic developments. These parameters are conditioning, rather than determining regional economic outcomes, and in those cases where resources are not easily locationally substitutable, regional and/or national authorities may even have the capacity to control the actions of firms.

Globalization is not a natural phenomenon, nor is it a one-way process. Regions and localities are not just passively producing responses to globalizing processes. Regional institutions are active participants in these processes and their effects are accommodated and integrated with regional economic, sociopolitical and sociocultural idiosyncrasies. It is this complex interaction between processes of global economic change and national and regional elements that should caution us in our conclusions as to the nature and course of globalization. Multilinear rather than unilinear conceptions of the evolutionary type should guide the study of globalization's effects. Recognizing the importance of processes of glocalization should restrain any tendency to generalize and should increase sensitivity to regional specificity.

Notes

1. For a systematic account of these theories, see Peter W. Preston, *Development Theory* (Oxford: Blackwell, 1996).
2. Michael Storper, *The Regional World, Territorial Development in a Global Economy* (New York: The Guilford Press, 1997).
3. Ibid., p. 181.
4. Mario Cerutti and Menno Vellinga, eds., *Burguesía e Industria en América Latina y Europa Meridional* (Madrid: Editorial Alianza, 1988).
5. Eric Van Young, "Are Regions Good to Think?" in *Mexico's Regions: Comparative History and Development*, ed. Eric Van Young (San Diego: Center for United States-Mexican Studies, 1992), p. 3.
6. Cerutti and Vellinga, *Burguesía e Industria en América Latina*, passim.
7. See Bryan Roberts, "The Place of Regions in Mexico," in Van Young, *Mexico's Regions*, pp. 228–230.
8. See the classic study by Gary Gereffi and Donald L. Wyman, eds. *Manufacturing Miracles: Paths of Industrialization in Latin America and East Asia* (Princeton: Princeton University Press, 1990.
9. Robert Wade, *Governing the Market: Economic Theory and the Role of Government in East Asian Industrialization* (Princeton: Princeton University Press, 1990).
10. Cf. Peter Evans, *Embedded Autonomy: States and Industrial Transformation* (Princeton: Princeton University Press, 1995); M. Douglass, "The Developmental State and the Newly Industrialized Economies of Asia" in *Environment and Planning*, 26, 1994, pp. 543–566.
11. William Glade, "The State in Retreat in the Economy" in *The Changing Role of the State in Latin America*, ed. Menno Vellinga (Boulder: Westview Press, 1998), pp. 93–113.
12. Stephan Haggard, *Pathways from the Periphery: the Politics of Growth in the Newly Industrializing Countries* (Ithaca, N.Y.: Cornell University Press, 1990), 223 ff; Vinod Ahuja et.al. *Everyone's Miracle? Revisiting Poverty and Inequality in East Asia* (Washington D.C.: World Bank, 1997), p. 6 ff.
13. Cf. Leslie Sklair, "Social Movements and Global Capitalism," in *The Cultures of Globalization*, eds. Fredric Jameson and Masao Miyoshi (Durham, N.C.: Duke University Press, 1998), p. 296.
14. Alberto Moreiras, "Global Fragments: A Second Latinamericanism," in Ibid., pp. 91–92.
15. Richard Kilminster, "Globalization as an Emergent Concept," in *The Limits of Globalization: Cases and Arguments*, ed. Alan Scott (London: Routledge, 1997), p. 276.
16. See Martin Khor, "Global Economy and the Third World," in *The Case Against The Global Economy and for a Turn Toward the Local*, eds. Jerry Mander and Edward Goldsmith (San Francisco: Sierra Club Books, 1996, pp.

47–59, also Wolfgang Sachs, "Neo-Development: Global Ecological Management," in Ibid., pp. 239–252.

17. V. Spike Peterson, "Shifting Ground(s): Epistemological and Territorial Remapping in the Context of Globalization(s)," in *Globalization: Theory and Practice*, eds. Eleonore Kofman and Gillian Youngs (London: Pinter, 1996), p. 11–28.

18. See the chapter by Egbert Wever in this volume.

19. Some good examples of this phenomena are: the movement Pro Antioquia in Medellin, Colombia; the historical mobilizations in support of the República del Sur in Arequipa, Peru; The industrial bourgeoisie— manipulated mobilizations in support of "the Regiomontano identity" in Monterrey, Mexico. These regionalist movements, like the others in Brazil and Argentina have long historical roots. See: Cerutti and Vellinga, *Burguesia e Industria en América Latina*, passim.

20. Sklair, "Social Movements and Global Capitalism," p. 303.

21. Cf. Amparo Menéndez-Carrión and Fernando Bustamante, "Purpose and Methods of Intraregional Comparison," in *Latin America in Comparative Perspective: New Approaches to Methods and Analysis*, ed. Peter H. Smith (Boulder: Westview Press, 1995), pp. 64–66.

About the Contributors

Stephanie Fahey is director of the Research Institute for Asia and the Pacific at the University of Sydney. She has published widely on the transition process in Vietnam.

Gary Gereffi is professor of sociology at Duke University. He has published extensively on the changing international division of labor, including *Manufacturing Miracles* (1990, with Donald Wyman) and *Commodity Chains and Global Capitalism* (1994, with Miguel Korzeniewicz).

Leo van Grunsven is lecturer in international economics at Utrecht University. He is the author of numerous publications on economic development in Southeast Asia, including *Regional Change in Industrializing Asia* (1998).

Robert Gwynne is reader in Latin American development at the University of Birmingham. He has written numerous books and articles on industrialization in the developing world and on the impacts of neoliberalism and globalization on regional development in Latin America, including *Industrialization and Urbanization in Latin America* (1985) and *Latin America Transformed: Globalization and Modernity* (1999, with Cristóbal Kay).

Paul Hirst is professor of social theory at Birkbeck College, University of London. He is the author of fourteen books, including *Globalization in Question* (1996, with Grahame Thompson) and *From Statism to Pluralism* (1997).

Ray Hudson is director of the Centre for European Studies of Territorial Development, University of Durham. His many publications focus on the relationships between economic change and territorial development strategies in Europe. His most recent book is *Divided Europe* (1998, with Allen Williams).

Kees Koonings is senior lecturer in social anthropology at Utrecht University. He has published extensively on the socioeconomic and sociopolitical aspects of regional development in Brazil, including *Industrialization, Industrialists and Regional Development in Brazil* (1995).

Terry McCoy is professor of political science at the University of Florida, where he has also served as director of the Center for Latin American Studies. He has published numerous articles on the changing nature of international relations in the Americas, the region's emerging sustainable development regime, and the impact of globalization on the Caribbean.

Helmut Nuhn is professor of economic geography at the Philipps University, Marburg am Lahn. He has published extensively on urbanization, decentralization, and the effects of economic policy reform in Central America, including *Apertura Comercial en Centroamérica* (1996, with Andreas Stamm).

Sam Ock Park is professor of economic geography at Seoul National University. He has published extensively on industrial and regional policy in Southeast Asia, including *The Asian Pacific Rim and Globalization* (1995, with Richard Le Heron).

Eike Schamp is professor in economic geography at the Johann Wolfgang Goethe University, Frankfurt am Main. He has published widely on the internationalization of industry in Europe and the effects on regional development, including *The New Map of Automobile Manufacturing in Europe* (1995, with Ray Hudson).

Tak-Wing Ngo is lecturer in political science at Leyden University, specializing in Chinese politics. He has published numerous books and articles on sociopolitical developments in Southeast and East Asia, including *Hongkong's History: State and Society Under Colonial Rule* (1998) and *The Cultural Construction of Politics in Asia* (1999, with Hans Ante).

Menno Vellinga is director of the Institute of Development Studies at Utrecht University. He is the author and editor of many books and articles on socioeconomic and sociopolitical aspects of development in Latin America, including *Social Democracy in Latin America* (1993) and *The Changing Role of the State in Latin America* (1998).

August van Westen is lecturer in international economics at Utrecht University. He has published on regional development in West Africa and Southeast Asia and is presently involved in a study of industrial restructuring in Malaysia and Thailand.

Egbert Wever is professor of economic geography at Utrecht University. His many publications in the areas of industrial restructuring and regional development in Europe include *The Corporate Firm in a Changing World Economy* (1990, with Marc de Smidt) and *Industrial Organization: The Firm and its Labour Market* (1994, with Bert van der Knaap).

Index